TALES OF THE GRIZZLY

D0884977

TALES OF THE GRIZZLY

THIRTY-NINE STORIES OF GRIZZLY BEAR ENCOUNTERS IN THE WILDERNESS

COMPILED BY TIM W. CLARK AND DENISE CASEY
WITH ILLUSTRATIONS BY BETH KROMMES

HOMESTEAD PUBLISHING
Moose, Wyoming

Copyright © 1992 Tim Clark and Denise Casey
All rights reserved.

ISBN 0-943972-14-0
Library of Congress Catalog Card Number 92-81304
Printed in the United States of America on ♻ recycled, acid free paper.

3 5 7 9 10 8 6 4 2

Published by
HOMESTEAD PUBLISHING
Box 193
Moose, Wyoming 83012

"Ute Creation Legend," by Nancy Wood. First published in *When Buffalo Free the Mountains* (Garden City: Doubleday, 1980). Copyright © 1980 by Nancy Wood. Reprinted by permission of the author.

"The Bears," by George Bird Grinnell. Published in *Blackfoot Lodge Tales: The Story of a Prairie People* (Lincoln: University of Nebraska Press, 1962).

"Mik-ápi—Red Old Man," by George Bird Grinnell. Published in *Blackfoot Lodge Tales: The Story of a Prairie People* (Lincoln: University of Nebraska Press, 1962).

"The Bear Helper," by George Bird Grinnell. Published in *By Cheyenne Campfires* (Lincoln: University of Nebraska Press, 1971). Copyright © 1926 by Yale Univeristy Press. Reprinted by permission of Yale University Press.

"How Devils Tower Came to Be—Kiowa and Cheyenne Legends," by Ray H. Mattison. Published in *Devils Tower National Monument—A History* (Sundance, Wyoming: Devils Tower Natural History Association, 1973; first published in *Annals of Wyoming*, April, 1956).

"How Devils Tower Came to Be—Sioux Legend," by Ella E. Clark. First published in *Indian Legends from the Northern Rockies* (Norman: University of Oklahoma Press, 1966). Copyright © 1966 by the University of Oklahoma Press. Reprinted by permission of the publisher.

"The Bear Man," by George Bird Grinnell. First published in *Pawnee Hero Stories and Folk-Tales* (Lincoln: University of Nebraska Press, 1961). First published by Forest and Stream Publishing Company, New York, 1889.

"The Medicine Grizzly Bear," by George Bird Grinnell. First published in *Harper's Monthly Magazine* (April, 1901).

"Into the Wilderness," by Captains Meriwether Lewis and William Clark, edited by Reuben Gold Thwaites. First published in *Original Journals of the Lewis and Clark Expedition, 1804-1806* (New York: Dodd, Mead and Company, 1904-1905). Reprinted by Antiquarian Press: New York, 1959.

"Astorian Anecdotes," by Washington Irving. Published in *Astoria, or Anecdotes of an Enterprise Beyond the Rocky Mountains*, edited and with an introduction by Edgeley W. Todd (Norman: University of Oklahoma Press, 1964). First published in 1836. Reprinted by permission of the publisher.

"Hugh Glass," by Aubrey L. Haines. Published in *The Mountain Men and the Fur Trade of the Far West*, v. 6, pp. 161-169, edited by LeRoy R. Hafen (Glendale, California: The Arthur H. Clark Company, 1968). Reprinted by permission of the publisher.

"A Lisson on the Charcter of the Grissly Baare," by Dale L. Morgan. Published in *Jedediah Smith and the Opening of the West* (New York: Bobbs-Merrill, 1953). Copyright © !953 by The Bobbs-Merrill Company, Inc., renewed © 1981 by James S. Morgan. Reprinted by permission of Macmillan Publishing Company.

"Prince Maximilian, Searcher for Knowledge," by Maximilian, Prinz von Wied. Published in *Travels in the Interior of North America*. First English publication in 1843. Reprinted in *Early Western Travels: 1748-1846*, v. XXIII, edited by Reuben Gold Thwaites. (Cleveland: The Arthur H. Clark Company, 1905).

"Greenhorn Meets Grizzly," by John K. Townsend. Published in *Narrative of a Journey Across the Rocky Mountains to the Columbia River*. First published in 1839. Reprinted in *Early Western Travels: 1748-1846*, v. XXI, edited by Reuben Gold Thwaites. (Cleveland: The Arthur H. Clark Company, 1905).

"A Dangerous Varmint," by Osborne Russell. First published in 1914. Published in *Journal of a Trapper, 1834-1843*, edited by Aubrey L. Haines (Lincoln: University of Nebraska Press, 1965).

"Black Robe Mission," by Father Pierre-Jean De Smet. First published in 1843 in *Letters and Sketches, with a Narrative of a Year's Residence Among the Indian Tribes of the Rocky Mountains*. Reprinted in *Early Western Travels: 1748-1846*, v. XXVII, edited by Reuben G. Thwaites (Cleveland: The Arthur H. Clark Company, 1906).

"Filled with the Beastly Thunder," by Overton Johnson and William H. Winter. First published in *Route Across the Rocky Mountains, with a Description of Oregon and California* (Lafayette, Indiana: John B. Semans, Printer, 1846). Reprinted with preface and notes by Carl L. Cannon, Princeton University Press, 1932.

"John C. Fremont, Tenderfoot," by John C. Thompson. First published in the *Wyoming State Tribune* (March, 1948). Reprinted by permission of the publisher.

"With Book in Hand," by Randolph B. Marcy. First published in *The Prairie Traveler: A Handbook for Overland Expeditions, with Maps, Illustrations, and Itineraries of the Principal Routes Between the Mississippi and the Pacific* (New York: Harper & Brothers, 1859).

"We See Bear Every Day or Two," by John C. Thompson. First published in the *Wyoming State Tribune* (March, 1948).

"A Savage Santa Claus," by Charles M. Russell. First published in *Trails Plowed Under: Stories of the Old West* (New York: Doubleday and Company, 1927). Copyright © 1927 by Doubleday and Company, a division of Bantam Doubleday Dell Publishing Group, Inc. Used by permission of Doubleday, a division of Bantam Doubleday Dell Publishing Group.

"Mrs. Bictoll and the Big Black Dog, " by G. E. Lemmon. Oral history from the Works Progress Administration Manuscripts Collection (#242), Wyoming Department of Commerce, Division of Parks and Cultural Resources, Museum Division, Historical Research and Publications, Cheyenne. Used with permission of Historical Research and Publications.

"General Sheridan Bags the Game," by General Philip Henry Sheridan. First published in *Personal Memoirs of P.H. Sheridan, General United States Army* (New York: Charles L. Webster & Company, 1888).

"Dr. Allen," by William A. Allen. First published in *Adventures with Indians and Game, or Twenty Years in the Rocky Mountains* (Chicago: A.W. Bowen, 1903).

"Grizzly Roping—A Great Cowboy Sport," by Peggy H. Benjamin. First published in *Wyoming Rural Electric News* (June, 1981). Reprinted with permission of the author.

"Seven Silvertips in Half an Hour," by G. B. McClellan. First published in the *Annals of Wyoming* (January, 1954). Reprinted with permission of Historical Research and Publications, Museum Division, Division of Parks and Cultural Resources, Department of Commerce, Cheyenne, Wyoming.

"Bear Hugs for Dan Blair," by Minnie A. Rietz. Oral history from the Works Progress Administration Manuscripts Collection (#9), Wyoming Department of Commerce, Division of Parks and

Cultural Resources, Museum Division, Historical Research and Publications, Cheyenne. Used with permission of Historical Research and Publications.

"Big Foot Wallace," by Bryant B. Brooks. First published in *Memoirs of Bryant B. Brooks: Cowboy, Trapper, Lumberman, Stockman, Oilman, Banker, and Governor of Wyoming* (Glendale, California: The Arthur H. Clark Company, 1939). Reprinted with permission of the publisher.

"A True Sportsman Speaks," by G.O. Shields. First published in *Harper's New Monthly Magazine* (1887).

"The Vetter Saga," by John C. Thompson. First published in the *Wyoming State Tribune* (February, 1948).

"The Vetter Saga," by Bob Edgar and Jack Turnell. First published in *The Brand of a Legend* (Cody, Wyoming: Stockade Publishing, 1978). Reprinted with permission of the authors.

"The Vetter Saga," by A.A. Anderson. First published in *Experiences and Impressions—The Autobiography of Colonel A.A. Anderson* (New York: Macmillan Company, 1933).

"Laramie River Grizzly," by Minnie A. Rietz. Oral history from the Works Progress Administration Manuscripts Collection (#9), Wyoming Department of Commerce, Division of Parks and Cultural Resources, Museum Division, Historical Research and Publications, Cheyenne. Used with permission of Historical Research and Publications.

"My Last Bear Hunt, by Joe III," by Joel Johnson. First published in the *Lovell Chronicle* (Lovell, Wyoming, date unknown).

"Wahb," by Ernest Thompson Seton. First published in *The Biography of a Grizzly* (New York: D. Appleton-Century Company, 1899).

"Wahb," by A.A. Anderson. First published in *Experiences and Impressions—The Autobiography of Colonel A.A. Anderson* (New York: Macmillan Company, 1933).

"A Photographic Expedition for the Yellowstone Grizzly," by William Wright. First published in *The Grizzly Bear: The Narrative of a Hunter-Naturalist* (New York: Charles Scribner's Sons, 1909).

" A Wildlife Crusader," by William T. Hornaday. Published in *Our Vanishing Wild Life: Its Extermination and Preservation* (New York: New York Zoological Society, 1913).

"The Yellowstone Sanctuary," by Stephen N. Leek. First published as "Grizzly and His Sanctuary" in *In the Open* (Pittsburgh, Pennsylvania; May, 1916). Manuscript from the Works Progress Administration Manuscripts Collection (#1335), Wyoming Department of Commerce, Division of Parks and and Cultural Resources, Museum Division, Historical Research and Publications, Cheyenne. Used with permission of Historical Research and Publications.

"New Environments," by Enos A. Mills. Published in *The Grizzly: Our Greatest Wild Animal* (Sausalito, California: Comstock Editions, 1976) First published in 1919. Reprinted with permission of the publisher.

"Wildwood Test," by Milton P. Skinner. Published in *Bears in the Yellowstone* (Chicago: A.C. McClurg and Company, 1925).

"Oh, Ranger," by Horace M. Albright and Frank J. Taylor. First published in *"Oh, Ranger!" A Book About the National Parks* (Stanford: Stanford University Press, 1928). Copyright © 1928 by Horace M. Albright and Frank J. Taylor.

"A Death in Yellowstone," by Dudley Hayden, recorded by Dave Aaberg. Cassette recording and transcript (#OH-99) collected by the Wyoming Department of Commerce, Division of Parks and and Cultural Resources, Museum Division, Historical Research and Publications, Cheyenne. Used with permission of Historical Research and Publications.

Dedicated
To Len Sargent, Cinnibar Ranch, Montana, who is committed to
conserving the grizzly bear in the Greater Yellowstone Ecosystem and
who aided our completion of this book.

CONTENTS

TALES OF THE GRIZZLY

PREFACE

THE Northern Rockies and the adjacent Great Plains of the western United States have a rich and fascinating history. Much of today's image of this territory formed as Indians, mountain men, explorers, and settlers adapted to its rigors—the long, snow-swept winters and brief summers, arid grass-sagebrush basins and rugged, forested mountains, relentless winds, open skies, unsurpassed vistas, and seemingly inexhaustible wildlife.

The grizzly bear, more than any other animal, lured the imagination of people. Stories about this fascinating animal abound. (As early as 1832, Prussian Prince Maximilian wrote, "Almost all the hunters of the prairie relate their adventures with the bears, and whole volumes might be filled with such stories.") They detail much more than simple encounters with the great bear. Accounts in journals and diaries, and later newspaper reports, oral histories, and books, reflect not only our view of the bear and its place in nature, but a view of *ourselves* and *our* place in nature as well. Once the grizzly symbolized untamed nature itself, and to some people it still does. But other views of the bear came about as they were decimated, as nature itself seemed to recede before the weight of Manifest Destiny. At first, humans lived in this region as a minor ecological element, but over the last 190 years we have come to dominate and alter many features of the landscape and, in fact, we have altered biological evolution itself.

Adding to the many volumes of American nature literature, these thirty-nine bear stories help chronicle this unfolding of ideas from the early 1800s through 1929. The stories are valuable because they record our history and because, collectively, they show a complex, changing relationship between man and nature. We hope this volume will make interesting reading for all who love the region, and we hope it encourages readers to ensure a living, healthy future for our few remaining grizzly bears.

Most of these tales have appeared in print before. Although there are a few famous bear encounters and a few famous authors here, we have tried to bring to light some lesser known stories from a variety of sources. Even though first published in the 1800s, the books from which some of our stories are taken are still readily available, including Washington Irving's *Astoria*,

Osborne Russell's *Journal of a Trapper*, Ernest Thompson Seton's *Biography of a Grizzly,* and several of George Bird Grinnell's collections of Native American legends. Other published sources are more obscure. For instance, the autobiography of the Civil War's General Sheridan is probably little read today. Two monumental series, *Original Journals of the Lewis and Clark Expedition, 1804-1806,* and *Early Western Travels, 1748-1846,* both edited by Reuben Gold Thwaites in the early 1900s, provide story sources. Time-Life Books republished many out-of-print western titles in its series Classics of the Old West. This series furnished sources for two stories. Old newspapers and magazines also provided stories; John C. Thompson wrote a column called "In Old Wyoming" for the *Wyoming State Tribune* in the 1940s, and we have reprinted accounts from his "bearana" series.

Four stories have never been published before. They were oral histories recorded, transcribed, and filed with the Wyoming Department of Commerce's Historical Research and Publications in Cheyenne. They give additional insight into the evolution of perspectives on bears as do the published accounts.

In all these stories, we have retained the original spelling and punctuation, unless otherwise noted. The inconsistent, phonetic spelling and casual punctuation make the reading somewhat slow in Lewis and Clark's excerpts, called "Into the Wilderness," and in two mountain men stories, but we feel that they preserve the original flavor. In a few other accounts, we have corrected occasional, obvious typographical errors without noting the changes. We have given our own titles to most of the stories, with the exception of Grinnell's Indian legends and a few others.

We would also like to warn readers not to accept these stories as scientific truth. During the entire period covered, from the early 1800s to 1929, scientific field research, as we know it today, was unknown, and so misinformation about grizzly bears passed down through the years. For instance, Seton asserts in his story "Wahb" that not one of the bears in Yellowstone "has ever yet harmed a man." Lewis and Clark remark that the male grizzly's testicles "are suspended in separate pouches from two to four inches asunder." Randolph Marcy was convinced that the grizzly was, on occasion, "one of the most stupid brutes imaginable." Of course, none of these statements are true.

This book began as an anthology of stories of bear and human encounters that took place in Wyoming. It now encompasses tales from adjacent states, but we have limited our territory to the northern Great Plains and northern Rocky Mountains.

Several people helped us collect the stories and complete the manuscript. We very much appreciate the assistance of Katherine A. Halverson and Jean Brainerd of the Historical Research and Publications Division, Wyoming Department of Commerce, in Cheyenne, in locating oral histories and early published materials. We are most grateful to Carl Schreier for his encouragement, his assistance in locating some stories, and his attention to detail. The staffs of the Teton County Library and the Teton County Historical Center were helpful in locating information about the stories and authors. We would also like to thank Anna Parks of Lovell, Wyoming, for researching the background of one story. We are grateful, too, for Walt Merschat's encouragement and review of an early version of the manuscript, and for Marcia Casey's assistance with an earlier version. Len Sargent and Catherine Patrick generously supported production of the manuscript via the Northern Rockies Conservation Cooperative, Jackson, Wyoming.

Tim W. Clark and Denise Casey
Jackson, Wyoming
August 1992

INTRODUCTION

 THE grizzly bear looms profoundly in the American psyche and evokes passionate responses, especially in the West where the bear once thrived and still hangs on in low numbers. Even though the great bear is gone from most of the region now, its memory and image linger on, suffusing our experience and expectations of the northern Plains and Rockies.

To many people, the bear's physical prowess and personality symbolize the dominion and capriciousness of nature; to others, the bear's wanderings signify the freedom of the wide open spaces; to still others, the bear's elusive ways typify the mystery and otherness of a natural world much studied but little known. As our interactions with nature itself have been a source of strength, character, and personal and societal definition, so too our encounters with grizzly bears have been a measure of ourselves—our sense of moral rightness, our ability to learn from nature, our wit and adaptability, and our insights into our own culture. No story about bears has ever been told without expressing these sensibilities, either directly or indirectly.

This anthology of stories of grizzly bear encounters spans the century from the pristine, pre-contact days of the Plains Indians to 1929. This period was pivotal in the history of the species. As grizzly hunter, naturalist, and later photographer William Wright wrote near the turn of the century: "When my grandfather was born, the grizzly had never been heard of. If my grandson ever sees one, it will likely be in the bear pit of a zoological garden." Most of these thirty-nine stories are arranged chronologically. The perspectives expressed by the people in the stories and by the storytellers clearly changed over time. We have grouped the stories to illustrate five distinct views of the bear and its place in nature that seem to emerge from the 125 years covered by these tales. The "periods" we have thus defined are not rigid or historically recognized; they reflect our selection of stories. We recognize that, in each period, a diversity of views departed in varying degrees from the dominant theme we discuss, and we have tried to avoid homogenizing these periods or stereotyping people's perspectives.

INDIAN LEGENDS: The oldest view is that of America's first people. Although Indians have sometimes been touted as the first environmentalists, most ethnologists would argue against viewing them as environmental "gurus." Yet if we hark back to the days before North American peoples were devastated by European diseases, market economies, and outright annihilation, most cultures had a way of life and a cosmology so intimately and intricately connected to the earth, its creatures, its foods, and its seasons as to be almost incomprehensible to most modern Americans. Each tribe and individual lived not only wholly within the natural physical world, but utterly enveloped within a cycle of myths, a set of ceremonies, and a code of behavior that bound the people to the earth.

The bear stories come from Ute, Cheyenne, Kiowa, Pawnee, Sioux, and Blackfeet tribes. It is one thing for us to state that Indians believed grizzly bears had great magic powers and wisdom, that they honored the grizzly in Bear Dance ceremonies, and they saw grizzlies as helpers, healers, teachers, or protectors. It is another thing entirely to read these powerful legends about bears that bring dead men back to life, chase little girls into the heavens, comfort wounded warriors, sing medicine songs, or give great gifts of power and healing, and thus to see the grizzly bear, in its myriad roles, as part of a world that was to the Indians wholly alive and articulate.

Early travelers in the northern Plains and Rockies remarked on the grizzly bear claw necklaces worn by some Indians. Using the name "white bear" that was common for grizzlies in the early nineteenth century, the Belgian-born Jesuit missionary Father De Smet wrote about these necklaces made of "the claws of the white bear; this is in their view the most costly and valuable decoration." Paintings by George Catlin and Karl Bodmer, both of whom traveled among the Plains tribes when their cultures were still relatively intact, show the bear claw necklaces.

LEARNING HARD LESSONS—EXPLORERS AND MOUNTAIN MEN: The next perspective on the grizzly bear to appear on the scene was that of the first white explorers and the mountain men, those legendary fur trappers of the 1820s and '30s. Although other explorers may have entered grizzly country earlier, Lewis and Clark were the first to record in detail their meetings with the white bear, reports from the Indians of the bear's habits and nature, and the physical characteristics of the two bear species of the region (grizzlies and black bears). We give several of their journal accounts as well as those of two scientific travelers to the region in the early 1830s. These early naturalists were curious about the grizzly bear and, at first, eager to meet it. Four stories in this section are from or about mountain men. The era of the free fur traders was brief, spanning primarily the 1820s to the 1840s. But it spawned a lasting, romantic American hero, the mountain man—living off the land, serving no man or government, dressed in buckskins, furs, and beads, kept company only by his horse and his gun. The mountain men's views of the wilderness were as varied as the men. Some argued that the Indians and animals would always occupy the land because only they could survive its rigors. Others, like the Indians, revered the land, the animals, and the freedom of wilderness life. Still others predicted that the wilderness that temporarily met their wants would eventually give way to advancing white civilization.

The earliest white men learned about the wilderness the hard way. The naturalists tried to be objective and accurate in their observations about the bear, and the mountain men certainly must have been open-minded in their approach to the wilderness, yet what both groups learned and what they could learn was limited in two respects: First, fear dominated their reactions to the grizzly. They met the grizzly on foot or horseback with small-bore, unrifled, single-shot guns, and their limited technology did not protect them from the bears' fearsome strength once provoked. Second, most of them came West with an ignorance of what was required of them and a presumptuous sense of their own dominance. Meeting a grizzly was an event that nothing in their previous lives had prepared them for. Nevertheless, these men traveled extensively and their combined experiences contributed significantly to knowledge of the species. What they wrote became scripture for later travelers.

OVERCOMING THE WILDERNESS—MISSIONARIES, SURVEYORS, EMIGRANTS, RAILROAD BUILDERS, PROSPECTORS AND THE ARMY: Another new perspective on the grizzly bear arrived on the landscape in the 1840s and persisted through the 1860s. It characterized the missionaries, surveyors, military men, railroad builders, and others who arrived to overcome the wilderness—to locate it, measure it, record its secrets, dig its riches, span it with roads and railroads and telegraph wires, to make it safe, comfortable, and usable. The emerging American paradigm of the inevitable destiny of purpose—commerce, domestication, exploitation—was a powerful tool in transforming wilderness into a human-dominated landscape.

In 1840, Father De Smet journeyed to the northern Rockies in the same way that the fur traders and explorers had—by river. The country was still a wilderness—a desert in De Smet's view. By 1870, General Sheridan was traveling by transcontinental railroad. The landscape of the West changed enormously within this thirty-year period. Military forts and new towns became linked by telegraph. The 1862 Homestead Act settled thousands of small farmers on the land. The wagon train era flourished and died. The land was divided into territories, explored, surveyed, and governing bodies set up. Nebraska and Kansas had already become states.

It was in those days a duty to kill grizzly bears. Bears stood in the way of business. The new human presence filling the land was simply antithetical to the free-roaming grizzly bear. This era also showed men beginning to seek and hunt grizzlies as a measure of themselves, to pit themselves against nature in yet another way. Although a few instances of this appeared in our previous section, the earlier explorers and mountain men tangled with grizzlies more from inexperience, while these continent-builders of the mid-century relished the challenge and the risks. They felt engaged in a worthy contest, and they took for granted that they were justified in the conquering.

RANCHERS AND SPORTSMEN: In the "Old West" of the 1870s, '80s, and '90s, an established livestock industry and a robust hunting industry held yet another outlook on the grizzly. Although not qualitatively different from the previous view of the bear, it stands as a separate chapter in history because it represented a widespread, organized effort to kill bears using rifles, traps, and poisons on a scale previously unknown.

Increasingly, grizzlies were seen as competitors for game and destroyers of livestock. To forge a successful ranch from the native short-grass prairies or intermountain basins in the early territorial days was difficult. Losses of cattle or sheep to grizzlies were not tolerated—too many other threats already made ranching precarious. By the time these enterprising individuals grew into a wealthy, well-organized, and influential industry at the end of the century, the destruction of bears and all other medium and large predators—sanctioned since the earliest days of colonial America—had become a dogma of hatred.

Ever-improving rifles and other technological advances facilitated the vast destruction of wildlife in these decades. Faster and better transportation to eastern markets and access to more and more remote hunting areas made market hunting lucrative (the bison and the passenger pigeon were both objects of market hunting). Game laws were minimal and little enforced. Many professional trappers made a living from the bounties paid for killing predators, including black and grizzly bears. As late as 1915, trappers in Wyoming were instructed "to use every possible means in destroying all species of predatory animals." State and federal monies were budgeted for this "animal damage control."

But grizzly bears were also viewed as the most magnificent game species of the continent and grizzly hunting as the "grandest sport." The last quarter of the nineteenth century saw development of a sport hunting ethic (see introduction to "A True Sportsman Speaks"). This period also witnessed the growth of a large hunting public, and for many of them, grizzly hunting was the ultimate test. As the bear's numbers dropped and remaining individuals held on in the mountains and forests, the status of hunting and killing a grizzly soared. Wealthy sportsmen in particular mounted large, well-supplied expeditions of their friends and associates to hunt grizzlies and other game in the mountains of Wyoming, Idaho, Montana, or the Canadian Rockies.

YELLOWSTONE—THE LAST REFUGE: The view illustrated by the final group of stories was the emerging recognition around the turn of the century that the bear, like the American wilderness, was fast becoming a thing of the past. In stories dating from 1899 to 1929, an appreciation and understanding of the grizzly emerged with a new notion that this mighty creature deserved protection.

Grizzly bears disappeared rapidly as we superimposed the American design on the western landscape. People realized that if the bears were to survive, they needed sanctuaries to protect them from hunting and provide food, shelter, and adequate living space. Although there were small remnant populations of grizzlies in other locations, we focused this group of stories on Yellowstone because of its key role in the evolution of the national park idea to encompass wildlife protection and because, throughout the twentieth century, it has been associated with grizzly bears in the public eye. During the early years of this century, Yellowstone National Park became a showcase of nature and the last stand for the grizzly bear in this region of the continent.

The idea of conservation, in part, grew out of the simple idea in the sportsmen's code of the late 1800s of leaving some game "for the next man and the next year." The ground swell of ideas and initiatives for better game laws and wildlife protection came not only from sportsmen, but also from nature lovers, bird watchers, and scientists. This protective sentiment was still unpopular in the northern Rockies and Plains in 1900, but gained public endorsement, scientific buttressing, and statutory muscle in the intervening decades.

▼▼▼

It is fascinating to see emerge from these thirty-nine stories the feelings of the people about their encounters with bears as expressions of their own situations and the times in which they lived. The fear and despair of an Indian woman toward the bear that is shadowing her turns to wonder, trust, and thanks in "The Bear Helper." A cocky young trapper is chastened by a close call in an episode from Osborne Russell's *Journal of a Trapper*. Mrs. Bictoll, from the story bearing her name, faints dead away when she learns that the critter she clobbered with an axe was a grizzly. In "Laramie River Grizzly," a rancher gathers his neighbors together to appreciate the bear he is about to shoot as the last in the region. "Big Foot Wallace" recounts the history of another rancher who finds in the bear his equal—in power, in will, in wit—and glories in crushing him. "Wildwood Test" follows a Yellowstone Park naturalist who tracks a grizzly for several days and admires its resourcefulness and elusiveness.

Although each tale is unique and many are told "with the vividness and tension that can be retained only when the details of an experience are seared into the human brain during seconds of great emotional activity," certain patterns emerge. We have tried in this anthology to demonstrate the evolution of characteristic attitudes of each period.

There are many, many more stories beyond the few recorded here. For instance, Martha Waln's account of the antics of a pet bear is recorded in the Wyoming Department of Commerce's Historical Research and Publications:

At sight of this five-month-old grizzly bounding toward them, the colt reared up in the air and snorted. When he came back down, the bear grabbed him lovingly by the front legs and things began to happen. The gentle horse was as bad as the colt. They jerked back breaking the rope they were tied with, wheeled at right angles and away they went, running as hard as they could. Down toward the stream they ran, dodged the trees and across the creek, to the opposite bank, turned and came back again, across the flat and up the hillside, and the bear right after them. They ran wildly in circles and in figures of eight all over the place, and finally ran into a tree and completely wrecked what was left of the wagon and harness, and the bear was right there with them when they stopped. Of course, this affair brought the pet bear idea to a swift climax.

A. A. Anderson, author of one segment of "Wahb" and one segment of "The Vetter Saga," noted that a German hunter spied the hindquarters of a bear feeding in the bushes near his ranch. He climbed the hill after him to get a shot and "was intensely amused, saying to himself, 'Vat a surprase I vill give dat bear!' Finally, he was so near that the bear heard him and turned around suddenly with a 'woof!' The German lost his nerve and started down the hill as fast as he could run, exclaiming, 'Mein Gott, vot a difference it makes vich end he looks at you mit!'" Anderson also claimed in his autobiography, "I could fill a book with my bear experiences. I have killed 39 grizzlies besides numerous black, brown and Alaskan bears."

Harry Yount was another of the "picturesque figures of Wyoming in the early days"—Union Army veteran, hunter and prospector, and "perennial beau for all the teachers who came into his neighborhood." One oral history claimed that he had killed forty grizzlies in his career and made a necklace of their claws. In his "bearana" series in the *Wyoming State Tribune,* John C. Thompson credits Yount with having "dispatched 57 of these mighty beasts."

These stories were not always funny or fearless. Trapper Ira ("Bearface") Dodge attacked a family of bears one spring in the 1890s in the Green River and Beaver Creek country of Wyoming. Having taken on more than he could handle, he was badly mauled—his left arm mangled and useless. But he made his way back to camp. His partner doctored his wounds, then went to the scene of the battle and retrieved all five bear skins as well as three of Dodge's fingers. The fate of Hank Mason, homesteader, hunter, and first road supervisor of Crook County in Wyoming's Black Hills, was sealed as soon as he surprised a big bear in its bed. The next day, his friends could only trace the signs of the struggle, bury him, and hunt and destroy the bear—and record his life and death with Wyoming's early history.

The bears were legendary, too. Men spent decades chronicling the stock depredations, the baiting and trapping efforts, the sightings and near-miss shots, and finally the triumphant kills of specific bears. Old Four Toes, for instance, in Jackson Hole at the turn of the century, was one such well-remembered grizzly.

The stories have remained. The bears have not. Overall, the grizzly bear has been reduced by about 90 percent in numbers and in range in the Northern Rockies of the U.S. That is why the United States Fish and Wildlife Service under the 1973 Endangered Species Act listed it as "threatened" with extinction. Today, it is estimated that perhaps 200 grizzlies remain in or around Yellowstone National Park, while another larger population resides in and near Glacier National Park, and smaller populations persist in Idaho and Washington.

In addition to revealing much about the people who met bears and the storytellers, these stories tell much about the grizzly bear's behavior and its haunts and habits. In most cases, the grizzly offered no real threat to human life until someone surprised it, deliberately attacked it, or approached a sow with cubs or a bear at a food cache. Of course, this generalization is accepted today partly because the people of earlier days proved it, sometimes the hard way, and set the stories down.

The book ends early in this century because no new generally-accepted views of bears have come forth since then. Although science has greatly improved our understanding of the ecology and behavior of grizzly bears and it has informed management decisions, it has contributed little to changing people's core values concerning bears and nature. Today in the West, the last two perspectives on the grizzly bear are both in evidence, and both still provide arguments for the controversy of "what to do about grizzly bears." We still live in the conflict of these two views: First, the attitude that we have the right—no, by God!—the duty to domesticate or kill every last remnant or living reminder of what is wild and uncontrollable, i.e., what threatens our illusions and our property (if less our lives). And, second, the attitude that wild nature is precious and necessary as the ultimate source of the material resources that sustain us as well as our spiritual and social well-being, worthy of all our efforts to protect and perpetuate it. The notion that we must kill all predators or provide hunting opportunities for a few sportsmen still clashes with our desire to preserve this important part of our biological diversity and our fear that, if we don't, we will lose a crucial element of our regional and historical identity and our integrity. The future of wild grizzly bears in the West remains uncertain. It will be the responsibility of future historians to chronicle what this generation did to or for the bear.

▼▼▼

William Wright, author of the story "A Photographic Expedition for the Yellowstone Grizzly," took great pains to clarify for posterity the image of the grizzly through his writings and his photos. We know of no more eloquent tribute to the greatness of the grizzly bear and the humility of humankind than these last lines from his book, *The Grizzly Bear*, first published in 1909.

I have dwelt so much upon the difference between the grizzly of popular imagination and the real grizzly of the wilds, that it may possibly appear that my traffic with this magnificent animal has not left me one of his admirers. As a matter of fact nothing could be farther from the truth.

First and last I have hunted and killed all the big game of this continent south of the Barren Grounds and Alaska. Later, as the years passed and I became less enamored of killing, I have been interested in the study of these animals, one and all. There is, indeed, no form of life in the open that is not beautiful, and I am not ashamed to own that I have spent many happy and silent hours watching the humblest of them. But not only as a sportsman did my interest in the grizzly survive the discovery that all my early and romantic ideas about him were ill-founded, but, as a student, I have steadily added to my admiration for him.

He is the one wild animal of our wilderness that owns no natural over-lord. With the exception of man he deigns to recognize no enemy. And if he is not, as he was once thought, the bloodthirsty and tyrannous autocrat of his vast domain, he is none the less its master. If, in sober truth, he is less terrible than he was painted, he only loses interest and dignity in the eyes of those whom fear alone impresses.

In short, just as the grizzly was in the beginning the lure that drew me to the wilderness, so now, to my mind, he remains the grandest animal our country knows.

INDIAN LEGENDS

THE grizzly bear was an immensely powerful creature that assumed many roles and many faces in the Native American universe. The following Indian legends illustrate an intimate and reciprocal relationship between human cultures and the natural world.

The first, a Ute creation legend, demonstrates the grizzly bear as the ultimate creation. Central to two of the stories are magical bears who adopt young men and impart great powers to them—powers to kill their enemies, to avoid being wounded, to use roots and herbs to heal their people's illnesses, and powers to lead their people as chiefs. Listen to the bears' words: "I want you to imitate us. This shall be a part of your greatness. I shall look after you. I shall give to you a part of myself. . . . As the fur that I am in has touched you it will make you great, and this will be a blessing to you." ("The Bear Man") "I wished you to come here, so that I might make you my son and give my power to you, so that you may become a great man among your people." ("The Medicine Grizzly Bear") In return, remembrances are made by the men, rites observed, and gifts offered. In two of the stories, Native Americans are in trouble, often alone, unequipped, pursued by enemies, or wounded. Grizzly bears come to them as helpers. "I am following you only to watch and protect you," says the grizzly in "The Bear Helper." But in the legends about Devils Tower, bears are dangerous pursuers, and in "The Bears," Old Man takes a long journey, changing the world as he goes.

It is not known how extensively this integrated view of man and nature was shared by all Native Americans of the West, but the diversity of stories from this range of tribes suggests that it was clearly a central feature of many native cultures.

UTE CREATION LEGEND

 THE Ute Indians, residents of Colorado and Utah, were hunters who spent most of the year in small hunting and gathering bands. But the tribe gathered annually in the springtime for the Bear Dance, a ritual of renewal. In The Beast That Walks Like Man: The Story of the Grizzly Bear *(Garden City, New York: Hanover House, 1955), Harold McCracken describes the Ute Bear Dance, as witnessed by anthropologist Verner Z. Reed in 1893 in southwestern Colorado. The Utes believed their first ancestors were grizzly bears and that grizzlies possessed "great magic powers and wisdom." The Bear Dance ceremony strengthened the Utes' friendship with bears, and protected the dancers from death by bears. It also facilitated communication with dead relatives, helped the grizzlies recover from their winter hibernation, and opened opportunities for courtship among the Indians, according to Reed's report.*

A large, circular enclosure, representing a bear's den, was fenced in with logs and pine boughs. Inside, a cave-like hole was dug in the ground; over its small entrance was placed a drum so the cave became a large sounding board to recreate the growls of the grizzly bears. After weeks of preparation and practice by musicians, singers, and storytellers, the families of the tribe gathered at the sacred site. They celebrated for four days. Their dancing, singing, and drumming—growing ever more intense—roused the bears from their months of sleep and helped them mate and come down from their mountain dens to find food. The Dance ended with a great feast. McCracken cites evidence that other tribes across North America, from tribes of the northeastern woodlands to the Blackfeet, also honored the great bear in Bear Dance ceremonies.

This wonderful legend, which tells the meaning of the Utes' reverence for the bear-spirit, comes from Nancy Wood's When Buffalo Free the Mountains *(Garden City, New York: Doubleday & Co., 1980).*

▼▼▼▼▼

IN the beginning there was nothing but the blue sky, clouds, sunshine, and rain. No mountains, plains, forest, or desert, no men either, red or white. The Manitou or great He-She spirit lived alone in the middle of the sky and was the ruler of all that was. There were no other powers or gods. He was alone.

After a while he became lonesome and wanted something new. He got tired of telling the sun to shine, the wind to blow, and the rain to fall. So he made a big stone drill and made a big hole through the heavens and kept on making it bigger and bigger until he could look down through onto the nothingness that was below. He was pleased with his work.

When the hole was as big as he wanted it, he took snow and rain and poured it through the hole into the void below. Then he took the dirt and stones that came out of the hole in the floor of heaven and poured them through. After he had poured all these things for a long time, he looked through the hole and saw a big mountain that he had made and all around the mountain there were other mountains, and to the east a great plain.

After looking at the top of the mountain the He-She thought he would like to see more, so he made the hole bigger and crawled through it and stepped down to the top of the mountain. When he finally got down, he found that all the stones, dirt, snow, and rain had formed an immense thing that was ugly and bald and that did not look nice. So he touched the earth with his fingers and there the trees and forests appeared. He swept his flat hand over the plains and there were grass and small plants. Then he told the sun to shine through the hole in the sky and as the snow melted, it made lakes and rivers and creeks. These flowed east and west and afterward went into great holes that formed the Sky Blue Waters, the Oceans. They stole their colors from the sky, which accounts for their name. It was all very pretty and every day the gentle rain fell and the earth blossomed.

The He-She came down every day from heaven and enjoyed the great creations. At that time there were no animals or men, only trees, grass, and water. After a while he got tired of it and wanted something else.

When the He-She came down from heaven he always carried his magic cane and as he sat and pondered, he broke off the small end of it. Out of this he made fishes, big ones and little ones, and of all sizes and shapes. Then he stroked them with his hands and breathed on them and they came alive. So he looked around to see what he would do with them and finally he put them in a stream and they swam away. That's how we have fishes in the streams now, but we don't eat them because some wicked people threw dead bodies in the water and they became fish. We don't know now who are real fish and who are dead people. Of course that was a longtime afterward.

Then the He-She went to the forests and he found lots of leaves that were on the ground and had pretty colors. These he took into his hands and making magic, blew on them and they grew wings and feathers and became birds. From the oak leaves he made eagles, ravens and hawks; from the red sumac the red bird and from the green aspen leaves the blue jay. Each leaf made its own kind of bird and the birds all sang nice songs.

From the middle of his magic cane the He-She made the antelope, buffalo, rabbits, squirrels, the coyote and all the other animals. They lived together in peace for a long time until the coyote got bad and caused a lot of mischief and then they began to fight. The strong killed the weak and soon there was lots of blood all over everything. The He-She looked on and was disgusted with his creations.

After a while he decided that he would make one big captain or wise animal who was to be chief and rule the rest of the animals with wisdom and strength. So he made the great grizzly bear. To him he gave all wisdom and power to govern the world and that's why the grizzly is such a wise old man today. He is the big chief of all the animals. He also explained to the animals that they must stop fighting and live at peace as those were the orders of the great He-She and that if they did not do it he would punish them. Most of them obey him excepting when the coyote makes mischief.

Then the He-She went back to the heavens to rest awhile and he left the bear to rule for him.

Chief Buckskin Charley and Chief Nanice
As told to Jean Allard Jeancon
Ignacio, Colorado 1904

THE BEARS

 "OLD Man" is a character who appears in many Native American stories. He is chief god and creator, but to those brought up in the Western European tradition, he often appears enigmatical and contradictory. George Bird Grinnell, who compiled Blackfoot Lodge Tales *(Lincoln: University of Nebraska Press, 1962), explained Old Man thus:*

> *The character of Old Man, as depicted in the stories told of him by the Blackfeet, is a curious mixture of opposite attributes. In the serious tales, such as those of the creation, he is spoken of respectfully, and there is no hint of the impish qualities which characterize him in other stories, in which he is powerful, but also at times impotent; full of all wisdom, yet at times so helpless that he has to ask aid from the animals. Sometimes he sympathizes with the people, and at others, out of pure spitefulness, he plays them malicious tricks that are worthy of a demon. He is a combination of strength, weakness, wisdom, folly, childishness, and malice.*

This story is about Old Man and why bears are so fat.

▼▼▼▼▼

NOW Old Man was walking along, and far off he saw many wolves; and when he came closer, he saw there the chief of the wolves, a very old one, and sitting around him were all his children.

Old Man said, "Pity me, Wolf Chief; make me into a wolf, that I may live your way and catch deer and everything that runs fast."

"Come near then," said the Wolf Chief, "that I may rub your body with my hands, so that hair will cover you."

"Hold," said Old Man; "do not cover my body with hair. On my head, arms, and legs only, put hair."

When the Chief Wolf had done so, he said to Old Man: "You shall have three companions to help you, one is a very swift runner, another a good runner, and the last is not very fast. Take them with you now, and others of my younger children who are learning to hunt, but do not go where the wind blows; keep in the shelter, or the young ones will freeze to death." Then they went hunting, and Old Man led them on the high buttes, where it was very cold.

At night, they lay down to sleep, and Old Man nearly froze; and he said to the wolves, "Cover me with your tails." So all the wolves lay down around him, and covered his body with their tails, and he soon got warm and slept. Before long he awoke and said angrily, "Take off those tails," and the wolves moved away; but after a little time he again became cold, and cried out, "Oh my young brothers, cover me with your tails or I shall freeze." So they lay down by him again and covered his body with their tails.

When it was daylight, they all rose and hunted. They saw some moose, and, chasing them, killed three. Now, when they were about to eat, the Chief Wolf came along with many of his children, and one wolf said, "Let us make pemmican of those moose"; and every one was glad. Then said the one who made pemmican, "No one must look, everybody shut his eyes, while I make the pemmican"; but Old Man looked, and the pemmican-maker threw a round bone and hit him on the nose, and it hurt. Then Old Man said, "Let me make the pemmican." So all the wolves shut their eyes, and Old Man took the round bone and killed the wolf who had hit him. Then the Chief Wolf was angry, and he said, "Why did you kill your brother?" "I didn't mean to," replied Old Man. "He looked and I threw the round bone at him, but I only meant to hurt him a little." Then said the Chief Wolf: "You cannot live with us any longer. Take one of your companions, and go off by yourselves and hunt." So Old Man took the swift runner, and they went and lived by themselves a long time; and they killed all the elk, and deer, and antelope, and moose they wanted.

One morning they awoke, and Old Man said: "Oh my young brother, I have had a bad dream. Hereafter, when you chase anything, if it jumps a stream, you must not follow it. Even a little spring you must not jump." And the wolf promised not to jump over water.

Now one day the wolf was chasing a moose, and it ran on to an island. The stream about it was very small; so the wolf thought: "This is such a little stream that I must jump it. That moose is very tired, and I don't think it will leave the island." So he jumped on to the island, and as soon as he entered the brush, a bear caught him, for the island was the home of the Chief Bear and his two brothers.

Old Man waited a long time for the wolf to come back, and then went to look for him. He asked all the birds he met if they had seen him, but they all said they had not.

At last he saw a kingfisher, who was sitting on a limb overhanging the water. "Why do you sit there, my young brother?" said Old Man. "Because," replied the kingfisher, "the Chief Bear and his brothers have killed your wolf; they have eaten the meat and thrown the fat into the river, and whenever I see a piece come floating along, I fly down and get it." Then said Old Man, "Do the Bear Chief and his brothers often come out? And where do they live?" "They come out every morning to play," said the kingfisher; "and they live upon that island."

Old Man went up there and saw their tracks on the sand, where they had been playing, and he turned himself into a rotten tree. By and by the bears came out, and when they saw the tree, the Chief Bear said: "Look at that rotten tree. It is Old Man. Go, brothers, and see if it is not." So the two brothers went over to the tree, and clawed it; and they said, "No, brother, it is only a tree." Then the Chief Bear went over and clawed and bit the tree, and although it hurt Old Man, he never moved. Then the Bear Chief was sure it was only a tree, and he began to play with his brothers. Now while they were playing, and all were on their backs, Old Man leaned over and shot an arrow into each one of them; and they cried out loudly and ran back on the island. Then Old Man changed into himself, and walked down along the river. Pretty soon he saw a frog jumping along, and every time it jumped it would say, *"Ni'-nah O-kyai'-yu!"* And sometimes it would stop and sing:

"Ni'-nah O-kyai'-yu! Ni'-nah O-kyai'-yu!
Chief Bear! Chief Bear!
Nap'-i I-nit'-si-wah Ni'-nah O-kyai'-yu!"
Old man kill him Chief Bear!

"What do you say?" cried Old Man. The frog repeated what he had said.

"Ah!" exclaimed Old Man, "tell me all about it."

"The Chief Bear and his brothers," replied the frog, "were playing on the sand, when Old Man shot arrows into them. They are not dead, but the arrows are very near their hearts; if you should shove ever so little on them, the points would cut their hearts. I am going after medicine now to cure them."

Then Old Man killed the frog and skinned her, and put the hide on himself and swam back to the island, and hopped up toward the bears, crying at every step, *"Ni'-nah O-kyai'-yu !"* just as the frog had done.

"Hurry," cried the Chief Bear.

"Yes," replied Old Man, and he went up and shoved the arrow into his heart.

"I cured him; he is asleep now," he cried, and he went up and shoved the arrow into the biggest brother's heart. "I cured them; they are asleep now"; and he went up and shoved the arrow into the other bear's heart. Then he built a big fire and skinned the bears, and tried out the fat and poured it into a hollow in the ground; and he called all the animals to come and roll in it, that they might be fat. And all the animals came and rolled in it. The bears came first and rolled in it, that is the reason they get so fat. Last of all came the rabbits, and the grease was almost all gone; but they filled their paws with it and rubbed it on their backs and between their hind legs. That is the reason why rabbits have two such large layers of fat on their backs, and that is what makes them so fat between the hind legs.

MIK-ÁPI—RED OLD MAN

 HERE is another story from George Bird Grinnell's Blackfoot Lodge Tales. *It is very different from the previous tale of Old Man; here is a grizzly bear helper, a healer.*

Almost half of Grinnell's book is devoted to describing the Blackfeet way of life in earlier days as well as their plight at the time of the book's publication in 1892. These Plains people, he tells us, venerated the bear and its powerful medicine second only to the buffalo, which was their chief source of food, shelter, clothing, and equipment, as well as a sacred beast. Grinnell points out that, "A reverence for the bear appears to be common to all North American tribes, and is based not upon anything that the animal's body yields, but perhaps on the fact that it is the largest carnivorous mammal of the continent, the most difficult to kill and extremely keen in all its senses. The Blackfeet believe it to be part brute and part human, portions of its body, particularly the ribs and feet, being like those of a man."

▼▼▼▼▼

I

IT was in the valley of "It fell on them" Creek, near the mountains, that the Pikŭn´i were camped when Mik-ápi went to war. It was far back, in the days of stone knives, long before the white people had come. This was the way it happened.

Early in the morning a band of buffalo were seen in the foot-hills of the mountains, and some hunters went out to get meat. Carefully they crawled along up the coulées and drew near to the herd; and, when they had come close to them, they began to shoot, and their arrows pierced many fat cows. But even while they were thus shooting, they were surprised by a war party of Snakes, and they began to run back toward the camp. There was one hunter, named Fox-eye, who was very brave. He called to the others to stop, saying: "They are many and we are few, but the Snakes are not brave. Let us stop and fight them." But the other hunters would not listen. "We have no shields," they said, "nor our war medicine. There are many of the enemy. Why should we foolishly die?"

They hurried on to camp, but Fox-eye would not turn back. He drew his arrows from the quiver, and prepared to fight. But, even as he placed an arrow, a Snake had crawled up by his side, unseen. In the still air, the Piegan heard the sharp twang of a bow string, but, before he could turn his head, the long, fine-pointed arrow pierced him through and through. The bow and arrows dropped from his hands, he swayed, and then fell forward on the grass, dead. But now the warriors came pouring from the camp to aid him. Too late! The Snakes quickly scalped their fallen enemy, scattered up the mountain, and were lost to sight.

Now Fox-eye had two wives, and their father and mother and all their near relations were dead. All Fox-eye's relatives, too, had long since gone to the Sand Hills [the Blackfoot future world, place of ghosts]. So these poor widows had no one to avenge them, and they mourned deeply for the husband so suddenly taken from them. Through the long days they sat on a near hill and mourned, and their mourning was very sad.

There was a young warrior named Mik-ápi. Every morning he was awakened by the crying of these poor widows, and through the day his heart was touched by their wailing. Even when he went to rest, their mournful cries reached him through the darkness, and he could not sleep. So he sent his mother to them. "Tell them," he said, "that I wish to speak to them." When they had entered, they sat close by the door-way, and covered their heads.

"*Kyi!*" Said Mik-ápi. "For days and nights I have heard your mourning, and I too have silently mourned. My heart has been very sad. Your husband was my near friend, and now he is dead and no relations are left to avenge him. So now, I say, I will take the load from your hearts. I will avenge him. I will go to war and take many scalps, and when I return, they shall be yours. You shall paint your faces black, and we will all rejoice that Fox-eye is avenged."

When the people heard that Mik-ápi was going to war, many warriors wished to join him, but he refused them; and when he had taken a medicine sweat, and got a medicine-pipe man to make medicine for him during his absence, he started from the camp one evening, just after sunset. It is only the foolish warrior who travels in the day; for other war parties may be out, or some camp-watcher sitting on a hill may see him from far off, and lay plans to destroy him. Mik-ápi was not one of these. He was brave but cautious, and he had strong medicine. Some say that he was related to the ghosts, and that they helped him. Having now started to war against the Snakes, he travelled in hidden places, and at sunrise would climb a hill and look carefully in all directions, and during the long day would lie there, and watch, and take short sleeps.

Now, when Mik-ápi had come to the Great Falls (of the Missouri), a heavy rain set in; and, seeing a hole in the rocks, he crawled in and lay down in the farther end to sleep. The rain did not cease, and when night came he could not travel because of the darkness and storm; so he lay down to sleep again. But soon he heard something coming into the cave toward him, and then he felt a hand laid on his breast, and he put out his hand and touched a person. Then Mik-ápi put the palm of his hand on the person's breast and jerked it to and fro, and then he touched the person with the point of his finger, which, in the sign language, means, "Who are you?"

The strange person then took Mik-ápi's hand, and made him feel of his own right hand. The thumb and all the fingers were closed except the forefinger, which was extended; and when Mik-ápi touched it the person moved his hand forward with a zigzag motion, which means "Snake." Then Mik-ápi was glad. Here had come to him one of the tribe he was seeking. But he thought it best to wait for daylight before attacking him. So, when the Snake in signs asked him who he was, he replied, by making the sign for paddling a canoe, that he was a Pend d'Oreille, or River person. For he knew that the Snakes and the Pend d'Oreilles were at peace.

Then they both lay down to sleep, but Mik-ápi did not sleep. Through the long night he watched for the first dim light, so he might kill his enemy. The Snake slept soundly; and just at daybreak Mik-ápi quietly strung his bow, fitted an arrow, and, taking aim, sent the thin shaft through his enemy's heart. The Snake quivered, half rose up, and with a groan fell back dead. Then Mik-ápi took his scalp and his bow and arrows, and also his bundle of moccasins; and as daylight had come, he went out of the cave and looked all about. No one was in sight. Probably the Snake, like himself, had gone alone to war. But, ever cautious, he travelled only a short distance, and waited for night before going on. The rain had ceased and the day was warm. He took a piece of dried meat and back fat from his pouch and ate them, and, after drinking from the river, he climbed on a high rock wall and slept. Now in his dream he fought with a strange people, and was wounded. He felt blood trickling from his wounds, and when he awoke, he knew that he had been warned to turn back. The signs also were bad. He saw an eagle rising with a snake, which dropped from its claws and escaped. The setting sun, too, was painted, [sun dogs]— a sure warning to people that danger is near. But, in spite of all these things, Mik-ápi was determined to go on. He thought of the poor widows mourning and waiting for revenge. He thought of the glad welcome of the people, if he should return with many scalps; and he thought also of two young sisters, whom he wanted to marry. Surely, if he could return and bring the proofs of brave deeds, their parents would be glad to give them to him.

II
It was nearly night. The sun had already disappeared behind the sharp-pointed gray peaks. In the fading light the far-stretching prairie was turning dark. In a valley, sparsely timbered with quaking aspens and cotton-woods, stood a large camp. For a long distance up and down the river rose the smoke of many lodges. Seated on a little hill overlooking the valley, was a single person. With his robe drawn tightly around him, he sat there motion-less, looking down on the prairie and valley below.

Slowly and silently something was crawling through the grass toward him. But he heard nothing. Still he gazed eastward, seeking to discover any enemy who might be approaching. Still the dark object crawled slowly onward. Now it was so close to him that it could almost touch him. The person thought he heard a sound, and started to turn round. Too late! Too late! A strong arm grasped him about the neck and covered his mouth. A long jagged knife was thrust into his breast again and again, and he died without a cry. Strange that in all that great camp no one should have seen him killed!

Still extended on the ground, the dark figure removed the scalp. Slowly he crawled back down the hill, and was lost in the gathering darkness. It was Mik-ápi, and he had another Snake scalp tied to his belt. His heart was glad, yet he was not satisfied. Some nights had passed since the bad signs had warned him, yet he had succeeded. "One more," he said. "One more scalp I must have, and then I will go back." So he went far up on the mountain, and hid in some thick pines and slept. When daylight came, he could see smoke rise as the women started their fires. He also saw many people rush up on the hill, where the dead watcher lay. He was too far off to hear their angry shouts and mournful cries, but he sung to himself a song of war and was happy.

Once more the sun went to his lodge behind the mountains, and as darkness came Mik-ápi slowly descended the mountain and approached the camp. This was the time of danger. Behind each bush, or hidden in a bunch of the tall rye grass, some person might be watching to warn the camp of an approaching enemy. Slowly and like a snake, he crawled around the outskirts of the camp, listening and looking. He heard a cough and saw a movement of a bush. There was a Snake. Could he kill him and yet escape? He was close to him now. So he sat and waited, considering how to act. For a long time he sat there waiting. The moon rose and travelled high in the sky. The Seven Persons [the constellation of the Great Bear] slowly swung around, and pointed downward. It was the middle of the night. Then the person in the bush stood up and stretched out his arms and yawned, for he was tired of watching, and thought that no danger was near; but as he stood thus, an arrow pierced his breast. He gave a loud yell and tried to run, but another arrow struck him and he fell.

At the sound the warriors rushed forth from the lodges and the outskirts of the camp; but as they came, Mik-ápi tore the scalp from his fallen enemy, and started to run toward the river. Close behind him followed the Snakes. Arrows whizzed about him. One pierced his arm. He plucked it out. Another struck his leg, and he fell. Then a great shout arose from the Snakes. Their enemy was down. Now they would be revenged for two lately taken lives. But where Mik-ápi fell was the verge of a high rock wall; below rushed the deep river, and even as they shouted, he rolled from the wall, and disappeared in the dark water far below. In vain they searched the shores and bars. They did not find him.

Mik-ápi had sunk deep in the water. The current was swift, and when at last he rose to the surface, he was far below his pursuers. The arrow in his leg pained him, and with difficulty he crawled out on a sand-bar.

Luckily the arrow was lance-shaped instead of barbed, so he managed to draw it out. Near by on the bar was a dry pine log, lodged there by the high spring water. This he managed to roll into the stream; and, partly resting on it, he again drifted down with the current. All night he floated down the river, and when morning came he was far from the camp of the Snakes. Benumbed with cold and stiff from the arrow wounds, he was glad to crawl out on the bank, and lie down in the warm sunshine. Soon he slept.

III

The sun was already in the middle when he awoke. His wounds were swollen and painful; yet he hobbled on for a time, until the pain became so great he could go no further, and he sat down, tired and discouraged.

"True the signs," he said. "How crazy I was to go against them! Useless now my bravery, for here I must stay and die. The widows will still mourn; and in their old age who will take care of my father and my mother? Pity me now, oh Sun! Help me, oh great Above Medicine Person! Look down on your wounded and suffering child. Help me to survive!"

What was that crackling in the brush near by? Was it the Snakes on his trail? Mik-ápi strung his bow and drew out his arrows. No; it was not a Snake. It was a bear. There he stood, a big grizzly bear, looking down at the wounded man. "What does my brother here?" he said. "Why does he pray to survive?"

"Look at my leg," said Mik-ápi, "swollen and sore. Look at my wounded arm. I can hardly draw the bow. Far the home of my people, and my strength is gone. Surely here I must die, for I cannot travel and I have no food."

"Now courage, my brother," said the bear. "Now not faint heart, my brother, for I will help you, and you shall survive."

When he had said this, he lifted Mik-ápi and carried him to a place of thick mud; and here he took great handfuls of the mud and plastered the wounds, and he sung a medicine song while putting on the mud. Then he carried Mik-ápi to a place where [there] were many sarvis berries, and broke off great branches of the fruit, and gave them to him, saying, "Eat, my brother, eat!" and he broke off more branches, full of large ripe berries, for him; but already Mik-ápi was satisfied and could eat no more. Then said the bear, "Lie down, now, on my back, and hold tight by my hair, and we will travel on." And when Mik-ápi had got on and was ready, he started off on a long swinging trot. All through the night he travelled on without stopping. When morning came, they rested awhile, and ate more berries; and again the bear plastered his wounds with mud. In this way they travelled on, until, on the fourth day, they came close to the lodges of the Pikun'i; and the people saw them coming and wondered.

. "Get off, my brother, get off," said the bear. "There are your people. I must leave you." And without another word, he turned and went off up the mountain.

All the people came out to meet the warrior, and they carried him to the lodge of his father. He untied the three scalps from his belt and gave them to the widows, saying: "You are revenged. I wipe away your tears." And every one rejoiced. All his female relations went through the camp, shouting his name and singing, and every one prepared for the scalp dance.

First came the widows. Their faces were painted black, and they carried the scalps tied on poles. Then came the medicine men, with their medicine pipes unwrapped; then the bands of the *I-kun-uh'-kah-tsi,* all dressed in war costume; then came the old men; and last the women and children. They all sang the war song and danced. They went all through the village in single file, stopping here and there to dance, and Mik-ápi sat outside the lodge, and saw all the people dance by him. He forgot his pain and was proud, and although he could not dance, he sang with them.

Soon they made the Medicine Lodge, and, first of all the warriors, Mik-ápi was chosen to cut the raw-hide which binds the poles, and as he cut the strands, he counted the *coups* he had made. He told of the enemies he had killed, and all the people shouted his name and praised him. The father of those two young sisters gave them to him. He was glad to have such a son-in-law. Long lived Mik-ápi. Of all the great chiefs who have lived and died, he was the greatest. He did many other great and daring things. It must be true, as the old men have said, that he was helped by the ghosts, for no one can do such things without help from those fearful and unknown persons.

THE BEAR HELPER

 THE quintessential American naturalist, George Bird Grinnell, spent parts of at least forty years with the Cheyenne Indians at the end of the nineteenth century and beginning of the twentieth. Among his many scientific and popular writings about them is By Cheyenne Campfires *(Lincoln: University of Nebraska Press, 1971), a wonderful collection of hero myths, war stories, trickster tales, as well as "stories of mystery," from which "The Bear Helper" comes. Although this tale dates "about 1835" and includes mention of guns, flint and steel, it is strongly evocative of the early life of the Cheyenne and their high regard for the grizzly bear.*

In this story, terror of the bear—this powerful, dangerous avatar of the wilderness—slowly changes to uncertainty, questioning, and supplication; to trust and recognition of the beast as a benevolent guardian and provider; and finally to a sense of obligation and gratitude.

▼▼▼▼

ONE autumn, about the year 1835, when the leaves were just beginning to turn yellow, a large village of Cheyennes and Arapahoes camped on Crow Creek, near the South Platte River. Game was scarce and there was not much to eat, so the people began to get hungry.

One day a man named Plenty Crows said to his wife, "I will take my gun and go up into the hills, where perhaps I may find a deer, or a bull, or an antelope, or something else to kill." He started out on foot and went up into the hills where a few pines grew, and after a time, as he was going along, he saw two bulls lying down. He crept up close to them and killed both where they lay, and then skinned and cut them up. He took a piece of meat to carry with him to the camp, put the rest in a pile and threw the hides over it, and putting his meat on his back went to the camp. When he reached his lodge, he told his wife that he had killed two bulls and butchered them, and that the next morning they would go after the meat. That night they tied their horses close by the lodge, and the next morning saddled a horse each, and took a pack horse, and went up to get the meat.

After Plenty Crows had butchered his meat, and gone to the camp, a war party of Crows had passed that way, and found the pile of meat. When they saw it, the Crows said to each other, "These persons will come back for this meat in the morning, and we will wait here for them, and kill them when they return." So they went over a little hill and stayed there all night.

Plenty Crows and his wife rode up to the meat, and got down from their horses, and packed all three of them with the meat, those that they were riding as well as the pack horse. The Crows were watching, and as soon as the horses were packed, they charged down on the man and his wife and began shooting. For some time Plenty Crows fought them off, but at last they killed him and took the woman prisoner, and went away with her and the horses.

They traveled north, and at last came to the Crow village on Sheep River [Big Horn River]. The Crow man who carried the pipe of this war party took the woman as his wife. He already had two Crow women, so she was his third wife. These two Crow wives did not like the Cheyenne woman, and whenever the man was not near they abused her, whipping her with quirts, and hitting her with sticks and stones. They made her work hard, packing wood, dressing hides, and making moccasins all the time.

In this lodge there lived a young man sixteen or seventeen years old, who was a servant, and herded the lodge man's horses. This young man took a liking to the Cheyenne woman, for he felt sorry for her. One day when no one was in the lodge except these two, he said to her: "These women abuse you, and it makes me angry. Go to work now and make moccasins for yourself, and hide them away. When you have made enough, you must run away and try to get back to your people. I will help you. If you get a chance to do it, wrap up some dried meat, and hide it away, so that you may have something to eat. Some time when they go out after buffalo, this man will take his women with him, and you can get away." The woman remained with the Crows all through the winter, and until the snow began to go off in the spring.

One day all the Crows went out for buffalo. The woman's husband went, and took with him his two Crow wives, and the young man also started with them. After the young man had gone a little way out from the camp he stopped, turned and went back. He rode around the Crow camp until he was on the other side of it, hid his riding horse in the timber, and tied him there. Then he caught another horse and rode into camp. Some of the people who saw him coming in on this horse said to him: "Why, what is the matter? We thought you went to kill buffalo."

He answered: "My horse threw me off and ran away, and I could not catch him. He has my blankets on the saddle."

He got off his horse and went into the lodge, and found the Cheyenne woman there. He said to her: "Hurry now, and get your things. I have hidden my horse in the timber down the creek, and you can get on him and go home. I will go with you and show you where the horse is. I have told these people a lie. I said my horse had thrown me off. I have a horse here, and I will get on him and ride down the creek a little way. Do you come on as soon as you can. I will wait for you."

He rode away out of sight of the camp, and stopped there and waited. Pretty soon he saw the woman coming, and at last she reached him. He said to her, "Jump up behind me quickly, before anyone sees you"; and they went on down the creek to where the horse was tied. Then he said to her: "Now tie your things on that saddle. There is my blanket. Take it. Get on now, and take this horse also, and lead him, so you will have two. You must go fast. I will go back to the camp, and will say that my horse has run off and I cannot find him; and when I look for the horses in the morning, I will tell them there is another one lost."

The woman started and traveled and traveled. When she got too tired, she got off and unsaddled, and let her horses feed. She went on and on, until she had passed the Pumpkin Buttes; then she made a camp and lay down and slept. That night her horses got frightened, and broke their ropes, and both of them ran off. She made up a bundle of her things, and started on afoot. All that day she walked on, frightened, and crying all the time. That night she lay down and went to sleep, and at daylight she started on again.

She had gone only a little way when she happened to look back, and there following close behind her was a great big bear. That frightened her still more, and she began to run, crying as she ran. She ran until she was exhausted and could go no further, and still the bear kept just about the same distance from her. At last she turned about and talked to the bear. She called him by name, saying: "O Bear, take pity on me. I am a poor woman, and am trying to get back to my own people." Then she would hurry on a little further, and turn around and talk to him again in the same way. At last she was so tired that she determined that she must sit down and rest, even if the bear should kill her.

She did so, and she was so tired that notwithstanding her fear of the bear she fell asleep at once. While she was lying there asleep, the bear spoke to her. She could hear his voice when he said: "Get up and go on to your people. I am following you only to watch and protect you. I am following you, stepping in your tracks, so the enemy cannot trail you."

After a time the woman got up and started on. The bear was sitting close to her looking at her; and even though he had spoken to her in this way she was still afraid of him. She walked on until it was a long time after dark, and then she lay down and went to sleep.

In the morning, when it was light enough to see, she got up and looked about her, and there, a little way off on top of a small butte, she saw the bear sitting. She started on her way, and as soon as she moved off, the bear came down from the place she had left, and followed in her tracks. That night she ate her last piece of meat, a very small one. Early the next day she reached the Platte River. The stream was full from bank to bank. She sat down on a hill a little way from the river, and looked and thought and thought, to see if there might be any way by which she could cross. She said, "If I were only on the other side now; but how can I ever get there?"

While she was sitting there, the bear came up and walked in front of her. Then he turned about and backed toward her. She could not think what he wanted. She turned aside to get away from him, but he walked around in front of her, and backed up to her as before. He did not speak. Suddenly she thought to herself: "I wonder if he does not want me to get on him and ride him. Now I will get up and go down to the river bank, and sit down close by the edge of the water, and see what he does." She walked down, and sat down close to the bank, and the bear came after her and got in front of her, and backed up toward her. He kept looking back at her over his shoulder, as if to see what she was doing. The woman said to herself: "I think he wants to carry me across the river. I believe I will get on him and try what he will do." Then she said aloud, "Bear, I am going to get on your back, if you will take me across the river." She prepared herself, and tied up her blanket. Then she crawled on his back, and put her arms around his neck, just in front of his shoulders. He looked back as if to see if she were ready, and then he gave a snort and jumped into the water. She held firmly to him, and he swam strongly, and took her safe across to the other side.

When she got off his back, the bear shook the water from himself and rolled on the ground, and the woman started on, and the bear followed her as before. She walked on and walked on, and at last got tired and sat down to rest. She looked around and saw that the bear had stopped close to her and then he sat down. She was feeling very tired and hungry, and she said, "Oh, I am hungry, and I am tired, and I think I shall starve to death before ever I get to my people." Then the bear spoke and said: "You will get there. Go on." She got up and started on, the bear following behind her. The woman walked and walked until she was very tired, and again she stopped to rest, sitting down on a little hill. Just beyond the hill was a creek, and along the creek were many buffalo. The woman said, "There are buffalo, but I cannot get any to eat."

The bear said to her: "Sister, you shall eat. Stay where you are until I go and kill a buffalo." The bear went down into the timber in the creek, where the buffalo were. He crept about for some little time, and at length he got close to a yearling and jumped on it, caught it, bit it, and killed it. The buffalo then all ran away, and the woman arose and went down to see what had happened.

When she got there, she found what the bear had killed, and saw him sitting on the ground a little way from it. She skinned and cut up the buffalo, and took her flint and steel and made a fire, and cooked and ate. While she was doing this, the bear went up to the top of a high hill and sat there watching.

When the woman had finished eating, she took what meat she could carry, and made a pack of it and put it on her back. "Now," she said, "I will leave the rest of this meat for the bear. Let him come down and eat it." She started on, and when she started, the bear came down and ate of what she had left. After he had eaten he followed on, and soon overtook her. They traveled on all that day, and at night she camped, cooked, and ate. She took a piece of meat out a little way from the camp and put it down on the ground, and the bear came and got it. He would not come up close to her and eat.

The next morning they set out again, and traveled all day, and then camped. The bear followed her all the time. The fourth morning she started on again. About noon that day they came to a hill, and from it she could see the

Laramie River. There she saw a big village—many lodges. She said, "There are many people, but I do not know whether they are my people or not." The bear went up close to her and said: "Those are your people. Go now into the camp, and I will go down into the thick timber below the camp. Go to your people and tell them that I brought you home safe. I want you to get a fat buffalo hump and have it cut into four pieces, and send it to me to eat. I will wait for it in the timber below the camp."

The woman went on into the camp, and when they saw her, all her relations were glad. She told the people that the bear had brought her home in safety, and that he was in the timber and wanted a fat buffalo hump. They got the hump, cut it into four pieces, and her relations and many other people in the camp went down to the timber. They took with them a fine robe, great strings of beads, and nice feathers. They found the bear there and gave him the meat, put the robe over him, and hung the strings of beads about his neck. Then they went away and left him.

HOW DEVILS TOWER CAME TO BE

 DEVILS Tower, a stunning landmark near Sundance, Wyoming, is a unique geological formation. It formed 60 million years ago by an upwelling of molten rock from beneath the earth's crust that cooled and solidified before reaching the surface; in the intervening eons, the softer earth around it eroded away, leaving an 865-foot tall, stump-shaped, columnar rock tower.

Or so says science. Here are three Native American legends on how the massive Devils Tower really came into being. The first two versions, Kiowa and Cheyenne legends, were reported by historian Ray H. Mattison in Devils Tower National Monument—A History *(Sundance, Wyoming: Devils Tower Natural History Association, 1973). The third tale, from the Sioux people, is taken from* Indian Legends from the Northern Rockies *by Ella E. Clark (Norman: University of Oklahoma Press, 1966).*

▼▼▼▼

Kiowa Legend by Mattison

ALL who have seen the gigantic stump-like formation, known as Devils Tower, rising some 1,200 feet above the Belle Fourche River, will understand why it inspired the imagination of the Indians. They called it Mateo Tepee, meaning Grizzly Bear Lodge, and had several legends regarding its origin. According to the Kiowas, who at one time are reputed to have lived in the region, their tribe once camped in a stream where there were many bears. One day seven little girls were playing at a distance from the village and were chased by some bears. The girls ran toward the village and when the bears were about to catch them, they jumped to a low rock about three feet in height. One of them prayed to the rock, "Rock, take pity on us—Rock, save us." The rock heard them and began to elongate itself upwards, pushing the children higher and higher out of reach of the bears. When the bears jumped at them they scratched the rock, broke their claws and fell back upon the ground. The rock continued to push the children upward into the sky while the bears jumped at them. The children are still in the sky, seven little stars in a group (the Pleiades). According to the legend, the marks of the bears' claws may be seen on the side of the rock.

Cheyenne Legend by Mattison

The Cheyenne version of the origin of the Tower is somewhat different. According to their legend, there were seven brothers. When the wife of the oldest brother went out to fix the smoke wings of her tipi, a big bear carried her away to his cave. Her husband mourned her loss deeply and would go out and cry defiantly to the bear. The youngest of the brothers was a medicine man and had great powers. He told the oldest one to go out and make a bow and four blunt arrows. Two arrows were to be painted red and set with eagle feathers; the other two were to be painted black and set with buzzard feathers. The youngest brother then took the bow and small arrows, told the older brothers to fill their quivers with arrows and they all went out after the big bear. At the entrance of the cave, the younger brother told the others to sit down and wait. He then turned himself into a gopher and dug a big hole in the bear's den. When he crawled in he found the bear lying with his head on the woman's lap. He then put the bear to sleep and changed himself back into an Indian. He then had the woman crawl back to the entrance where the six brothers were waiting. Then the hole closed up. After the Indians hurried away, the bear awoke. He started after them taking all the bears of which he was the leader.

The Indians finally came to the place where Devils Tower now stands. The youngest boy always carried a small rock in his hand. He told his six brothers and the woman to close their eyes. He sang a song. When he had finished the rock had grown. He sang four times and when he had finished singing the rock was as high as it is today. When the bears reached the Tower, the brothers killed all the bears except the leader, who kept jumping against the rock. His claws made the marks that are on the rock today. The youngest brother then shot two black arrows and a red arrow without effect. His last arrow killed the bear. The youngest brother then made a noise like a bald eagle. Four eagles came. They took hold of the eagles' legs and were carried to the ground.

Sioux Legend by Clark

The Devils Tower is the chief feature in Devils Tower National Monument, which is located in the northeast corner of Wyoming. The Tower rises 1,280 feet above the bed of the Belle Fourche River and about 865 feet above its apparent base.

Considered "a geological mystery," it looks like a "huge, fluted monumental shaft set upon a mound." At its base are fragments of fallen columns.

The Sioux Indians used to say that the Thunderbird takes his gigantic drums to the top of the Tower, beats them, and thus causes the noise of thunder and the storms that follow.

Chief Sitting Bull is said to have gone near it for supernatural power and to have received assurance from the spirits there that he would be victorious in one of his biggest campaigns.

The Sioux called the Tower *Mateo Tipi,* meaning "Grizzly Bear's Lodge," and related the following legend about it. The Kiowa Indians, who, according to their traditions, once lived along the Montana-Wyoming border, also had a legend about the Tower: the seven little girls who climbed the rock became the stars we know as the Pleiades. The Cheyennes related a very different story about the Tower.

One day in early summer, three girls went out on the prairie to pick flowers. Just as they were starting home, they were frightened by three bears. They ran to the top of the nearest rock, which at that time was only a few feet above the ground. The bears also started to climb the rock.

Frightened still more, the girls called on the spirits for help, and the spirits caused the rock to grow. Higher and higher it rose. Again and again the bears tried to reach the top where the girls were, but the surface was so smooth and the rock so steep that they could make no headway. At last the three bears were so tired that they could try no longer. They fell down the giant rock and were killed on the broken rocks at its base.

The three girls, safe at the top of the column, had watched all the actions of the bears. When they saw that the bodies moved no more, the girls took the flowers they had gathered and braided them into a rope. This they fastened to the top of the rock and then, one by one, they climbed down the rope and reached the ground.

This happened a long time ago, but on the sides of the Grizzly Bear's lodge you can still see the marks of the bear's claws. They were made while the three bears were struggling to reach the three girls on the top of the rock.

THE BEAR MAN

 THIS folktale comes from George Bird Grinnell's Pawnee Hero Stories and Folk Tales, *first published in 1889. In a prefatory note, Grinnell writes that after he explained to Eagle Chief, of the Pawnee Agency in the Indian Territory, that he had come to write a book about "how things used to be in the olden times," the Chief considered and answered, " It is good and it is time. Already the old things are being lost, and those who knew the secrets are many of them dead. If we had known how to write, we would have put all these things down, and they would not have been forgotten, but we could not write, and these stories were handed down from one to another. The old men told their grandchildren, and they told their grandchildren, and so the secrets and the stories and the doings of long ago have been handed down. It may be that they have changed as they passed from father to son, and it is well that they should be put down, so that our children, when they are like the white people, can know what were their fathers' ways." Grinnell, too, felt strongly "when [the old men] shall die much of the unwritten lore will perish too, for with them will cease that sympathetic and perfect credence, which alone gives to folk-lore vitality and lastingness."*

"The Bear Man" illustrates the profound spiritual life of the Pawnees and the role of the animals that shared their grassland home as helpers, as intermediators, as fellow beings endowed with "intelligence, knowledge and power far beyond those of man." The man in the story lived with the bears until he "had come to understand all their ways" and they had "taught him everything that they knew." We recommend the book in its entirety for its evocation of the Pawnee people through their stories as recorded accurately by Grinnell and through his 200 pages of notes about their origins, relationships, customs, daily lives, warfare, religion, and recent history as of 1889.

▼▼▼▼

THERE was once a young boy, who, when he was playing with his fellows, used often to imitate the ways of a bear, and to pretend that he was one. The boys did not know much about bears. They only knew that there were such animals.

Now, it had happened that before this boy was born his mother had been left alone at home, for his father had gone on the warpath toward the enemy, and this was about five or six months before the babe would be born. As the man was going on the warpath, he came upon a little bear cub, very small, whose mother had gone away; and he caught it. He did not want to kill it because it was so young and helpless. It seemed to him like a little child. It looked up to him, and cried after him, because it knew no better; and he hated to kill it or to leave it there. After he had thought about this for a while, he put a string around its neck and tied some medicine smoking stuff, Indian tobacco, to it, and said, *"Pi-rau'*—child, you are a *Nahu'rac; Ti-ra'-wa* made you, and takes care of you. He will look after you, but I put these things about your neck to show that I have good feelings toward you. I hope that when my child is born, the *Nahu'rac* will take care of him, and see that he grows up a good man, and I hope that *Ti-ra'-wa* will take care of you and of mine." He looked at the little bear for quite a long time, and talked to it, and then he went on his way.

When he returned to the village from his warpath, he told his wife about the little bear, and how he had looked at it and talked to it.

When his child was born it had all the ways of a bear. So it is among the Pawnees. A woman, before her child is born, must not look hard at any animal, for the child may be like it. There was a woman in the Kit-ke-hahk'-i band, who caught a rabbit, and, because it was gentle and soft, she took it up in her hands and held it before her face and petted it, and when her child was born it had a split nose, like a rabbit. This man is still alive.

This boy, who was like a bear, as he grew up, had still more the ways of a bear. Often he would go off by himself, and try to pray to the bear, because he felt like a bear. He used to say, in a joking way, to the other young men, that he could make himself a bear.

After he had come to be a man, he started out once on the warpath with a party of about thirty-five others. He was the leader of the party. They went away up on the Running Water, and before they had come to any village, they were discovered by Sioux. The enemy pursued them, and surrounded them, and fought with them. The Pawnees were overpowered, their enemies were so many, and all were killed.

The country where this took place is rocky, and much cedar grows there. Many bears lived there. The battle was fought in the morning; and the Pawnees were all killed in a hollow. Right after the fight, in the afternoon, two bears came traveling along by this place. When they came to the spot where the Pawnees had been killed, they found one of the bodies, and the she bear recognized it as that of the boy who was like a bear. She called to the he bear, and said, "Here is the man that was very good to us. He often sacrificed smokes to us, and every time he ate he used always to take a piece of food and give it to us, saying, 'Here is something for you to eat. Eat this.' Here is the one that always imitated us, and sung about us, and talked about us. Can you do anything for him ?" The he bear said, "I fear I cannot do it. I have not the power, but I will try. I can do anything if the sun is shining. I seem to have more power when the sun is shining on me." That day it was cloudy and cold and snowing. Every now and then the clouds would pass, and the sun come out for a little while, and then the clouds would cover it up again.

The man was all cut up, pretty nearly hacked in small pieces, for he was the bravest of all. The two bears gathered up the pieces of the man, and put them together, and then the he bear lay down and took the man on his breast, and the she bear lay on top of it to warm the body. They worked over it with their medicine, and every now and then the he bear would cry out, and say, "*A-tí-us*—Father, help me. I wish the sun was shining." After a while the dead body grew warm, and then began to breathe a little. It was still all cut up, but it began to have life. Pretty soon the man began to move, and to come to life, and then he became conscious and had life.

When he came to himself and opened his eyes he was in the presence of two bears. The he bear spoke to him, and said, "It is not through me that you are living. It was the she bear who asked for help for you, and had you brought back to life. Now, you are not yet whole and well. You must come away with us, and live with us for a time, until all your wounds are healed." The bears took him away with them. But the man was very weak, and every now and then, as they were going along, he would faint and fall down; but still they would help him up and support him; and they took him along with them, until they came to a cave in the rocks among the cedars, which was their home. When he entered the cave, he found there their young ones that they had left behind when they started out.

The man was all cut up and gashed. He had also been scalped, and had no hair on his head. He lived with the bears until he was quite healed of his wounds, and also had come to understand all their ways. The two old bears taught him everything that they knew. The he bear said to him, "None of all the beings and animals that roam over the country are as great and as wise as the bears. No animal is equal to us. When we get hungry, we go out and kill something and eat it. I did not make the wisdom that I have. I am an animal, and I look to one above. He made me, and he made me to be great. I am made to live here and to be great, but still there will be an end to my days, as with all of us that *Ti-rá-wa* has created upon this earth. I am going to make you a great man; but you must not deceive yourself. You must not think that I am great, or can do great things of myself. You must always look up above for the giver of all power. You shall be great in war and great in wealth.

"Now you are well, and I shall take you back to your home, and after this I want you to imitate us. This shall be a part of your greatness. I shall look after you. I shall give to you a part of myself. If I am killed, you shall be killed. If I grow old, you shall be old.

"I want you to look at one of the trees that *Ti-rá-wa* made in this earth, and place your dependence on it. *Ti-rá-wa* made this tree (pointing to a cedar). It never gets old. It is always green and young. Take notice of this tree, and always have it with you; and when you are in the lodge and it thunders and lightens, throw some of it on the fire and let the smoke rise. Hold that fast."

The he bear took the skin of a bear, and made a cap for him, to hide his naked skull. His wounds were now all healed, and he was well and strong. The man's people had nearly forgotten him, it had been so long ago, and they had supposed that the whole party had been killed.

Soon after this the he bear said, "Now we will take that journey." They started, and went to the village, and waited near it till it was night. Then the bear said to him, "Go into the village, and tell your father that you are here. Then get for me a piece of buffalo meat, and a blue bead, and some Indian tobacco, and some sweet smelling clay."

The man went into the village, and his father was very much surprised, and very glad to see him again. He got the presents, and brought them to the bear, and gave them to him, and the bear talked to him.

When they were about to part, the bear came up to him, and put his arms about him, and hugged him, and put his mouth against the man's mouth, and said, "As the fur that I am in has touched you it will make you great, and this will be a blessing to you." His paws were around the man's shoulders, and he drew them down his arms, until they came to his hands, and he held them, and said, "As my hands have touched your hands, they are made great, not to fear anything. I have rubbed my hands down over you, so that you shall be as tough as I am. Because my mouth has touched your mouth you shall be made wise." Then he left him, and went away.

So this man was the greatest of all warriors, and was brave. He was like a bear. He originated the bear dance which still exists among the tribe of Pawnees. He came to be an old man, and at last died of old age. I suspect the old bear died at the same time.

THE MEDICINE GRIZZLY BEAR

 HERE is yet another tale recorded directly from its Native American storytellers by George Bird Grinnell. Although Grinnell's name is associated with Western ethnography, natural history, and conservation, it also often touched on the history of grizzly bears in the Northern Plains and Rockies. The grizzly bear tales collected here from his publications were among scores of stories that might have been lost forever without his lifetime efforts to record and publish them. Grinnell first visited the West in 1870 (after graduating from Yale University) and was part of an expedition to Yellowstone in 1875. From 1876 until 1911 he managed Forest and Stream, *a sporting magazine credited with organizing hunters, spreading a "sportsmen's code," and pressing for responsible game laws and wildlife protection, which benefited grizzly bears as well as numerous other species. In the 1880s, he was one of the founders of the Audubon Society and the Boone and Crockett Club, a sportsmen's organization that was one of the early prime movers for wildlife conservation. (Theodore Roosevelt, whose name is closely associated with bears and Yellowstone, was another founder of the Boone and Crockett Club.) Grinnell was also a staunch supporter of the national parks, which, particularly in the case of Yellowstone, have been instrumental in maintaining grizzly bear populations to the present. Along with Enos Mills (author of "New Environments"), he was instrumental in creating Glacier National Park, another haven for grizzlies. He was truly a remarkable man whose vision, intellect, and life's work kept alive much of what we today in the West cherish—including grizzly bears and their lore.*

This story first captivated readers in April, 1901, in Harper's Monthly Magazine *(v. 102, pp. 736-744). The grizzly bear in this story is a source of power and wisdom.*

▼▼▼▼

A long time ago there lived in a camp of Pawnees a certain poor boy. His father had only one pony. Once he had been a leading man in the tribe, but now he seemed to be unlucky. When he went on the war-path he brought back nothing, and when he fought he did nothing, and the people did not now look up to him.

There was a chief's son who loved the poor boy, and these two went together all the time. They were like brothers; they used to hunt together and go courting together, and when they were travelling, the poor boy often rode one of the ponies of the chief's son, and the latter used to go to the poor boy's lodge and sleep there with him.

Once the camp went off to hunt buffalo, and the poor boy and the chief's son rode together all the time. After the people had made camp at a certain place, the chiefs decided to stop here for four days, because the buffalo were close by, and they could kill plenty and dry the meat here. North of the camp was a hill on which grew many cedar-trees, and during the day the poor boy had overheard people saying that many Indians had been killed on that hill, among those trees. They said that no one ought to go there, for it was a dangerous place.

That night the chief's son went over to his friend's lodge to sleep there, but before they went to bed he left the lodge for a time, and while he was gone the poor boy, as he sat there waiting, began to think about himself and how unhappy he was. He remembered how poor he and his father were, and how everybody looked down on them and despised them, and it did not seem to him that things would ever be any better for them than they were now. For a long time he sat there thinking about all these things, and the more he thought of them the worse they seemed, and at last he felt that he was no longer glad to live, and he made up his mind to go up into those cedars.

He went out of the lodge and started to go up toward the trees. It was bright moonlight, so that he could see well. Just before he reached the edge of the timber he crossed a ravine, and saw there many skeletons of people who had been killed. The ground was white with these bones. He went on into the cedars, and came to a ravine leading up the hill, and followed it. As he went on he saw before him a trail and followed it, and when he came to the head of the ravine there was a big hole in the bank, and the trail led to it. He stopped for a moment when he came to this hole, but then he went in, and when he had entered he saw there, sitting by the fire, a big she-bear and some little cubs.

As the boy stood there looking at her, the she-bear said to him: "I am sorry that you have come here. My husband is the one who kills persons and brings them here for the children and me to eat. You had better go back to your people quickly, or he will eat you up. He has gone hunting, but he will soon be back again. If he finds you here, he will kill you."

The poor boy said: "Well, I came here on purpose to be killed, and I give myself up to you. I shall be glad to be eaten by you. I am here ready to be killed. I am yours. Take me."

The she-bear said: "Oh, I wish I could do something to save you, but I cannot. He's one of those bad bears—a grizzly—medicine. I can do nothing for you, but I will try. As soon as you hear any noise outside—any one coming—pick up that cub, the littlest one, and hold it in your arms. When he comes in he will tell you to put it down, but do not do so. Hold it tight; he loves that one best of all."

All at once the boy heard outside the cave the noise of a bear snorting and grunting. The she-bear said, "Pick up the cub, quick; he is coming." The boy caught up the little bear, and held it tight to his breast. All at once the noise came to the mouth of the den and stopped. It was the Bear. The boy could hear him talking. He said: "Here! somebody has been about my house. I smell human beings. Yes, he even came in. Where is he? Let me see him, so that I may jump upon him and kill him." When he came in he saw the boy, and seemed very angry. He stood up on his hind feet and threw up his hands, and then came down again and struck his paws on the ground, and then rose up and snorted "*whoof,*" and blew out red dust from his nostrils, and then came down and jumped about, and sometimes sprang toward the boy, as though he were going to seize him. He was very terrible, and the boy was very much afraid.

The Bear called out to the boy in a loud voice: "How dare you take up my child and hold it? Let it go, or I will tear you to pieces and eat you." But the boy still held the cub. No matter what the Bear said or what he did, the boy held fast to the cub.

When the Bear saw that the boy would not let the cub go, he became quiet, and no longer seemed angry. He said: "Boy, you are my son. Put down your brother, for now he is your brother. He shall go with you, he shall be your companion, and shall be with you always as your guide and helper. He has told me your story, and how you are poor, unhappy, and now he has kept you from being eaten up. I have taken pity on you, and we will send you back to your people, where you may do some good among them. My son, I am at the head of all these animal lodges, down at Pahuk and at Pahur and everywhere else. I am at the head; there is no animal living that is stronger than I; none that I cannot kill. If a man shoots at me, I make the arrow to fall from my skin without hurting me. Look up around my lodge. See these arrows, these guns, these leggings, these beads, and the medicine that men have brought, thinking to kill me; but I have killed them, and have taken these things, and keep them here.

"I knew that your people were coming to this place to hunt. I drove the buffalo over, so that the people should stop here and hunt and kill meat, in order so you might come to my lodge. I know all your feelings. I know that you are sorry for your poor father, my brother, and I wished you to come here, so I might make you my son and give my power to you, so you may become a great man among your people. I know that they are now killing buffalo, and that they will be camped here for four days.

"Now, my son, set your brother free. All the power that I have I give to you. I shall kill my son, your little brother there, and give you his skin to keep and to carry away with you, so that he may be your companion and may be with you always. Your brother, your friend at the camp, is looking for you, mourning for you, for he thinks you dead, but to-morrow night you shall see him, and shall tell him to rejoice for you and not to mourn. You shall tell him where you have been."

The little bear that he was holding said to the boy: "It is all right now, brother; put me down. My father means what he says. I am glad that I am going to be with you, my brother." The boy put him down.

Then the Bear said to his wife: " Get up. Take that gun." The she-bear took the gun, and they walked around the fireplace in a circle, and sang, and the boy looked on. The Bear took the gun and told the boy to look at them, and to watch carefully everything that they did. After a little he stopped, and shot his wife, and she fell down dead. Then he put down the gun, and went to the she-bear and put his mouth on the wound, and breathed on it and snorted *"whoof,"* and sucked in his breath and took the bullet out, and went around the lodge, singing and making motions, and then he took hold of the she-bear and lifted her to her feet, and supported her, and pushed her around, and helped her, and at last she walked, and was well. Then he called the boy to him and said, "Now I will do the same thing to you." And he did the same thing to the boy, and brought him to life in the same way. Then he said, "That is one power I give you to-night."

Then he gave the gun to the boy and went to the other side of the lodge, and sat up, and said, "Now I will open my mouth, and you shoot me right in the mouth." He opened his mouth, and the boy shot him, and he fell over. After a moment he got up on his feet and slapped his paws on his chest several times, and the bullet came out of his mouth; and he walked around the fireplace two or three times, and made motions and grunted, and then he was well. Then he took the boy in his arms, and hugged him and kissed him and breathed on him, and said: "Now I give you my power. Go over there and I will shoot you as you shot me. Do just as I did." The boy went over there, and the Bear shot him, and the boy did just as the Bear had done, and made himself well.

The Bear then put an arrow in the gun and shot it at the boy, and when the smoke cleared away the boy found the arrow fast in his throat, the feather end sticking out. The Bear took it out and made him well, and gave him also this power. Then the Bear told him to load the gun with a ball and to shoot it at him, and he did so, and shot the Bear, but the lead was made flat and dropped to the ground. The bullet did not go into the Bear.

The Bear now told the boy to take the bow and arrow and to shoot at him with all his strength. The boy did this, but the arrow did not go through the Bear, but the spike rolled up and the shaft was split. The Bear said: "Now you see, my son, that the gun and the bow, the bullet and the arrow, cannot harm me. You shall have the same power. When you go into battle you shall not carry a gun nor arrows, for they are not mine, but you shall take this paint, and put it all over your body, then put this feather on your head and take this club, which is part of my jawbone. All these things have my power and medicine. When you are carrying these things your enemy cannot hurt you, even if you run right on to him; but with one stroke of this club you shall kill your enemy."

The next morning the Bear took the boy out on the prairie and showed him the different roots and leaves of medicines, and told him how to use them; how he should eat some medicine and then he could cure the wounded by just breathing on the wound.

That night the Bear said to him: "Hereafter you shall have the same feelings as the bear. When you get angry, you will have a grunt like a bear; and if you get too fierce, tushes [tusks] like a bear's will stick out of your mouth, so that the people will know that you are very angry. You shall have my power, and you can go into any of the lodges of the animals, of which I am the chief." And he told him how to get into these lodges.

That day they staid in the Bear's lodge, and the Bear took the claw off from his little finger and gave it and a little bundle of medicine to the boy. He said, "Take this claw and this bundle of medicine and put them on a string and wear them on your neck always, the claw hanging in front." He taught him how to make plums grow on trees, and how to make ground-cherries come out of his mouth.

That night he sent the boy back to the camp. He said: "Tell your father and mother not to mourn for you, for you will return in two days more. I have driven plenty of buffalo to this place, and they will kill them and dry the meat. Now go to the camp and get a pipe and some tobacco, and bring them here."

The boy went back to the camp. When he went into the lodge his father and mother were glad to see him. He told them not to be anxious about him, and not to say anything about his having been away. Then he went out and found his brother, the chief's son, asleep. He said to him: "Wake up, brother. I want you to get some tobacco and a pipe from your father. Tell no one that it is for me. Bring it here. I want to smoke with you. I am going away again, but you must stay in camp. I will he back in a few days." The chief's son got the things and gave them to the boy. He wanted to go with him, but the poor boy would not let him.

That same night the boy went back to the Bear's den, carrying with him the pipe and tobacco. After he went into the lodge he filled his pipe and lighted it, and he and the Bear smoked together. The Bear said to him: "After you have gone home, whenever you smoke, always point your pipe toward my den and ask me to smoke with you. After lighting your pipe, point it first to Atíus Tiráwat, and then blow a few whiffs to me. Then I shall know that you still remember me. All my power comes from Atíus. He made me. There will be an end to my days as there is to those of every mortal. So long as I live I shall protect you; when I die of old age, you shall die too."

After this he said, "Now bring my youngest boy here." The boy brought the little cub, and the Bear said, "Now kill him." The boy hesitated to do this. He did not want to kill the little bear, but it said to him: "Go on, my brother, kill me. After this I am going to be a spirit, and always to be with you." Then the boy killed him, and skinned him, and tanned his hide. After it was tanned he put come red medicine paint on the hide. When this was done the Bear told him to put his paint, his feathers, and his war-club in this hide, and to wrap them up and make a bundle of them. Then he said: "Now, my son, go to your people, and when you get home hang your bundle up at the back of the lodge, and let the people know nothing of all this. Keep it secret. Wherever you go, or wherever you are, I shall be with you."

The boy went home to the camp, and told his mother to hang up his bundle, as the Bear had said. Next morning he was in camp and all the people saw him. They were surprised, for they had thought that he had been killed. By this time the Pawnees had all the buffalo they wanted, and the next day they started back to their village.

After they had reached their home, the boy told the chief's son that he wanted him to go off with him on the war-path. His brother said: "It is good. I will go." The poor boy took his bundle, and they started. After travelling many days they came to a camp of the enemy. They went into the village in the daytime, and took many horses and started away with them, riding hard. Soon the enemy pursued them, and at length they could see them coming, and it seemed as if they must soon overtake them. Then the poor boy got off his horse and stopped, telling his brother to go on, driving the horses.

The boy had painted himself red over his whole body. He held his war-club in his hand, and had his feather tied on his head and the little bear-skin on his hack. The enemy soon came up and tried to kill him, but they could not. He would run after one and kill him, and all the others would shoot at him with their arrows, but they could not hurt him, and at last they left him and went back, and he went on and overtook the chief's son. Then his brother saw that he had great power. After this they travelled on slowly, and at last reached the village. His brother told the people that this man was powerful, that they had taken the horses in broad daylight, and the young man had staid behind on foot and fought the enemy off, while he drove on the horses.

A few days after they reached home a war-party of the enemy

attacked the village. All the Pawnees went out to fight them, but the poor boy staid behind in the lodge. He took down his bundle, filled the pipe, and pointed it first to Atíus, and then toward the Bear's lodge, and smoked. Then he took the paint and mixed it with grease, and rubbed it all over his body except his face: that he painted black. Then he put the feather on his head and the little bear-robe on his back, and took his war-club in his hand and started out. The Bear had told him that in going into battle he must never start toward the east, but must attack going toward the west. So he went around, and came on the battle-field from one side.

As he came up he saw that his people were having a hard time, and were being driven back. There was one of the enemy who seemed to be the bravest of all. The poor boy rushed at this man and killed him with his club, and then ran back to his own line. When his people looked at him, and saw that it was really the poor boy who had just done so brave a deed, they knew that what the chief's son had said was true. When he started again to rush toward the enemy's line, all the Pawnees followed him. He ran among the enemy, and with his club killed one here and one there, and the enemy became afraid and ran, and the Pawnees followed and killed many of them. That night they returned to the village, rejoicing over the victory. Everybody was praising the young man. Old men were calling his name, young women were singing about him, and old women dancing before him. People no longer made fun of his father or mother, or of him. Now they looked upon him as a great and powerful person.

The Bear had told him that when he wanted his name changed he must call himself Ku ruks la war uks ti, Medicine Bear.

That night the Bear came to the boy in his sleep and spoke to him. He said: "My son, to-morrow the chief of the tribe is going to ask you to take his daughter for your wife, but you must not do this yet. I wish you to wait until you have done certain things. If you take a wife before that time, your power will go from you."

The next day the chief came to Medicine Bear and asked him to marry his daughter, and told him the people wanted him to be their head chief. He refused.

Some time after this all the different tribes that had been attacked by him joined forces and came down together to fight the Pawnees. All the people went out to meet them, but he staid in his lodge and painted himself, and put his feather in his head and the bear-claw on his neck and his bear-skin on his back, and smoked as he always did, and took his club and went out. When he came to the battle, the Pawnees were having a hard time, because the enemy were so many. Medicine Bear charged, and killed a man, and then came back, and the second time he charged the people charged all together, following him, and they killed many and drove the enemy off, and those who had the fastest horses were the only ones who got away. The Pawnees went home to the village. Everybody rejoiced, and there were many scalp-dances. Now the poor boy was more highly thought of than ever. Even the chiefs bowed their heads when they saw him. They could not equal him. This time he called himself Ku ruks ti carish, Angry Bear.

After the excitement had quieted down, one day the head chief said: "Medicine Bear, in all this tribe there is no chief who is equal to you. Sit down by my daughter. Take her for your wife, and take my place as chief. I and my wife will go out of this lodge, and it shall be yours. You shall be the chief of the tribe. Whatever you say we will abide by." The poor boy said: "My father, I will think about this. By morning I will let you know." In the night, before he slept, he filled the pipe and smoked as the Bear had told him to do, and then he went to bed. In dreams the Bear said to him: "My son, you have done what I wished you to do. Now the power will remain with you as long as you shall live. Now you can marry, if you will."

But the boy was not yet ready to do this. The girl was very pretty, and he liked her, but he felt that before he married there were still some things that he must do. He called his brother and said to him, "Go, kill the fattest of the buffalo; bring it to me, and I will take a long journey with you."

His brother went hunting and killed a buffalo, and brought the meat home, and they dried it and made a bundle of it. Medicine Bear told his brother to carry this bundle and a rawhide rope and a little hatchet, and they started on a journey toward the Missouri River. One day toward evening they reached the river, and they found themselves on top of a steep-cut bluff. The river ran at its foot. The poor boy cut a cottonwood pole and drove it into the ground, and tied the rope to it, and then tied the other end of the rope about his brother's body. Then he sharpened a stick and gave it to his brother and said: "Now take the bundle of meat, and I will let you down over the bank. You must put the meat on a ledge of the cliff, and when the birds come you must feed them. Give a piece to the first one that comes, and then take your sharp stick and get another piece, and so feed all the birds. They are the ones that have power, and they can take pity on you." So he let the chief's son down.

The first bird that came was a buzzard, then an eagle, then hawks and owls, all kinds of birds that kill their prey. He fed them all. While he was doing this, the poor boy was above lying on top of the bank. Late in the afternoon, as the sun was going down, he saw, far up the river, what looked like a flock of geese coming. They came nearer and nearer, and at last passed out of sight under the bank. Afterward, when he looked down on the river, he could see in the water red light as if it were all on fire, and as he lay on the bank he could hear down below him the sound of drumming and singing just as plain as could be, and all the time the chief's son was hanging there in front of the bank, and the poor boy would call down to him to cry and ask the animals to take pity on him. When Medicine Bear had done this, he started back and went home, leaving the chief's son hanging there.

The chief's son staid there all the night and all the next day, and for three days and nights, and on the night of the fourth day he fell asleep. When he awoke he was in a lodge. It was under the Missouri River. When he looked about him, he saw that those in the lodge were all animals. There was the beaver, there was the otter, two buffalo, the antelope, hawks, owls, ermines, bears, frogs, woodpeckers, catfish—all kinds of animals. On each side of the lodge was a little pool, and in each pool sat a goose, and every time they sang, the geese would shake their wings on the water, and it sounded just like drumming. The chief of the animals spoke to him, saying: "My son, at this time we can do nothing for you. We must first send our messenger up to the Bear's lodge to ask him what we may do for you." While he was saying this the Bear's servant entered the lodge and said: "My father, it is all right. Our father the Bear told me to say to you that his son has sent this young man to you, and you must exert all your power for him."

Now the animals began to make ready to use their power to help the chief's son. First the Beaver talked to the young man, to tell him of his powers and his ways, so he might perform wonderful acts. How he should take the branch of a tree and strike a man with its point and it would go through him, and then how to draw it out and to make the man well again. He gave him the power to do this. He taught him how to take a stick two feet long and swallow it, and then take it out again from his throat, and gave him this power.

The Otter gave him the power, if his enemies ever attacked him, to break their arrows with his teeth and shoot back the shaft without a spike, and if he hit an enemy with the shaft, it would kill him. "The poison from your mouth will kill him," he said.

The Ground-dog said: "My son, here is my little one. I give him to you. Take him, and if you have an enemy among the doctors in your tribe, take this little one down to the water early in the morning and dip his nose in the water, and when you take it out it will have a piece of liver in its mouth. The man who has tried to kill you will be found dead."

The Owl said: "My son, I give you power to see in the night. When you go on the war-path and want to take horses, the night will be like daytime for you."

The Hawk said: "My son, I give you power to run swiftly, and I give you my war-club, which is my wing. You shall strike your enemy with it only once, and the blow shall kill him. Take also this little black rope; you shall use it when you go on the war-path to catch horses. Take also this scalp which you see hanging down from my claw. You shall be a great man for scalping."

Each of the other animals gave him all his kinds of power.

For two days and two nights they taught him the kinds of power, and for two days and two nights they taught him the kinds of roots and herbs for healing the sick. They said to him: "You shall be the great doctor of your people. Every now and then you must bring us tobacco, so that we can smoke." They further told him that at this time they could teach him only a little, but that afterward, one at a time, they would meet him out on the prairie, and would teach him more. At last they said: "Now it is time for you to go. Your friend has come, and is waiting for you out on the prairie."

The Buffalo now stood up and said: "My son, I want to be with you always. I give you my robe. Wear it wherever you go, that the people may know that you come from this place." All the animals said, "We want to be with you too." Each of the birds took off a feather and put it on the robe, and each animal put one of its claws on it, and some put medicine on it. In one of the holes the Beaver tied a little sweet-grass, and others did the same. By the time they were through, the robe was all covered with feathers and claws and smelt sweet. The animals had put their medicine on it so that it smelt sweet. Then the animals said, "Go, my son, to your people, and bring us something to smoke, so we may be satisfied."

Presently the chief's son found himself upon the bluff, facing his brother. His brother grasped him in his arms and said: "Oh, my brother, you smell nice. What a fine robe you have on! Look at all these feathers." They hugged each other. Then they went home together. The chief's son had a bundle that the animals had given him.

Soon after this the Pawnees had a big doctors' dance. These boys went into the doctors' lodge and said: "Doctors, you are the head doctors, but we have come tonight to visit you. We want to do a few things ourselves." The doctors all said *"Lau-a."* The young men took seats close to the door, which is the most important place in this dance. All the doctors were surprised, and said " *Uh!*"

The Bear boy got up first and began shooting at the chief's son, just as he had done with the Bear, and all the doctors thought he was powerful, shooting at this young man and curing him. When he got through, it was the other boy's turn. He would take a long sharp stick and thrust it through his brother, and then heal him again, and then take a knife and stab him, and then cure him. He did some powerful things, more so than his brother had done. After the doctors had seen all these things they all said, "Let us have these two for our head doctors." But the poor boy said: "Not so. This one who is sitting by me has more power than I have. He ought to be the head doctor, for I am a warrior, and can never stay in the camp to doctor people. My brother has gone into the animals' lodge, and they have given him more power than I possess." So the chief's son was chosen to be the head doctor.

When the doctors' dance was over, the two brothers at once started to go to the animals' lodge, carrying with them tobacco and a pipe. When they got there, the chief's son told his brother to wait on the bank, that he was going down to take the tobacco and the pipe to his fathers. He jumped off the steep bank into the river, down into the door of the lodge, and went in. When they saw him all the animals slapped their mouths and called out. They were glad to see him. After smoking with them, he went back to his friend. After that the chief's son would go off by himself and would meet the animals on the hills. They would tell him about different roots, and how to doctor this disease and that. He would come back with some roots and herbs and put them away.

Finally the head chief sent for the Bear man and said to him: "My son, I offered you my lodge, my daughter, and the whole tribe. Now take all this. Let me go out of this lodge and look for another one, and you stay here with my daughter." The young man said: "What of my brother? Send for the other chief. Let him give his daughter, his lodge, his people, to him, and this day we will accept your gifts to us. My brother will after this be the head doctor of this tribe." The other chief when asked to do this agreed, and it was so done.

The Bear man went often on the war-path, but his brother staid at home, and fought against the enemy only when they attacked the village. He took charge of the doctors' lodge. The Bear man after this had some children, and when they had grown up he told his son the secrets of his power. He was now beginning to grow old, and his son went on the war-path, while he staid at home.

One night he had a dream about his father the Bear. The Bear said to him: "My son, I made you great and powerful among your people. The hairs of my body are falling and soon I shall die. Then you too will die. Tell your son all the secret powers that I gave you. He shall keep the same power that you have had."

Soon after this the old Bear must have died, for the man died. Before he died he said to his brother: "Do not mourn for me, for I shall always be near you. Take care of your people. Cure them when they are sick, and always be their chief."

When the enemy came and attacked these people and wounded any, the chief's son was always there and always cured them. He was a great doctor. At last he also died, but his son had the same kind of power. But these two sons never had so great a power as their fathers.

LEARNING HARD LESSONS
Explorers and Mountain Men

THE seven stories in this section span the years from 1804 to 1838. They capture a fundamental transition between Native American views described earlier and what was to come later in the century. At first, the explorers and mountain men carried eastern values into the vast western wilderness; these were to be changed by the rigors of survival, the demands of making a living in a land very different from the East, as well as by encounters with grizzlies.

Men came to understand the bear more realistically after spending some time in the West. Two men were mauled; both Hugh Glass's and Jedediah Smith's ("A Lisson on the Charcter of the Grissly Baare") stories have come down to us as memorable epics. There were numerous close calls. Confrontations like some of Lewis and Clark's earliest encounters ("Into the Wilderness") were still being repeated by trappers thirty years later ("A Dangerous Varmint")—nearly all precipitated by men, not bears. A surprising amount about the grizzly's behavior was revealed in the accounts of the Astorian venturers, even though their story was told second-hand. Surprisingly, less was revealed about the bear than the men's attitudes in the two accounts from naturalists ("Maximilian" and "Greenhorn Meets Grizzly").

In a sense, the explorers and mountain men were at a stand-off with the grizzly bears. Regardless of their values and how they viewed the bear, the men were too few and their weaponry too primitive to have a major impact on the bear. But they were the first wave of a radical change.

INTO THE WILDERNESS
1804-06

 THE Lewis and Clark Expedition of 1804 to 1806 needs no introduction, of course. Long-term initiatives by Thomas Jefferson to undertake exploration of the land west of the Mississippi River culminated during his presidency. The need to learn more about the new Louisiana Purchase of 1803 was added to the needs of finding a route to the Pacific Ocean and strengthening the U.S.'s hold on the Oregon territory. Thus, a band of a few men, under the leadership of Captains Meriwether Lewis and William Clark, traveled up the Missouri River, crossed the Continental Divide, and continued down the Columbia River to the Pacific.

Among its many historic accomplishments, this military/scientific expedition is credited with recording a wealth of natural history information, not the least of which was the habits and distribution of a species new to the scientific world, the grizzly bear. Although this impressive animal had been reported by earlier explorers, Lewis and Clark were the first to encounter it with naturalists' interests, collect skins, and inquire about its habits from the local Indians. It was with great anticipation that they entered grizzly range, saw the first enormous tracks, and met their first "white bear," as the grizzly was commonly called in those days. Although they were at first confident that their weapons would protect them, their curiosity about the grizzly soon diminished as its tremendous size and tenacity of life intimidated them. By July of 1806, on the return voyage, Lewis wrote that "it seems that the hand of providence has been most wonderfully in our favor with rispect to them, or some of us would long since have fallen a sacrifice to their farosity."

The following excerpts are taken from Reuben Gold Thwaites, ed., Original Journals of the Lewis and Clark Expedition, 1804-1806 *(New York: Antiquarian Press, 1959; first published by Dodd, Mead & Company 1904-1905). We have retained the original spelling and punctuation.*

▼▼▼▼

OCTOBER 7, 1804

at the mouth of this river we Saw the Tracks of white bear which was verry large.

October 20, 1804

our hunters killed 10 Deer & a Goat to day and wounded a white Bear, I saw several fresh tracks of those animals which is 3 times as large as a mans track.

April 13, 1805

we found a number of carcases of the Buffaloe lying along shore, which had been drowned by falling through the ice in winter and lodged on shore by the high water when the river broke up about the first of this month. we saw also many tracks of the white bear of enormous size, along the river shore and about the carcases of the Buffaloe, on which I presume they feed. we have not as yet seen one of these anamals, tho' their tracks are so abundant and recent. the men as well as ourselves are anxious to meet with some of these bear. the Indians give a very formidable account of the streng[t]h and ferocity of this anamal, which they never dare to attack but in parties of six eight or ten persons; and are even then frequently defeated with the loss of one or more of their party. the savages attack this anamal with their bows and arrows and the indifferent guns with which the traders furnish them, with these they shoot with such uncertainty and at so short a distance, that *(unless shot thro' head or heart wound not mortal)* they frequently mis their aim & fall a sacrefice to the bear. Two Minetaries were killed during the last winter in an attack on a white bear. This anamal is said more frequently to attack a man on meeting with him, than to flee from him. When the Indians are about to go in quest of the white bear, previous to their departure, they paint themselves and perform all of those supersticious rights commonly observed when they are about to make war uppon a neighboring nation.

April 29, 1805

I walked on shore with one man. about 8. A.M. we fell in with two brown or yellow [white] bear; both of which we wounded; one of them made his escape, the other after my firing on him pursued me seventy or eighty yards, but fortunately had been so badly wounded that he was unable to pursue so closely as to prevent my charging my gun; we again repeated our fir[e] and killed him. it was a male not fully grown, we estimated his weight at 300 lb^s. not having the means of ascertaining it precisely. The legs of this bear are somewhat longer than those of the black, as are it's tallons and tusks incomparably larger and longer. the testicles, which in the black bear are placed pretty well back between the thyes and contained in one pouch like those of the dog ad most quadrupeds, are in the yellow or brown bear placed much further forward, and are suspended in separate pouches from two to four inches asunder; it's colour is yellowish brown, the eyes small, black, and piercing; the front of the fore legs near the feet is usually black; the fur is finer thicker and deeper than that of the black bear. these are all the particulars in which this anamal appeared to me to differ from the black bear; it is a much more furious and formidable anamal, and will frequently pursue the hunter when wounded. it is asstonishing to see the wounds they will bear before they can be put to death. the Indians may well fear this anamal equiped as they generally are with their bows and arrows or indifferent fuzees, but in the hands of skillful riflemen they are by no means as formidable or dangerous as they have been represented.

May 5, 1805

Capt. Clark and Drewyer killed the largest brown bear this evening which we have yet seen. it was a most tremendious looking anamal, and extreemly hard to kill notwithstanding he had five balls through his lungs and five others in various parts he swam more than half the distance across the river to a sandbar, & it was at least twenty minutes before he died; he did not attempt to attack, but fled and made the most tremendous roaring from the moment he was shot. We had no means of weighing this monster; Capt. Clark thought he would weigh 500 lb^s. for my own part I think the estimate too small by 100 lb^s. he measured 8. Feet 7 1/2 Inches from the nose to the extremety of the hind feet, 5 F. 10 1/2 In^s. arround the breast, 1 F. 11. I. arround the middle of the arm, & 3.F. 11.I. arround the neck; his tallons which were five in number on each foot were 4 3/8 Inches in length.

May 6, 1805

saw a brown bear swim the river above us, he disappeared before we can get in reach of him; I find that the curiossity of our party is pretty well satisfyed with rispect to this anamal, the formidable appearance of the male bear killed on the 5th added to the difficulty with which they die when even shot through the vital parts, has staggered the resolution [of] several of them, others however seem keen for action with the bear; I expect these gentlemen will give us some amusement sho[r]tly as they soon begin now to coppolate.

May 11, 1805

About 5. P. M. my attention was struck by one of the Party running at a distance towards us and making signs and hollowing as if in distress, I ordered the perogues to put too, and waited untill he arrived; I now found that it was Bratton the man with the soar hand whom I had permitted to walk on shore, he arrived so much out of breath that it was several minutes before he could tell what had happened; at length he informed me that in the woody bottom on the Lar^d. side about 1 1/2 [miles] below us he had shot a brown bear which immediately turned on him and pursued him a considerable distance but he had wounded it so badly that it could not overtake him; I immediately turned out with seven of the party in quest of this monster, we at length found his trale and persued him about a mile by the blood through very thick brush of rosbushes and the large leafed willow; we finally found him concealed in some very thick brush and shot him through the skull with two balls; we proceeded [to] dress him as soon as possible, we found him in good order; it was a monstrous beast not quite so large as that we killed a few days past but in all rispects much the same   the hair is remarkably long fine and rich tho' he appears parshally to have discharged his winter coat; we now found that Bratton had shot him through the center of the lungs, notwithstanding which he had pursued him near half a mile and had returned more than double that distance and with his tallons had prepared himself a bed in the earth of about 2 feet deep and five long and was perfectly alive when we found him which could not have been less than 2 hours after he received the wound; these bear being so hard to die reather intimedates us all; I must confess that I do not like the gentlemen and had reather fight two Indians than one bear; there is no other chance to conquer them by a single shot but by shooting them through the brains, and this becomes difficult in consequence of two large muscles which cover the sides of the forehead and the sharp projection of the center of the frontal bone, which is also of a pretty good thickness. the flece and skin were as much as two men could possibly carry.

May 14, 1805

one of the party wounded a brown bear very badly, but being alone did not think proper to pursue him. In the evening the men in two of the rear canoes discovered a large brown bear lying in the open grounds about 300 paces from the river, and six of them went out to attack him, all good hunters; they took the advantage of a small eminence which concealed them and got within 40 paces of him unperceived, two of them reserved their fires as had been previously conserted, the four others fired nearly at the same time and put each his bullet through him, two of the balls passed through the bulk of both lobes of his lungs, in an instand this monster ran at them with open mouth, the two who had reserved their fir[e]s discharged their pieces at him as he came towards them, boath of them struck him, one only slightly and the other fortunately broke his shoulder, this however only retarded his motion for a moment only, the men unable to reload their guns took to flight, the bear pursued and had very nearly overtaken them before they reached the river; two of the party betook themselves to a canoe and the others seperated an[d] concealed themselves among the willows, reloaded their pieces, each discharged his piece at him as they had an opportunity they struck him several times again but the guns served only to direct the bear to them, in this manner he pursued two of them seperately so close that they were obliged to throw aside their guns and pouches and throw themselves into the river altho' the bank was nearly twenty feet perpendicular; so enraged was this anamal that he plunged into the river only a few feet behind the second man he had compelled [to] take refuge in the water, when one of those who still remained on shore shot him through the head and finally killed him; they then took him on shore and butch[er]ed him when they found eight balls had passed through him in different directions.

June 13, 1805

I am induced to believe that the Brown, the white and the Grizly bear of this country are the same species only differing in colour from age or more probably from the same natural cause that many other anamals of the same family differ in colour. one of those which we killed yesterday was of a creem-coloured white while the other in company with it was of the common bey or r[e]dish brown, which seems to be the most usual colour of them. the white one appeared from it's tallons and teath to be the youngest; it was smaller than the other, and although a monstrous beast we supposed that it had not yet attained it's growth and that it was a little upwards of two years old. the young cubs which we have killed have always been of a brownish white, but none of them as white as that we killed yesterday. one other that we killed sometime since which I mentioned sunk under some driftwood and was lost, had a white stripe or list of about eleven inches wide entirely arround his body just behind the shoalders, and was much darker than these bear usually are. the grizly bear we have never yet seen. I have seen their tallons in possession of the Indians and from their form I am preswaded if there is any difference between this species and the brown or white bear it is very inconsiderable.

June 14, 1805

    I [Lewis] decended the hill and directed my course to the bend of the Missouri near which there was a herd of at least a thousand buffaloe; here I thought it would be well to kill a buffaloe and leave him untill my return from the river and if I then found that I had not time to get back to camp this evening to remain all night here there being a few sticks of drift wood lying along shore which would answer for my fire, and a few s[c]attering cottonwood trees a few hundred yards below which would afford me at least the semblance of a shelter. under this impression I scelected a fat buffaloe and shot him very well, through the lungs; while I was gazing attentively at the poor anamal discharging blood in streams from his mouth and nostrils, expecting him to fall every instant, and having entirely forgotten to reload my rifle, a large white, or reather brown bear, had perceived and crept on me within 20 steps before I discovered him; in the first moment I drew up my gun to shoot, but at the same instant recolected that she was not loaded and that he was too near for me to hope to perform this opperation before he reached me, as he was then briskly advancing on me; it was an open level plain, not a bush within miles nor a tree within less than three hundred yards of me; the river bank was sloping and not more than three feet above the level of the water; in short there was no place by means of which I could conceal myself from this monster untill

I could charge my rifle; in this situation I thought of retreating in a brisk walk as fast as he was advancing untill I could reach a tree about 300 yards below me, but I had no sooner terned myself about but he pitched at me, open mouthed and full speed, I ran about 80 yards and found he gained on me fast, I then run into the water the idea struk me to get into the water to such debth that I could stand and he would be obliged to swim, and that I could in that situation defend myself with my espontoon [a short spear]; accordingly I ran haistily into the water about waist deep, and faced about and presented the point of my espontoon, at this instant he arrived at the edge of the water within about 20 feet of me; the moment I put myself in this attitude of defence he sudonly wheeled about as if frightened, declined the combat on such unequal grounds, and retreated with quite as great precipitation as he had just before pursued me. as soon as I saw him run of[f] in that manner I returned to the shore and charged my gun, which I had still retained in my hand throughout this curious adventure. I saw him run through the level open plain about three miles, till he disappeared in the woods on medecine river; during the whole of this distance he ran at full speed, sometimes appearing to look behind him as if he expected pursuit.

June 28, 1805

The White bear have become so troublesome to us that I do not think it prudent to send one man alone on an errand of any kind, particularly where he has to pass through the brush. we have seen two of them on the large Island opposite to us today but are so much engaged that we could not spare the time to hunt them but will make a frolick of it when the party return and drive them from these islands. they come close arround our camp every night but have never yet ventured to attack us and our dog gives us timely notice of their visits, he keeps constantly padroling all night. I have made the men sleep with their arms by them as usual for fear of accedents.

May 31, 1806

Goodrich and Willard visited the indian Villages this morning and returned in the evening. Willard brought with him the dressed skin of a bear which he had purchased for Capt. C. this skin was an uniform pale redish brown colour, the Indians informed us that it was not the *Hoh-host* or white bear. that it was the Yâck-kâh. this distinction of the indians induced us to make further enquiry relative to their opinions of the several speceis of bear in this country. we produced the several skins of the bear which we had killed at this place and one very nearly white which I had purchased. The white, the deep and pale red grizzle, the dark bro[w]n grizzle, and all those which had the extremities of the hair of a white or frosty colour without regard to the colour of the ground of the poil, they designated Hoh-host and assured us that they were the same with the white bear, that they associated together, were very vicisious, never climbed the trees, and had much longer nails than the others. the black skins, those which were black with a number of intire white hairs intermixed, the black with a white breast, the uniform bey, brown and light redish brown, they designated the *Yâck-kâh;* said that they climbed the trees, had short nails and were not vicious, that they could pursue them and kill them with safety, they also affirmed that they were much smaller than the white bear. I am disposed to adopt the Indian distinction with respect to these bear and consider them two distinct speceis.

ASTORIAN ANECDOTES BY WASHINGTON IRVING
1811

 IN 1811, an expedition under Wilson Price Hunt was on its way to the mouth of the Columbia River to set up a trading empire based on furs, as conceived by John Jacob Astor. The group unwittingly camped in the middle of a grizzly bear feeding area; we know today how dangerous this mistake can be, partly from experiences such as those of Hunt's party. The second brief encounter comes from later in the journey; it shows one possible way of avoiding conflict with the unpredictable grizzly.

These anecdotes come from Washington Irving's book, Astoria, or Anecdotes of an Enterprise Beyond the Rocky Mountains, *edited by Edgeley W. Todd (Norman: University of Oklahoma Press, 1964; first published in 1836). Irving did not take part in the Astorian ventures, but as a renowned literary man and a long-time friend of John Jacob Astor, he was asked in the early 1830s by Astor himself to write a book about Astoria, "something that might . . . secure to him [Astor] the reputation of having originated the enterprise and founded the colony that are likely to have such important results in the history of commerce and colonization." Irving was offered abundant documentation—letters, journals, and discussions with some of the original participants, as well as numerous published sources. Although his book appeared 25 years after the events he wrote about, historians consider that he produced an accurate account, and certainly, it is as readable today as when it first delighted readers in the 1830s.*

▼▼▼▼

FAR off in the west they descried a range of lofty mountains printing the clear horizon, some of them evidently capped with snow. These they supposed to be the Bighorn Mountains, so called from the animal of that name, with which they abound. They are a spur of the great Rocky chain. The hill from whence Mr. Hunt had this prospect was, according to his computation, about two hundred and fifty miles from the Arickara village.

On returning to the camp, Mr. Hunt found some uneasiness prevailing among the Canadian voyageurs. In straying among the thickets they beheld tracks of grizzly bears in every direction, doubtless attracted thither by the fruit. To their dismay, they now found that they had encamped in one of the favorite resorts of this dreaded animal. The idea marred all the comfort of the encampment. As night closed, the surrounding thickets were peopled with terrors; insomuch that, according to Mr. Hunt, they could not help starting at every little breeze that stirred the bushes.

The grizzly bear is the only really formidable quadruped of our continent. He is the favorite theme of the hunters of the far West, who describe him as equal in size to a common cow and of prodigious strength. He makes battle if assailed, and often, if pressed by hunger, is the assailant. If wounded, he becomes furious and will pursue the hunter. His speed exceeds that of a man but is inferior to that of a horse. In attacking he rears himself on his hind legs, and springs the length of his body. Woe to horse or rider that comes within the sweep of his terrific claws, which are sometimes nine inches in length, and tear everything before them.

At the time we are treating of, the grizzly bear was still frequent on the Missouri and in the lower country, but, like some of the broken tribes of the prairie, he has gradually fallen back before his enemies, and is now chiefly to be found in the upland regions, in rugged fastnesses like those of the Black Hills and the Rocky Mountains. Here he lurks in caverns, or holes which he has digged in the sides of hills, or under the roots and trunks of fallen trees. Like the common bear, he is fond of fruits, and mast, and roots, the latter of which he will dig up with his foreclaws. He is carnivorous also, and will even attack and conquer the lordly buffalo, dragging his huge carcass to the neighborhood of his den, that he may prey upon it at his leisure.

The hunters, both white and red men, consider this the most heroic game. They prefer to hunt him on horseback, and will venture so near as sometimes to singe his hair with the flash of the rifle. The hunter of the grizzly bear, however, must be an experienced hand, and know where to aim at a vital part; for of all quadrupeds, he is the most difficult to be killed. He will receive repeated wounds without flinching, and rarely is a shot mortal unless through the head or heart.

That the dangers apprehended from the grizzly bear, at this night encampment, were not imaginary, was proved on the following morning. Among the hired men of the party was one William Cannon, who had been a soldier at one of the frontier posts, and entered into the employ of Mr. Hunt at Mackinaw. He was an inexperienced hunter and a poor shot, for which he was much bantered by his more adroit comrades. Piqued at their raillery, he had been practicing ever since he had joined the expedition, but without success. In the course of the present afternoon, he went forth by himself to take a lesson in venerie, and, to his great delight, had the good fortune to kill a buffalo. As he was a considerable distance from the camp, he cut out the tongue and some of the choice bits, made them into a parcel, and slinging them on his shoulders by a strap passed round his forehead, as the voyageurs carry packages of goods, set out all glorious for the camp, anticipating a triumph over his brother hunters. In passing through a narrow ravine, he heard a noise behind him, and looking round beheld, to his dismay, a grizzly bear in full pursuit, apparently attracted by the scent of the meat. Cannon had heard so much of the invulnerability of this tremendous animal, that he never attempted to fire, but, slipping the strap from his forehead, let go the buffalo meat and ran for his life. The bear did not stop to regale himself with the game, but kept on after the hunter. He had nearly overtaken him when Cannon reached a tree, and, throwing down his rifle, scrambled up it. The next instant Bruin was at the foot of the tree; but, as this species of bear does not climb, he contented himself with turning the chase into a blockade. Night came on. In the darkness Cannon could not perceive whether or not the enemy maintained his station; but his fears pictured him rigorously mounting guard. He passed the night, therefore, in the tree, a prey to dismal fancies. In the morning the bear was gone. Cannon warily descended the tree, gathered up his gun, and made the best of his way back to the camp, without venturing to look after his buffalo meat.

While on this theme we will add another anecdote of an adventure with a grizzly bear, told of John Day, the Kentucky hunter, but which happened at a different period of the expedition. Day was hunting in company with one of the clerks of the Company, a lively youngster, who was a great favorite with the veteran, but whose vivacity he had continually to keep in check. They were in search of deer, when suddenly a huge grizzly bear emerged from a thicket about thirty yards distant, rearing himself upon his hind legs with a terrific growl, and displaying a hideous array of teeth and claws. The rifle of the young man was leveled in an instant, but John Day's iron hand was as quickly upon his arm. "Be quiet, boy! Be quiet!" exclaimed the hunter between his clenched teeth, and without turning his eyes from the bear. They remained motionless. The monster regarded them for a time, then, lowering himself on his forepaws, slowly withdrew. He had not gone many paces before he again returned, reared himself on his hind legs, and repeated his menace. Day's hand was still on the arm of his young companion; he again pressed it hard, and kept repeating between his teeth, "Quiet, boy!—Keep quiet!—Keep quiet!"—though the latter had not made a move since his first prohibition. The bear again lowered himself on all fours, retreated some twenty yards further, and again turned, reared, showed his teeth, and growled. This third menace was too much for the game spirit of John Day. "By Jove!" exclaimed he, "I can stand this no longer," and in an instant a ball from his rifle whizzed into the foe. The wound was not mortal; but, luckily, it dismayed instead of enraging the animal, and he retreated into the thicket.

Day's youthful companion reproached him for not practicing the caution which he enjoined upon others. "Why, boy," replied the veteran, "caution is caution, but one must not put up with too much, even from a bear. Would you have me suffer myself to be bullied all day by a varmint?"

▼▼▼

On the 2d of November, . . . they pitched their camp for the winter, on the woody point, and their first thought was to obtain a supply of provisions. Ben Jones and the two Canadians accordingly sallied forth, accompanied by two others of the party, leaving but one to watch the camp. Their hunting was uncommonly successful. In the course of two days, they killed thirty-two buffaloes, and collected their meat on the margin of a small brook, about a mile distant. Fortunately, a severe frost froze the river, so that the meat was easily transported to the encampment. On a succeeding day, a herd of buffalo came trampling through the woody bottom on the river banks, and fifteen more were killed.

It was soon discovered, however, there was game of a more danger-ous nature in the neighborhood. On one occasion, Mr. Crooks had wandered about a mile from the camp, and had ascended a small hill commanding a view of the river. He was without his rifle, a rare circumstance, for in these wild regions, where one may put up a wild animal, or a wild Indian, at every turn, it is customary never to stir from the camp-fire unarmed. The hill where he stood overlooked the place where the massacre of the buffalo had taken place. As he was looking around on the prospect, his eye was caught by an object below, moving directly towards him. To his dismay, he discovered it to be a grizzly bear, with two cubs. There was no tree at hand into which he could climb; to run, would only be to provoke pursuit, and he should soon be overtaken. He threw himself on the ground, therefore, and lay motionless, watching the movements of the animal with intense anxiety. It continued to advance until at the foot of the hill, when it turned, and made into the woods, having probably gorged itself with buffalo flesh. Mr. Crooks made all haste back to camp, rejoicing at his escape, and determining never to stir out again without his rifle. A few days after this circumstance, a grizzly bear was shot in the neighborhood, by Mr. Miller.

HUGH GLASS
1823

 THE saga of Hugh Glass—a mountain man who suffered a terrible grizzly mauling, was abandoned by his fellows, and returned alone and unarmed across hundreds of miles to civilization—has in recent decades acquired sufficient documentation to be considered as true in basic form as it is mythic in scale. This most terrible and awe-inspiring tale was given its proper setting by Glass biographer John Myers Myers: "Deep in the medicine bag of every nation is the tale of a warrior pitted against a beast of dread proportions. In the lore of America, this alpha of epics takes the form of a struggle between a mountain man called Hugh Glass and an outsize grizzly." (The Saga of Hugh Glass: Pirate, Pawnee, and Mountain Man, *Lincoln: University of Nebraska Press, 1963). Here, more than in any other story in this collection, is the grizzly bear the incarnation of a raw and pitiless wilderness, against which one man struggles alone and, through incredible will and ability, survives. Glass's journey is not so much a struggle against nature, an overpowering of natural forces, as a triumph of the human spirit within nature.*

This account of the Glass "cycle," as it's called, was prepared by historian Aubrey L. Haines; it is one of the many fascinating biographies in The Mountain Men and the Fur Trade of the Far West, *edited by LeRoy R. Hafen (Glendale, California: The Arthur H. Clark Co., 1968).*

▼▼▼▼

THE enraged grizzly bear which set upon and mauled a trapper named Hugh Glass near the headwaters of Nebraska's [South Dakota's] Grand River in 1823, laid the basis for a fascinating and durable tale which has only recently been rescued from the limbo of the legendary. It is a saga typifying the independence, hardihood, perseverance and raw courage of the trappers who first penetrated the vast territory opened to American enterprise through the Louisiana Purchase.

Nothing is known with certainty concerning the background of the hero of this sketch prior to the savage encounter through which he came to fame. However, there is a surmise that his ancestry was Irish, while the reminiscence of George C. Yount, a fellow trapper, indicates Glass may once have played the roles of sailor, unwilling pirate and adopted Indian.

As the story goes, the nautical career of Glass was diverted from honest seafaring when his ship was captured by a pirate crew of the notorious Jean LaFitte. For the unfortunate sailors there was only one alternative to immediate death—they could join their captors; and, in that way, Glass and one other preserved their lives. Yet, the business of piracy was so repugnant to both that they soon fell under suspicion and were marked for death.

That fate was avoided by swimming from the pirate vessel under cover of darkness as it lay in a sheltering bay on the coast of Texas. Wandering inland, they were at last captured by Indians identified by our informant as Pawnees. A few days later, Glass' comrade was ceremoniously burned to death, a fate Glass escaped by pleasing a chief with a present of vermilion. Thereafter, he was accepted as a member of the tribe, living as a Pawnee and learning wilderness craft until mid-year of 1822, when a tribal visit to St. Louis gave him an opportunity to escape. That the foregoing is probable has been amply demonstrated by John Myers Myers in his excellent study of Hugh Glass.

On January 16, 1823, the *Missouri Republican* carried an advertisement seeking "One Hundred MEN, to ascend the Missouri to the Rocky Mountains." It was an offer of employment to the liking of Hugh Glass, who joined the expedition which General William Ashley led up river on March 7. What should have been merely a laborious ascent of the great waterway, to a juncture with the band of trappers wintering at the mouth of the Yellowstone River under Major Andrew Henry, developed differently.

Unexpected losses of men and horses in the course of trapping operations on the upper Missouri had so crippled the band at "Fort Henry" that the Major sent a courier to General Ashley seeking replacements. Ashley was met a few miles below the Arikara towns, and the great need for horses led him to trade with those unpredictable river Indians. That business ended with a dawn attack on Ashley's men as they lay encamped on the beach before the towns. The ensuing battle was a debacle for the trappers, costing them eleven dead and thirteen wounded—among the latter, Hugh Glass.

Ashley's defeat at the Arikara towns also led to the writing of a letter which is the only communication known to have been penned by Glass. In that letter he gave notice, to a father in Virginia, of the death of his son; he did so with such tact and literacy there can be no doubt he was reasonably well-educated by the standard of the time. Here, too, is a coincidence which is most striking. The young man for whom he did that last, sad chore was John S. Gardner, while the man who avenged the death of Glass a decade later was Johnson Gardner. But, more of that later.

Far from being able to send the men and horses so desperately needed at Fort Henry, General Ashley found it necessary to draw upon the slender resources of that post in order to assist Colonel Henry Leavenworth in a punitive effort against the Arikaras. It was a campaign which accomplished next to nothing, and, at its conclusion, Ashley was left with only thirty men who were willing to continue to the mountains.

Recognizing that the tiny garrison left at Fort Henry had to be reinforced as soon as possible, it was decided that Major Henry should lead a party overland by way of the Grand River. Yet, after a sufficient crew was allowed the supply boat, "Rocky Mountain," to move it up the river, the overland party was dangerously small—only thirteen men. Hugh Glass was among those who took up the march, afoot and leading a few packhorses, on August 16,1823.

Perhaps a week later and not far from the present town of Grand River, South Dakota, Glass met his grizzly bear. That encounter, and its aftermath, was subsequently reported in three forms which differ sufficiently to be indicative of separate reporting. The essential story goes thus:

Hugh Glass was somewhat separated from his comrades when attacked by a bear which he failed to stop with his one shot. When rescued he was so severely mauled it was thought he could not live. The party could neither take him along nor await his demise; so it was arranged for two volunteers to stay with him until he could be buried, after which they were to hasten after the party.

But Glass took too long in dying, the two volunteers became nervous and finally abandoned their helpless comrade, who was left without his gun or other essentials. Bolstered by his anger at such heartlessness, Glass refused to die; instead he crawled back down the Grand River to the Missouri, was befriended by Sioux Indians, and eventually delivered safely at Fort Kiowa.

From there, he took up the pursuit of his faithless comrades. Traveling up the Missouri on a trader's boat, he went ashore just before the crew was attacked by Arikaras and killed. Fortuitously rescued by the Mandans (after a desperate, hand-to-hand encounter with an Arikara scout, in [one] version), he continued from their town on foot, reaching the mouth of the Yellowstone, and the abandoned Fort Henry, early in winter. He continued up the Yellowstone River to the Big Horn, arriving at the new post to find only the younger, and least responsible, of the two he sought yet there. The older man had gone down the river to Fort Atkinson; so Glass took up the trail once more, traveling with three comrades by way of the Platte River. On that stream they were treacherously attacked by Arikaras and two were killed, but Glass escaped and eventually reached the fort. Yet he was denied his vengeance because the man he sought had joined the army and was beyond his reach.

It is a tale with enough "Hair-breadth-Harry" escapes to sound impossible, and so it has been considered by many, historians included. Yet, diligent research has confirmed so many salient points of the story that it is no longer possible to explain it away as the product of an overly fertile imagination. Here are the facts which support the Glass cycle in its essential details:

The star role of Glass in the bear incident is attested by James Clyman, a fellow trapper, whose diary for September, 1823, states:

> Amongst this party was a Mr. Hugh Glass who could not be restrained . . . and kept under subordination. He went off the line of march one afternoon and met with a large grizzly bear, which he shot at and wounded. The bear as is usual, attacked Glass. He attempted to climb a tree but the bear caught him and hauled him to the ground tearing and lacerating his body in fearful rate.
>
> By this time several men were in close gun shot but could not shoot for fear of hitting Glass. At length the bear appeared to be satisfied and turned to leave, when two or three men fired. The bear turned immediately on Glass and gave him a second mutilation. On turning again several more shot him, when for the third time he pounced on Glass and fell dead over his body. This I have from information, not being present. [Charles L. Camp, ed., *James Clyman, American Frontiersman,* San Francisco, 1928, p. 35.]

Confirmation of the abandonment of Glass comes from another trapper, Daniel T. Potts, who speaks of "One man who [was] also tore nearly all to peases by a White Bear and was left by the way without any gun who afterwards recovered." Dale Morgan has supplied the proof that Fitzgerald (the older man left to care for Glass) was a real person. He says:

> I have established Fitzgerald's identity through War Department records in the National Archives, which shows that John S. Fitzgerald enlisted at Fort Atkinson April 19, 1824, in Brevet Major Daniel Ketchum's Company I of the Sixth Regiment. The place of his birth is stated to have been Albermarle Co., Va., date not given. At the end of his five-year hitch he was mustered out April 19, 1829, at Jefferson Barracks, St. Louis, being then a private in Company C, his occupation stated as carpenter. [*Jedediah Smith and the Opening of the West,* Indianapolis, 1953, p. 97.]

Those who would argue against the identification of the younger man as Jim Bridger (this has rested upon Captain Joseph LaBarge's statement, as reported by Chittenden, and upon Edmund Flagg's slightly garbled surnaming as "Bridges"), must now deal with a third witness—James Stevenson. He came to know Bridger quite well while expeditioning under G. K. Warren, W. F. Raynolds and F. V. Hayden and he states, in a letter to Professor J. D. Butler, that Bridger told him the story of Hugh Glass, but *without the desertion.* The most likely explanation for such omission of a salient feature of the story is that it remained too embarrassing.

As for the Odyssey which forms so colorful a sequel to the abandonment of Glass, there is no documentary evidence to link him indisputably to the action until the false report of his death at the hands of the Arikaras while descending the Platte River. And yet, the careful analysis of Myers in the work previously cited, indicates the traditional tale is likely correct in its broad details: the timing is logical and, except for the deadly encounter with the Arikara scout (a possible literary accretion), the events are probable. Indeed, the details of the destruction of the boat sent up to the Mandans by Brazeau agree so well with the contemporary reports as to inspire confidence in the probity of the whole tale.

According to George Yount, whose reminiscence supplies most of what is known about the life of Hugh Glass following the scene in which he forgave Fitzgerald at Fort Atchinson, the old trapper entered a partnership and traded into New Mexico. After laboring for a year "with but indifferent success," he returned to trapping by leading a band of his fellows from Taos into the country of the Ute Indians. There, he had another adventure which came near ending his life in a lingering fashion.

The trappers had taken many beaver along a river down which they were drifting in canoes. Seeing a squaw digging roots on the shore, and having more beaver meat with them than could be used, they thought to land and give her the surplus. But their approach was too quiet; the three trappers who stepped ashore—each with a beaver carcass—were not seen until they came up the bank. The surprised squaw screamed, arousing an Indian sleeping nearby, and he jumped up and shot an arrow into one of the trappers who killed him in return.

The mortally wounded trapper asked to be left with a charged gun, and, it was while preparing the firearm for his helpless comrade that Hugh Glass received an arrow in his back from one of the Indians who came crowding up. The trappers escaped down-river, but Hugh was in serious condition, with the broken off arrowhead firmly imbedded near his spine. In that condition he traveled seven hundred miles before the point was cut out by another trapper who used a razor for the operation. That trip, with his flesh "swollen & inflamed to an astonishing degree," must have been as painful as his return to civilized care following the abandonment on Grand River.

After several years during which his movements are unknown, Hugh Glass came to prominence in 1828 as the spokesman for those free trappers who rebelled at the tyranny of "mountain prices" imposed upon them at the annual rendezvous. He left Bear Lake as an emissary to the American Fur Company, arriving at Fort Floyd at the mouth of the Yellowstone River, that fall. Dale Morgan has likened the proposal of the free trappers—that McKenzie should send goods to the next rendezvous—as resembling the invitation of the frogs to King Stork; all too soon he gobbled them up.

Hugh Glass remained in the vicinity of Fort Floyd (Union), where he found employment as a meat hunter during much of his few remaining years. In fact, the bluffs across the Missouri River, below the mouth of the Yellowstone, were for a time known as Glass' Bluffs from his hunting of big horn sheep there.

During the winter of 1832-33, Hugh Glass went with some companions to take beaver along the Yellowstone River in the vicinity of Fort Cass, and, while crossing on the ice a few miles below the mouth of the Big Horn, he was ambushed by his old enemies, the Arikaras, and killed along with Edward Rose and a man named Menard. So perished a man of whom a comrade would say: "He had his failings—But his fellow trappers bear testimony to his honor, integrity & fidelity—He could be relied on."

Perhaps it was that high regard for the eccentric old trapper which caused Johnson Gardner to take such terrible vengeance upon the Indians suspected of doing him in. As Maximilian, Prince of Weid, had the story from Gardner in the course of a boat trip down the Missouri River, Gardner's band of twenty trappers were on the headwaters of Powder River when some Indians identified as Arikaras came into their camp. Being suspicious that their object was to steal his horses, and seeing that they had in their possession items known to have belonged to Hugh Glass, Gardner took precautions which allowed the trappers to seize three Indians as hostages when the stock was run off. But subsequent bargaining for return of the horses failed, and two Indians were killed in an attempt to "escape." Such was Gardner's version in polite company; quite another was current on the frontier.

George Catlin noted, "But a few weeks before I left the mouth of Yellow Stone, the news arrived at that place, that a party of trappers and traders had burnt two Riccarees to death, on the prairies." Sanford's letter... identifies Gardner as the perpetrator of that inhuman act, which was probably a bit more inhuman than the statement implies because Gardner had a scalp to give the German prince. Obviously, it must have been taken before its owner was consigned to the flames. Hugh Glass was certainly avenged; but vengeance is a two-edged sword, and Edmund Flagg was able to add, "Not long afterwards Gardiner himself fell into the hands of the Erickeraws, who inflicted upon him the same dreadful death."

A LISSON ON THE CHARCTER OF THE GRISSLY BAARE
1824

 JIM Clyman was a frontiersman whose remarkable life spanned almost the entire nineteenth century and the entire North American continent. He joined Ashley's second expedition up the Missouri in 1823 and was wounded in the battle with the Arikara Indians, as was Hugh Glass. He spent a few years in the mountains on this first trip, during which he was one of the first white men to cross South Pass, was separated from his companions and walked 600 miles alone back to Fort Atkinson on the Missouri River, and was one of the first whites to circumnavigate Great Salt Lake. He spent some years in Illinois and Wisconsin, served in the Black Hawk War, traveled to Oregon and California, returned east, returned west, and established a ranch in the Napa Valley where he spent his last thirty years. Perhaps most significantly, he chronicled all his travels, his adventures, and his fights. His biographer and editor of his journals, Charles L. Camp (James Clyman, Frontiersman, Portland, Oregon: Champoeg Press, 1960), wrote: "The moving force in his career was in intense love of the freedom of the wilderness. . . . He wandered restlessly for forty-one years over the breadth of the continent and into the farthest recesses of the mountains."

This 1824 account from Jim Clyman's journal stands out as one of the classic mountain men stories. Jedediah Smith's fortitude and endurance were an inspiration to his frightened men, and they remain a compelling memory in the history of the West. This story comes from Dale L. Morgan's Jedediah Smith and the Opening of the West *(New York: Bobbs-Merrill Co., 1953).*

▼▼▼▼▼

INCLINING more to the west, Jedediah and his men reached better going. They were approaching the Black Hills, which rose at first only slightly above the rolling plains, but presently became a pleasant, undulating region of pointed dark pines, refreshingly different from the hot and dusty land they had thus far seen. The hills grew higher and near the dividing ridge were more brushy, with scrubby pine and juniper. Beyond the divide the ravines were steeper, rugged and rocky. The western slope of the Black Hills was undiscovered country, and Jedediah thought it probable he was on the eastern heads of the Powder. But this was singular terrain, the beginnings of his education in mountain travel. One evening late, Clyman says:

> . . . gowing d[o]wn a small stream we came into a Kenyon and pushed ourselves down so far that our horses had no room to turn while looking for a way out it became dark by unpacking and leading our animals down over Slipery rocks three of us got down to a n[i]ce open glade whare we killed a Buffaloe and fared Sumpiously that night while the rest of the Company remained in the Kenyon without room to lie down.

It would not do to follow the streams. Jedediah climbed a ridge and was lucky enough to emerge upon a main divide, which he followed a considerable distance before descending again. But the ridges yielded no feed for the horses, which became weak and emaciated. Five of the animals had to be given a chance to recruit, and Jedediah left three men to look after them while he took the rest of the company on; the young captain hoped to find beaver in numbers sufficient to justify the whole party in stopping. At the same time he ordered Edward Rose to go ahead and find the Crows. If they were really on the waters of the Powder, they had reached Crow country, and Rose might be able to get fresh horses.

Five days later, toward evening, the little company was threading its way through a brushy bottom, the men on foot leading the horses. A large grizzly came down the valley. He struck the line nearly in the center, turned and ran parallel with it. Jedediah, being in advance, ran to the open ground, and as he emerged from the thicket met the bear face to face.

Jim Clyman tells the story:

> Grissly did not hesitate a moment but sprang on the cap^t taking him by the head first pitc[h]ing sprawling on the earth he gave him a grab by the middle fortunately cat[c]hing by the ball pouch and Butcher K[n]ife which he broke but breaking several of his ribs and cutting his head badly none of us having any su[r]gical Knowledge what was to be done one Said come take hold and he wuld say why not you so it went around I asked the Capt what was best he said one or 2 [go] for water and if you have a

needle and thread git it out and sew up my wounds around my head which was bleeding freely I got a pair of scissors and cut off his hair and then began my first Job of d[r]essing wounds upon examination I [found] the bear had taken nearly all his head in his capcious mouth close to his left eye on one side and clos[e] to his right ear on the other and laid the skull bare to near the crown of the head leaving a white streak whare his teeth passed   one of his ears was torn from his head out to the outer rim after stitching all the other wounds in the best way I was capabl[e] and according to the captains directions the ear being the last I told him I could do nothing for his Eare   O you must try to stitch up some way or other said he   then I put in my needle sti[t]ching it through and through and over and over laying the lacerated parts togather as nice as I could with my hands   water was found in about ame mille when we all moved down and encamped the captain being able to mount his horse and ride to camp whare we pitched a tent the onley one we had and made him as comfortable as circumstances would permit   this gave us a lisson on the charcter of the grissly Baare which we did not forget.

Lying torn and bleeding at the feet of his men, Jedediah retained a power of decision and a clarity of mind which illustrated clearly why he was their captain. Tradition has persisted in the Smith family that Jedediah killed his bear, but it seems unlikely. Mountain tradition was that Arthur Black, Jedediah's later companion in the adventures on the Pacific slope, once saved him from the attack of a bear, and, if so, this may have been the occasion, though Black's presence in the party of 1823 has not been proved. Jedediah bore the marks of this encounter to the end of his life, eyebrow ripped away, ear scarred and torn. These were honorable scars, but of a kind to give men pause when they looked at him, and Jedediah wore his hair long thereafter, hanging down over his ears.

PRINCE MAXIMILIAN, SEARCHER FOR KNOWLEDGE
1833

THAT indefatigable historian, Reuben Gold Thwaites, who made so many documents of early western history available to twentieth-century readers, introduced the author this way:

In the early nineteenth century, scientific collection was the chief object of ambition among thoughtful explorers—to secure for the world a complete catalogue of its plants and animals was worth much toil and hardship, heroic endeavor, and mighty daring. To such, the still unknown regions of the New World offered strong attractions. There were in the trans-Mississippi and in South America, spread out upon mountains and prairies and bordering far-flowing streams, fresh races of barbarians yet uncontaminated by civilized contact, beasts of prey, birds of brilliant plumage, and unknown plant species.

Just such a naturalist/scholar/explorer was Alexander Philip Maximilian, Prince of Wied-Neuwied, in Prussian Germany. Although he was a soldier in his early career, scholarly interests in natural history had occupied him from childhood. He spent 1815 to 1817 in Brazil, studying its flora and fauna and its native peoples. Then, in 1833 and 1834, he traveled up the Missouri on the annual steamboat of the American Fur Company, spent two months at Fort McKenzie on Marias River in northern Montana and the winter at Fort Clark in what is now North Dakota among the Mandans and Minitarees. His writings and Karl Bodmer's paintings formed a valuable ethnographic record of these people, who were devastated by smallpox not long after their visit, and of the landscapes, plants, and animals of the upper Missouri.

In mid-summer, the party met its first grizzlies. Although they clearly had a strong scientific interest in these animals (in fact, Maximilian made observations on two grizzly cubs he kept in cages for part of his journey), there was also an undeniable interest in the sport of "collecting" these specimens. This excerpt is taken from Maximilian's Travels in the Interior of North America, *its 1843 English translation reprinted by Reuben Gold Thwaites, ed., in his series* Early Western Travels: 1748-1846, v. XXIII," (Cleveland: The Arthur H. Clark Co., 1905).

▼▼▼▼▼

DURING our voyage, on the 18th of July, I could not help making comparisons with my journeys on the Brazilian rivers. There, where nature is so infinitely rich and grand, I heard, from the lofty, thick, primeval forests on the banks of the rivers, the varied voices of the parrots, the macaws, and many other birds, as well as of the monkeys, and other creatures; while here, the silence of the bare, dead, lonely wilderness is but seldom interrupted by the howling of the wolves, the bellowing of the buffaloes, or the screaming of the crows. The vast prairie scarcely offers a living creature, except now and then, herds of buffaloes and antelopes, or a few deer and wolves. These plains, which are dry in summer, and frozen in winter, have certainly much resemblance, in many of their features, with the African deserts. Many writers have given them the name of savannahs, or grassy plains; but this expression can be applied, at most, to those of the Lower Missouri, and is totally inapplicable to the dry, sterile tracts of the north-west, where a more luxuriant growth of grass may be expected, at best, only in a few moist places, though various plants, interesting to the botanist, are everywhere to be found.

On this day, at noon, we reached, on the south bank, an Indian fort, an expression which I shall often have occasion to use in the sequel; it is a kind of breastwork, which Indian war-parties construct in haste of dry trunks of trees. When such parties intend to stop for the night, they erect a breastwork, sufficiently large, according to their number, composed of trunks of trees, or thick branches, laid one on the other, generally either square or triangular. In this bulwark they lie down to sleep, after having placed sentinels, and are there able to repel an attack. This fort consisted of a fence, and several angles, enclosing a rather small space, with the open side towards the river. In the centre of the space there was a conical hut, composed of wood. Near this fort, on the same bank of the river, there was a beaver's den made of a heap of brushwood.

After our hunters had returned, with the flesh of a buffalo, we had a favourable wind, which allowed us to use our sail. At a turn of the river we suddenly saw a couple of bears running backwards and forwards on a sand bank before the willow thickets. One of them at length went away, and the other ran along the strand, and fell on the dead body of a buffalo cow, which was half buried in the mud. While the keel-boat sailed against the stream in the middle of the river, a boat was put out, into which Messrs. Mitchell and Bodmer, and the hunters, Dechamp and Dreidoppel, threw themselves, and rowed along the bank towards the ravenous animal. The sight of this first bear chase was interesting, and we that remained as spectators on deck awaited the result with impatience. Dechamp, a bold and experienced hunter, and an excellent marksman, was put on shore, and crept unperceived along the strand, till he got to the branch of a tree, about eighty paces from the bear, in order, in case of need, to intercept his retreat to the thickets. The ravenous bear sometimes raised his colossal head, looked around him, and then greedily returned to his repast; doubtless, because the wind was in our favour, and these animals are not remarkably quick-sighted. The boat had got to within fifty paces, when the pieces were levelled. Mr. Mitchell fired the first mortal shot, behind the shoulder blade. The other shots followed in quick succession, on which the bear rolled over, uttered fearful cries, tumbled about ten steps forwards, scratched the wounded places furiously with his paws, and turned several times completely over. At this moment Dechamp came up, and put an end to his misery by shooting him through the head. The huge beast lay stretched out: it was fastened by ropes to the boat, and conveyed in triumph to the ship, where it was measured, and a drawing made of it. I much regretted that I had not taken part in the sport; but I had not believed that it was possible, in such an open, unprotected spot, to get so near the bear.

This grizzly bear was a male, about three years old, and, therefore, not of the largest size: he was six feet two inches and two lines in length, from the nose to the tip of the tail; the latter being eight inches. His colour was dark brown, with the point of the hair of a rusty colour, but new hair already appeared of a lighter grey, with yellow tips. This bear is known to be a very dangerous beast of prey, and is willingly avoided by the hunters: if fired at, he very frequently attacks, even if not wounded, when they suddenly come too near him. If he perceives a man in time, he generally gets out of the way, especially when he has the wind. Almost all the hunters of the prairie relate their adventures with the bears, and whole volumes might be filled with such stories. It is certain that many white men and Indians have been torn to pieces by these dangerous animals, especially in former times, when they were very numerous, and lived to a great age, as may be seen in Lewis and Clarke's Travels. Even last year, five of Mr. Mitchell's hunters, who had wounded one of these animals, were so quickly pursued by him, that they were obliged to take refuge in the Missouri. This species of bear cannot climb, and therefore a tree is a good means to escape their attacks. The true country of these animals on the Missouri, where they are at present the most numerous, is the tract about Milk River. Here there is no wood of any extent in which they are not found, but they are likewise seen everywhere in a north-westerly direction. In these solitudes, the long claws of this bear serve to dig up many kinds of roots in the prairie, on which he chiefly subsists, but he is especially fond of animal food, particularly the flesh of dead animals. There is no other species of bear on the Upper Missouri, for the black bear is not found so high up. At the place where we had killed the bear, it would have been easy to shoot many of these animals, by posting ourselves near the dead buffalo cow: the whole sand bank was covered with the prints of bears' footsteps, and trodden down like a threshing-floor; but our time was too short and too precious: we, therefore, proceeded on our voyage till a violent thunder-storm threatened us, and we lay to, by the high bank of the prairie, where our bear was skinned. During the night, torrents of rain fell, which wetted our books and plants in the cabin.

On the following day, the 19th, we had another chase after a colossal bear, which swam through the Missouri to a dead buffalo; but our young hunters were this time too eager, and fired too soon, so that the animal escaped, though probably wounded, as fifteen rifles were discharged at him. Afterwards we saw several beaver lodges. The people towed the steamer in the afternoon, making their way along the bank, through a dense willow thicket. All of a sudden they cried that there were bears close to them; on which the hunters immediately leaped on shore. Mr. Mitchell had scarcely arrived at the head of the towers, when he perceived a she bear with two cubs. Dechamp came to his aid, and in a few minutes the three animals were in our power. Mr. Mitchell had killed the mother, which was of a pale yellowish-red colour; one of the cubs, which was brought alive on board, was whitish about the head and neck, and brownish grey on the body; the other was dark brown. The females of these animals are generally of a lighter colour than the males, which is the case with many beasts of prey, particularly the European fox. The live cub was in a great rage, and growled terribly; it was impossible for me to save his life.

GREENHORN MEETS GRIZZLY
1834

 IN 1834, 25-year-old John K. Townsend set out on Nathaniel J. Wyeth's second wagon train expedition to the Oregon country with a commission to collect birds for the American Philosophical Society and the Academy of Natural Sciences at Philadelphia. Townsend was a Philadelphia physician and an avid student of birds. *Along with fellow traveler Thomas Nuttall, a naturalist, botanist, and Harvard professor, he amassed a valuable collection of both birds and mammals. John James Audubon used Townsend's collections for descriptions and paintings of wildlife of the Oregon country in his two monumental series,* Birds of America *and* Viviparous Quadrupeds of North America. *In honor of his discoveries, Townsend's name has been given to numerous species. Today, for instance, Townsend's ground squirrel, Townsend's vole, Townsend's warbler, and Townsend's solitaire—all species of the northwestern U.S.—remind us of this pioneering naturalist, his historic journey, and his enormous contribution to our early knowledge of the region's biota.*

Townsend kept a journal of his travels and adventures, which lasted more than three and a half years and took him as far afield as Hawaii and Chile. He published them in 1839 as Narrative of a Journey Across the Rocky Mountains to the Columbia River. *His text was reprinted in the classic series* Early Western Travels: 1748-1846, v. XXI, *edited by Reuben Gold Thwaites (Cleveland: The Arthur H. Clark Co., 1905), from which these three segments are taken.*

It was from early encounters such as these that the grizzly acquired its ugly reputation for ferocity, aggression, "malignity," and savagery. Today's readers can easily point out the blunders in human behavior that brought on these attacks— wounding a bear, leaving "piles of meat" in camp, surprising a bear in a thicket—yet these early travelers, with their unquestioned, human-centered world view and little understanding of animal behavior, always blamed the bear.

▼▼▼▼

IN the afternoon, one of our men had a somewhat perilous adventure with a grizzly bear. He saw the animal crouching his huge frame in some willows which skirted the river, and approaching on horseback to within twenty yards, fired upon him. The bear was only slightly wounded by the shot, and with a fierce growl of angry malignity, rushed from his cover, and gave chase. The horse happened to be a slow one, and for the distance of half a mile, the race was hard contested; the bear frequently approaching so near the terrified animal as to snap at his heels, while the equally terrified rider,—who had lost his hat at the start,—used whip and spur with the most frantic diligence, frequently looking behind, from an influence which he could not resist, at his rugged and determined foe, and shrieking in an agony of fear, "shoot him, shoot him?" The man, who was one of the greenhorns, happened to be about a mile behind the main body, either from the indolence of his horse, or his own carelessness; but as he approached the party in his desperate flight, and his lugubrious cries reached the ears of the men in front, about a dozen of them rode to his assistance, and soon succeeded in diverting the attention of his pertinacious foe. After he had received the contents of all the guns, he fell, and was soon dispatched.

▼▼▼

Towards evening, we struck Blackfoot river, a small, sluggish, stagnant stream, heading with the waters of a rapid rivulet passed yesterday, which empties into the Bear river. This stream passes in a north-westerly direction through a valley of about six miles in width, covered with quagmires, through which we had great difficulty in making our way. As we approached our encampment, near a small grove of willows, on the margin of the river, a tremendous grizzly bear rushed out upon us. Our horses ran wildly in every direction, snorting with terror, and became nearly unmanageable. Several balls were instantly fired into him, but they only seemed to increase his fury. After spending a moment in rending each wound, (their invariable practice,) he selected the person who happened to be nearest, and darted after him, but before he proceeded far, he was sure to be stopped again by a ball from another quarter. In this way he was driven about amongst us for perhaps fifteen minutes, at times so near some of the horses, that he received several severe kicks from them. One of the pack horses was fairly fastened upon by the terrific claws of the brute, and in the terrified animal's efforts to escape the dreaded gripe, the pack and saddle were broken to pieces and disengaged. One of our mules also lent him a kick in the head while pursuing it up an adjacent hill, which sent him rolling to the bottom. Here he was finally brought to a stand.

The poor animal was so completely surrounded by enemies that he became bewildered. He raised himself upon his hind feet, standing almost erect, his mouth partly open, and from his protruding tongue the blood fell fast in drops. While in this position, he received about six more balls, each of which made him reel. At last, as in complete desperation, he dashed into the water, and swam several yards with astonishing strength and agility, the guns cracking at him constantly; but he was not to proceed far. Just then, Richardson, who had been absent, rode up, and fixing his deadly aim upon him, fired a ball into the back of his head, which killed him instantly. The strength of four men was required to drag the ferocious brute from the water, and upon examining his body, he was found completely riddled; there did not appear to be four inches of his shaggy person, from the hips upward, that had not received a ball. There must have been at least thirty shots made at him, and probably few missed him; yet such was his tenacity of life, that I have no doubt he would have succeeded in crossing the river, but for the last shot in the brain. He would probably weigh, at the least, six hundred pounds, and was about the height of an ordinary steer. The spread of the foot, laterally, was ten inches, and the claws measured seven inches in length. This animal was remarkably lean; when in good condition, he would, doubtless, much exceed in weight the estimate I have given. Richardson, and two other hunters, in company, killed two in the course of the afternoon, and saw several others.

▼▼▼

This evening the roaring of the bulls in the *gang* near us is terrific, and these sounds are mingled with the howling of large packs of wolves, which regularly attend upon them, and the hoarse screaming of hundreds of ravens flying over head. The dreaded grizzly bear is also quite common in this neighborhood; two have just been seen in some bushes near, and they visit our camp almost every night, attracted by the piles of meat which are heaped all around us. The first intimation we have of his approach is a great *grunt* or *snort*, unlike any sound I ever heard, but much more querulous than fierce; then we hear the scraping and tramping of his huge feet, and the snuffing of his nostrils, as the savory scent of the meat is wafted to them. He approaches nearer and nearer, with a stealthy and fearful pace, but just as he is about to accomplish the object of his visit, he suddenly stops short; the snuffing is repeated at long and trembling intervals, and if the slightest motion is then made by one of the party, away goes *"Ephraim,"* like a cowardly burglar as he is, and we hear no more of him that night....

This afternoon I observed a large flock of wild geese passing over; and upon watching them, perceived that they alighted about a mile and a half from us, where I knew there was a lake. Concluding that a little change of diet might be agreeable, I sallied forth with my gun across the plain in quest of the birds. I soon arrived at a thick copse of willow and currant bushes, which skirted the water, and was about entering, when I heard a sort of angry growl or grunt directly before me—and instantly after, saw a grizzly bear of the largest kind erect himself upon his hind feet within a dozen yards of me, his savage eyes glaring with horrible malignity, his mouth wide open, and his tremendous paws raised as though ready to descend upon me. For a moment, I thought my hour had come, and that I was fated to die an inglorious death away from my friends and my kindred; but after waiting a moment in agonizing suspense, and the bear showing no inclination to advance, my lagging courage returned, and cocking both barrels of my gun, and presenting it as steadily as my nerves would allow, full at the shaggy breast of the creature, I retreated slowly backwards. Bruin evidently had no notion of braving gunpowder, but I did not know whether, like a dog, if the enemy retreated he would not yet give me a chase; so when I had placed about a hundred yards between us, I wheeled about and flew, rather than ran, across the plain towards the camp. Several times during this run for life, (as I considered it,) did I fancy that I heard the bear at my heels; and not daring to look over my shoulder to ascertain the fact, I only increased my speed, until the camp was nearly gained, when, from sheer exhaustion I relaxed my efforts, fell flat upon the ground, and looked behind me. The whole space between me and the copse was untenanted, and I was forced to acknowledge, with a feeling strongly allied to shame, that my fears alone had represented the bear in chase of me.

When I arrived in camp, and told my break-neck adventure to the men, our young companion, Mr. Ashworth, expressed a wish to go and kill the bear, and requested the loan of my double-barrelled gun for this purpose. This I at first peremptorily refused, and the men, several of whom were experienced hunters, joined me in urging him not to attempt the rash adventure. At length, however, finding him determined on going, and that rather than remain, he would trust to his own single gun, I was finally induced to offer him mine, with a request, (which I had hoped would check his daring spirit,) that he would leave the weapon in a situation where I could readily find it; for after he had made one shot, he would never use a gun again.

He seemed to heed our caution and advice but little, and, with a dogged and determined air, took the way across the plain to the bushes, which we could see in the distance. I watched him for some time, until I saw him enter them, and then, with a sigh that one so young and talented should be lost from amongst us, and a regret that we did not forcibly prevent his going, I sat myself down, distressed and melancholy. We all listened anxiously to hear the report of the gun; but no sound reaching our ears, we began to hope that he had failed in finding the animal, and in about fifteen minutes, to my inexpressible relief, we saw him emerge from the copse, and bend his steps slowly towards us. When he came in, he seemed disappointed, and somewhat angry. He said he had searched the bushes in every direction, and although he had found numerous footprints, no bear was to be seen. It is probable that when I commenced my retreat in one direction, bruin made off in the other, and that although he was willing to dispute the ground with me, and prevent my passing his lair, he was equally willing to back out of an engagement in which his fears suggested that he might come off the loser.

A DANGEROUS VARMINT
1834-1838

 OSBORNE Russell set off from Independence, Missouri, in April 1834 on the same expedition that carried the previous author, John Townsend. But these were two very different journal-keepers: in contrast to Townsend's extensive education and scholarly pursuits, Russell had run away to sea at sixteen, deserted, then trapped in the Great Lakes area for three years before joining Wyeth's emigrant party. He remained in the Rocky Mountains as a fur trapper. Nine years later, at the end of his trapping days, he became part of the Great Migration of 1843 to Oregon (as did the authors of the story "Filled With the Beastly Thunder"), where he became active in establishing a civil government for the Oregon Territory, studied law, and was appointed a judge.

His journals cover the years 1834 to 1843, the peak of the fur trade, and recount travels in the Northern Rockies, including what later became Yellowstone National Park. Bears were more common in the early days of western exploration; travelers, trappers, and pioneers accepted them as part of the landscape, observing their behavior, killing and eating them, calling their meat "preferable to Pork." Yet in Russell's nine-year journal, he mentions grizzlies specifically on only nine occasions, including a note in his appendix of the bear's foods, behavior, size, and so on. The original spelling and punctuation have been retained in these four excerpts, which come from Journal of a Trapper 1834-1843, *edited by Aubrey L. Haines (Lincoln: University of Nebraska Press, 1965).*

▼▼▼▼

[W]E left the Fort and travelled abot 6 miles when we discovered a Grizzly Bear digging and eating roots in a piece of marshy ground near a large bunch of willows. The Mullattoe approached within 100 yards and shot him thro. the left shoulder he gave a hideous growl and sprang into the thicket. The Mullattoe then said "let him go he is a dangerous varmint" but not being acquainted with the nature of these animals I determined on making another trial, and persuaded the Mullattoe to assist me we walked round the bunch of willows where *where* the Bear lay keeping close together, with our Rifles ready cocked and presented towards the bushes untill near the place where he had entered, when we heard a sullen growl about 10 ft from us, which was instantly followed by a spring of the Bear toward us; his enormous jaws extended and eyes flashing fire. Oh Heavens! was ever anything so hideous? We could not retain sufficient presence of mind to shoot at him but took to our heels, separating as we ran the Bear taking after me, finding I could out run him he left and turned to the other who wheeled about and discharged his Rifle covering the Bear with smoke and fire the ball however missing him he turned and bounding toward me—I could go no further without jumping into a large quagmire which hemmed me on three sides, I was obliged to turn about and face him he came within about 10 paces of me then suddenly stopped and raised his ponderous body erect, his mouth wide open, gazing at me with a beastly laugh at this moment I pulled trigger and I knew not what else to do and hardly knew that I did this but it accidentally happened that my Rifle was pointed towards the Bear when I pulled and the ball piercing his heart, he gave one bound from me uttered a deathly howl and fell dead: but I trembled as if I had an ague fit for half an hour after, we butchered him as he was very fat packed the meat and skin on our horses and returned to the Fort with the trophies of our bravery, but I secretly determined in my own mind never to molest another wounded Grizzly Bear in a marsh or thicket.

▼▼▼

This is a beautiful country the large plains widely extending on either side of the river intersected with streams and occasional low spurs of Mountains whilst thousands of Buffaloe may be seen in almost every direction and Deer Elk and Grizzly bear are abundant. The latter are more numerous than in any other part of the mountains. Owing to the vast quantities of cherries plums and other wild fruits which this section of country affords. In going to visit my traps a distance of 3 or 4 mils early in the morning I have frequently seen 7 or 8 standing about the clumps of Cherry bushes on their hind legs gathering cherries with surprising dexterity not even deigning to turn their Grizzly heads to gaze at the passing trapper but merely casting a sidelong glance at him without altering their position.

▼▼▼

The place where we struck the River is called Cache Valley so called from its having been formerly a place of deposit for the Fur Traders. The country on the north and west side of the river is somewhat broken uneven and covered with wild Sage. The snow had disappeared only upon the South sides of the hills. On the South and East sides of the river lay the valley but it appeared very white and the river nearly overflowing its banks insomuch that it was very difficult crossing: and should we have been able to have crossed, the snow would have prevented us gaining the foot of the mountain on the East side of the valley. This place being entirely destitute of game we had to live chiefly upon roots for ten days. On the 11th of April we swam the river with our horses and baggage and pushed our way thru. the snow accross the Valley to the foot of the mountain: here we found the ground bare and dry. But we had to stay another night without supper. About 4 oclk the next day the meat of two fat Grizzly Bear was brought into Camp. Our Camp Kettles had not been greased for some time: as we were continually boiling thistle roots in them during the day: but now four of them containing about 3 gallons each were soon filled with fat bear meat cut in very small pieces and hung over a fire which all hands were employed in keeping up with the upmost impatience: An old experienced hand who stood six feet six and was never in a hurry about anything was selected by a unanimous vote to say when the stew (as we called it) was done but I thought with my comrades that it took a longer time to cook than any meal I ever saw prepared, and after repeated appeals to his long and hungry Stewardship by all hands he at length consented that it might be seasoned with salt and pepper and dished out to cool. But it had not much time for cooling before we commenced operations: and all pronounced it the best meal they had ever eaten as a matter of course where men had been starving.

▼▼▼

　　　My intentions were to set my traps on Rocky fork which we reached about 3 oclk P.M. our party having diminished to three men beside myself. In the meanwhile it began to rain and we Stopped to approach a band of Buffaloe and as myself and one of My comrades (a Canadian) were walking along half bent near some bushes secreting ourselves from the Buffaloe a large Grizzly Bear who probably had been awakened from his slumbers by our approach sprang upon the Canadian who was 5 or 6 feet before me and placing one forepaw upon his head and the other on his left shoulder pushed him one side about 12 ft. with as little ceremony as if he had been a cat still keeping a direct course as tho. nothing had happened. I called to the Cannadian and soon found the fright exceeded the wound as he had received no injury except what this impudent stranger had done by tearing his coat but it was hard telling which was the most frightened the man or the Bear. We reached Rocky fork about Sunset and going along the edge of the timber saw another Bear lying with a Buffaloe Calf lying between his forepaws which he had already killed while the Mother was standing about 20 paces distant Moaning very pitifully for the loss of her young. The bear on seeing us dropped the calf & took to his heels into the brush.

OVERCOMING THE WILDERNESS
Missionaries, Surveyors, Emigrants, Railroad Builders, Prospectors, and the Army

DURING the period from 1840 to 1870 many of the people who came to the West did not come to stay and settle. They were not disposed to accommodate themselves to the distinctive character of the West and its rigors. Instead they were bent, for the most part, on imposing their will upon it and transforming it. Missionaries bearing their versions of truth ("Black Robe Mission"), surveyors mapping landscapes ("John C. Fremont, Tenderfoot"), emigrants on their way to the West Coast and a new life ("Filled With the Beastly Thunder"), railroad crews in self-contained camps ("Mrs. Bictoll and the Big Black Dog"), a few prospectors hoping to leave with their fortunes ("A Savage Santa Claus"), and, of course, the Army ("We See Bear Every Day or Two," "With Book in Hand" and "General Sheridan Bags the Game"), which had among its mandates the protection of all these people and their ventures by eliminating threats from Indians—all these people were simply passing through.

The people of this era valued their enterprises and their property. They differed from the explorers and mountain men in that they did not live close to the land; mountain men had to accommodate themselves to bears, these people did not. By the end of this period, the infrastructure was in place for the massive changes that were to come.

BLACK ROBE MISSION
1840-41

 IN 1840-41, Father Pierre-Jean De Smet, an eager Jesuit missionary, was sent west to report on the prospects for missions to the Indians of the Rocky Mountains. He journeyed indefatigably for the next thirty plus years throughout the Great Plains, American and Canadian Rockies, and the Pacific Northwest. He is said to have been a zealous missionary, physically robust, and a friendly, open, and trustworthy man—traits that made him an important mediator in the growing hostilities between the native inhabitants and the invading whites. In fact, his biographer John Upton Terrell (Black Robe: The Life of Pierre-Jean De Smet, Missionary, Explorer & Pioneer, *Garden City, New York: Doubleday & Co., 1964) wrote:*

> *For more than thirty years he was the most influential man in the western wilderness. These were the years when the era of the fur trader was drawing to a close and being supplanted by the era of mass migration and settlement— the years of transition, when the juggernaut of civilization smashed across the plains, deserts and mountains, and the call of the wild was lost in the ensuing uproar.*
>
> *During this critical time no man was more trusted and revered by the Indians, and no man was a better friend to them.*

Terrell argues that if De Smet's advice concerning the Indians had been followed by federal authorities, many of the bloody conflicts of the last half of the nineteenth century would have been avoided.

Father De Smet's Letters and Sketches, with a Narrative of a Year's Residence among the Indian Tribes of the Rocky Mountains *(reprinted in Reuben Gold Thwaites, ed.,* Early Western Travels: 1748-1846, *v. XXVII, Cleveland: The Arthur H. Clark Co., 1906) "throws much light," editor Thwaites affirms, "upon wilderness travel, the topography and scenery of the Rocky Mountain region, and above all upon the habits and customs, modes of thought, social standards, and religious conceptions of the important tribes of the interior."*

Although his reports on grizzly bears were few, it is clear that these "most terrible animals" constituted one of the more salient features of the wilderness through which De Smet traveled. Lewis and Clark's journals remained valuable guides to wilderness travelers for many decades, as indicated by De Smet's repeating one of their most memorable bear encounters.

▼▼▼▼

THIS region is the retreat of grizzly bears, the most terrible animals of the desert, whose strength equals their daring and voracity. I have been assured that by a single stroke of his paw, one of these animals tore away four ribs of a buffalo, which fell dead at his feet. He seldom attacks man, unless when he has been surprised and wounded. An Indian, however, belonging to my escort, in passing by a thick wood of sallow trees, was assailed by one of these ferocious beasts, that sprung furiously upon his horse, fixed his formidable claws in his back, and brought him to the ground. The horseman fortunately was not mounted at the time, and having his gun in his hand, the bear instantly disappeared in the depths of the forest.

▼▼▼

There are also four kinds of bears, distinguished by the colors: white, black, brown and grey. The white and grey bears are what the lion is in Asia, the kings of the mountains: they are scarcely inferior to the lion in form and courage. I have sometimes joined in the chase of this animal, but I was in good company—safe from danger. Four Indian hunters ran around the bear and stunned him with their cries—they soon despatched him. In less than a quarter of an hour after this, another fell beneath their blows. This chase is perhaps the most dangerous for the bear, when wounded, becomes furious, and unless he be disabled, as was the case in the two instances mentioned, he attacks and not unfrequently kills his pursuers. Messrs. Lewis and Clarke, in their expedition to the sources of the Missouri, adduce a striking proof of the physical strength of this animal, which shows that he is a most formidable enemy. One evening, the men who were in the hindmost canoe, discovered a bear, crouched in the prairie, at a distance of about three hundred yards from the river. Six of them, all skilful hunters, left the canoe, and advanced to attack him. Protected by a little eminence, they approached without being perceived, till they were but forty steps from the animal. Four of the men discharged their guns, and each one lodged a ball in his body—two of the balls had pierced the lungs. The bear, frantic with rage, starts up and rushes upon his enemies, with wide extended jaws. As he approached, the two hunters who had kept their fire, inflicted two wounds on him; one of the balls broke his shoulder, which for a few moments retarded his progress, but before they could re-load their guns, he was so close upon them that they had to run with the greatest speed to the river. Here he was at the point of seizing them—two of the men threw themselves into the canoe, the four others scattered and hid themselves among the willows, where they loaded and fired with the greatest expedition. They wounded him several times, which only served to increase his fury; at last he pursued two of them so closely, that they were compelled to provide for their safety by leaping into the river from a perpendicular bank nearly twenty feet high. The bear followed them, and was but a few feet from them, when one of the hunters who had come from his lurking place, sent a ball through his head and killed him. They dragged him to the shore, and there ascertained that not less than eight balls passed through his body.

▼▼▼

In the following lyrical passage from Father De Smet's later travels, recorded in Oregon Missions and Travels Over the Rocky Mountains, in 1845-46 (R. G. Thwaites, ed., *Early Western Travels: 1748-1846, v. XXIX, Cleveland: The Arthur H. Clark Co., 1906), he describes the grizzly bear as well as numerous other species of the American prairie.*

▼▼▼

A monstrous animal, the grey bear, which replaces on our mountains, the African lion, is not content with growling and menacing the intrepid venturer, who dares infringe on his cavernous dominions, but grinds his teeth, expressive of his rage. Suddenly, a well-aimed gun-shot forces him to make a lowly reference; the formidable beast rolls in the dust, biting the sand saturated with his blood, and expires.

The ordinary music of the desert is, the shrill cry of the panther, and the howling of the wolf. The diminutive mountain hare, six inches high, and whose biography has not yet found a place in natural history, amuses itself amidst the stony rubbish, and exhibits wonderful activity, whilst his neighbor, the lubberly porcupine, clambers up, seats himself upon a branching cypress and gnaws bark. He views the eager huntsman with a careless and indifferent air, unconscious that his tender flesh is regarded as a most delicious morsel. The industrious beaver like a wary sentinel, warns his family of man's approach by striking the water with his tail. The muskrat, or musquash, plunges immediately into the water. The otter quits his sports and slides upon his belly among the reeds—the timid squirrel leaps from bough to bough, until it reaches the topmost shade of the cypress, the marten jumps from tree to tree, and buries itself in the foliage—the whistler and weasel repair to their respective domicils:—a precipitous flight alone saves the fox his rich silvery pelisse—the badger, or the ground hog, too remote from his dwelling, digs the sandy soil and buries himself alive, to avoid pursuit—his magnificent skin is destined to adorn the loins of an Indian—it requires the joint efforts of two men to force him from his hiding place, and to kill him.

FILLED WITH THE BEASTLY THUNDER
1843

 OVERTON Johnson and William H. Winter were young men from Indiana who made up part of the Great Migration of 1843 to Oregon and California. According to Carl L. Cannon, who provided a preface and notes to a reprint of their book, Route Across the Rocky Mountains, with a Description of Oregon and California; Their Geographical Features, Their Resources, Soil, Climate, Productions, &c., &c. *(LaFayette, Indiana: John Semans, 1846), theirs was the voice of "sensible young men, no doubt filled with Western land fever, but not too easily impressed." They produced a lively narrative for readers back home, describing not just the commercial prospects of the coastal territories but also their own day-to-day activities, hardships, encounters with Indians, and the myriad novelties and curiosities of travel on the frontier.*

▼▼▼▼

HAVING what meat we could carry, we proceeded West, along the foot of the Mountain, for a deep gap, which we had seen from the other side, in the evening. About sunset, as we were going along, we saw three Bears, up in the breaks of the Mountain, busily engaged scratching in the earth for roots. Having taken advantage of the ground, we approached near to them, and again leaving our partner, who was not a very good shot, a little distance behind with the horses and mules, we climbed up to the brink of the ridge between us and the Bears, and fired at the largest one. It fell, and supposing that we had given it a dead shot, we borrowed our companion's gun, intending to serve the second in the same way; but finding the first still alive, we gave him the contents of the second gun; upon receiving which, he sprang upon one of the others, and cuffed him until he squalled for dear life. We returned and were hastily reloading our rifles, and had only poured down the powder, when all three came rushing to the top of the hill, roaring most furiously, and so loud that the answering hills and hollow caves were filled with the beastly thunder. They stopped within forty yards of us, and in open view, rearing up on their hinder feet, the wounded one in the middle—which, as he stood, was about eight feet high—with the blood streaming from his mouth and down his side, snuffing the air on every side, to catch some tainted breath of us; but the wind was ours, and being blind with rage and pain, he did not discover us. Our companion became dreadfully frightened, so that he lost all reason, and commenced running around his horse, and exclaiming loudly, "Oh Lord! what shall we do?" We told him to mount; but he still continued running around his horse, bawling at the top of his voice: "Good God Almighty! what shall we do?" "Mount! mount!" said we again; but he paid no attention, and was making about the twentieth trip around his horse, crying aloud, "Oh Lord!" "Oh Lord!" at every step; when we gave a loud whoop, and the two Bears that were not wounded wheeled and ran off, and the wounded one tumbled back down the hill. This set our partner a little to rights, and turning to us, with a look of most perfect simplicity, he exclaimed, in a half weeping tone, "Good God! we can't fight them three Bears." You were frightened, were you not? said we. "O no, no, not bad scared," said he; "but stop—stop—look here," he continued, "may such another beautiful roar as that we just now heard, be my music from this on, if you ever catch me in a bear fight again," he added, shaking his head.

JOHN C. FREMONT, TENDERFOOT
1843

 JOHN C. Fremont was a soldier, surveyor, and politician, best remembered for his exploring expeditions throughout the West in the 1840s. On the incredibly long second expedition in 1843-44, he crossed the prairies, the Northern and Central Rockies, the Cascades, the Great Basin, the Sierra Nevadas, and the south-western deserts. These journeys, largely planned and promoted by influential politicians in Washington, were significant in opening the Far West to settlement and ousting the Mexican government from the region.

Despite the long period he spent in Wyoming Territory, Fremont encountered very few grizzlies. By the 1840s, it appears, grizzly bears were avoiding contact with people. Interestingly, Fremont's encounter doesn't conclude with the same humble, I-learned-my-lesson attitude expressed in the earlier stories by Jim Clyman and Osborne Russell.

This March 1, 1948, installment of John C. Thompson's In Old Wyoming series continued his decade-long "bearana" tales in the Wyoming State Tribune. *Fremont's adventures can be followed in his* Narrative of the Exploring Expedition to the Rocky Mountains in the Year 1842, and to Oregon and North California in the Years 1843-'44 *(Washington: H. Polkinhorn, 1845). Several biographies chronicle his travels and adventures.*

▼▼▼▼▼

JULY 11, 1843, a young man who 13 years later was to be the first Republican candidate for president of the United States, ignorant of the character of the beast took a long chance on being eliminated by a grizzly bear. He was Brevet Captain John Charles Fremont, United States topographical engineer, on his way to his second traverse of the region now encompassed within the boundaries of the state of Wyoming. His foolhardy adventure with the grizzly occurred on the South Platte river around 50 miles due south of where Cheyenne stands. He sketched it in his journal as follows:

"As we were riding quietly along, eagerly searching every hollow in search of game, we discovered, at a little distance in the prairie, a large grizzly bear so busily engaged in digging roots that he did not perceive us until we were galloping down a little hill fifty yards from him, when he charged upon us with such sudden energy, that several of us came near losing our saddles. Being wounded, he commenced retreating to a rocky piney ridge near by, from which we were not able to cut him off, and we entered the timber with him. The way was very much blocked up with fallen timber; and we kept up a running fight for some time, animated by the bear charging among the horses. He did not fall until after he had received six rifle balls. He was miserably poor, and added nothing to our stock of provisions."

Fremont at the time was little more than a tenderfoot in the West. His previous experience had been a journey up the North Platte and Sweetwater to South Pass, a climb up a peak which he christened with his own name, Fremont, then back along the Sweetwater and Platte. Had he, in 1843, known grizzly bear nature better, he would as lief have jumped off Fremont peak as pursue the wounded bear into the South Platte covert. Lady Luck certainly rode with him into the timber.

Although he traveled 1,000 or more miles in the grizzly-infested Wyoming country in 1842 and 1843, his journal relates that he saw only two grizzlies, the one he killed on the South Platte and another which he hardly more than glimpsed. His journal entry of Aug. 3, 1842, notes that about 15 miles up the Sweetwater from Devil's Gate, "several bands of buffalo made their appearance today, with herds of antelope; and a grizzly bear—the only one we encountered during the journey—was seen scrambling up among the rocks." Earlier the journal, under date of July 29, noted that while the party was near the Red Buttes, beside which flows the Platte, "on the banks were willow and cherry trees. The cherries were not yet ripe, but in the thickets are numerous fresh tracks of the grizzly bear, which are very fond of this fruit."

WITH BOOK IN HAND
1858

 IN 1859, Randolph B. Marcy, Captain U.S. Army, authored The Prairie Traveler: A Handbook for Overland Expeditions, with Maps, Illustrations, and Itineraries of the Principal Routes Between the Mississippi and the Pacific *(New York: Harper & Brothers). In this volume, reprinted in 1981 by Time-Life Books in the series* Classics of the Old West, *the Captain attempted "to explain and illustrate, as clearly and succinctly as possible, the best methods of performing the duties devolving upon the prairie traveler, so as to meet their contingencies under all circumstances, and thereby to endeavor to establish a more uniform system of marching and campaigning in the Indian country." The book was, in other words, a cookbook for conestogas.*

Numerous other guidebooks, journals, and advertising tracts had described the adventures of the emigrants, given advice on both traveling and settling in the West, and offered promises of a new future. But Marcy felt that not only his quarter century of personal experience on the frontier but also the unique role of the Army itself could help turn the wagon train traveler into a "master spirit in the wilderness."

In fact, The Prairie Traveler *was probably extremely valuable to its readers. It provided advice on the foods, clothing, and camp equipage suitable for such a journey, discussed methods of finding and purifying water, recommended ways of herding mules, repairing wagons, and fording rivers, and offered detailed itineraries complete with mileages, camping sites, and AAA-like ratings ("Good grass, wood, and water. Mail station. United States bridge for high water; no toll.")*

The author discussed the habits of the grizzly bear and other wild animals, including "secrets of the hunter's and warrior's strategy, which [he] endeavor[s] to impress more forcibly upon the reader by introducing illustrative anecdote." Unfortunately, the captain's experiences and sources were not only limited but in some cases wrong, and despite the late date of this work, considerable misinformation about the grizzly was passed along to trusting readers.

▼▼▼▼

BESIDES the common black bear of the Eastern States, several others are found in the mountains of California, Oregon, Utah, and New

Mexico, viz., the grizzly, brown, and cinnamon varieties; all have nearly the same habits, and are hunted in the same manner.

From all I had heard of the grizzly bear, I was induced to believe him one of the most formidable and savage animals in the universe, and that the man who would deliberately encounter and kill one of these beasts had performed a signal feat of courage which entitled him to a lofty position among the votaries of Nimrod. So firmly had I become impressed with this conviction, that I should have been very reluctant to fire upon one had I met him when alone and on foot. The grizzly bear is assuredly the monarch of the American forests, and, so far as physical strength is concerned, he is perhaps without a rival in the world; but, after some experience in hunting, my opinions regarding his courage and his willingness to attack men have very materially changed.

In passing over the elevated table-lands lying between the two forks of the Platte River in 1858, I encountered a full-grown female grizzly bear, with two cubs, very quietly reposing upon the open prairie, several miles distant from any timber. This being the first opportunity that had ever occurred to me for an encounter with the ursine monster, and being imbued with the most exalted notions of the beast's proclivities for offensive warfare, especially when in the presence of her offspring, it may very justly be imagined that I was rather more excited than usual. I, however, determined to make the assault. I felt the utmost confidence in my horse, as she was afraid of nothing; and, after arranging every thing about my saddle and arms in good order, I advanced to within about eighty yards before I was discovered by the bear, when she raised upon her haunches and gave me a scrutinizing examination. I seized this opportune moment to fire, but missed my aim, and she started off, followed by her cubs at their utmost speed. After reloading my rifle, I pursued, and, on coming again within range, delivered another shot, which struck the large bear in the fleshy part of the thigh, whereupon she set up a most distressing howl and accelerated her pace, leaving her cubs behind. After loading again I gave the spurs to my horse and resumed the chase, soon passing the cubs, who were making the most plaintive cries of distress. They were heard by the dam, but she gave no other heed to them than occasionally to halt for an instant, turn around, sit up on her posteriors, and give a hasty look back; but, as soon as she saw me following her, she invariably turned again and redoubled her speed. I pursued about four miles and fired four balls into her before I succeeded in bringing her to the ground, and from the time I first saw her until her death-wound, notwithstanding I was often very close upon her heels, she never came to bay or made the slightest demonstration of resistance. Her sole purpose seemed to be to make her escape, leaving her cubs in the most cowardly manner.

Upon three other different occasions I met the mountain bears, and once the cinnamon species, which is called the most formidable of all, and in none of these instances did they exhibit the slightest indication of anger or resistance, but invariably ran from me.

Such is my experience with this formidable monarch of the mountains. It is possible that if a man came suddenly upon the beast in a thicket, where it could have no previous warning, he might be attacked; but it is my opinion that if the bear gets *the wind* or sight of a man at any considerable distance, it will endeavor to get away as soon as possible. I am so fully impressed with this idea that I shall hereafter hunt bear with a feeling of as much security as I would have in hunting the buffalo.

The grizzly, like the black bear, hybernates in winter, and makes his appearance in the spring with his claws grown out long and very soft and tender; he is then poor, and unfit for food.

I have heard a very curious fact stated by several old mountaineers regarding the mountain bears, which, of course, I can not vouch for, but it is given by them with great apparent sincerity and candor. They assert that no instance has ever been known of a female bear having been killed in a state of pregnancy. This singular fact in the history of the animal seems most inexplicable to me, unless she remain concealed in her brumal [i.e., winter] slumber until after she had been delivered of her cubs.

I was told by an old Delaware Indian that when the bear has been traveling against the wind and wishes to lie down, he always turns in an opposite direction, and goes some distance away from his first track before making his bed. If an enemy then comes upon his trail, his keen sense of smell will apprise him of the danger. The same Indian mentioned that when a bear had been pursued and sought shelter in a cave, he had often endeavored to eject him with smoke, but that the bear would advance to the mouth of the cave, where the fire was burning, and put it out with his paws, then retreat into the cave again. This would indicate that Bruin is endowed with some glimpses of reason beyond the ordinary instincts of the brute creation in general, and, indeed, is capable of discerning the connection between cause and effect. Not withstanding the extraordinary intelligence which this quadruped exhibits upon some occasions, upon others he shows himself to be one of the most stupid brutes imaginable. For example, when he has taken possession of a cavern, and the courageous hunter enters with a torch and rifle, it is said he will, instead of forcibly ejecting the intruder, raise himself upon his haunches and cover his eyes with his paws, so as to exclude the light, apparently thinking that in this situation he can not be seen. The hunter can then approach as close as he pleases and shoot him down.

WE SEE BEAR EVERY DAY OR TWO
1862

 ON July 26, 1865, 20-year-old Lieutenant Caspar Collins led a small party of soldiers from the Platte Bridge Telegraph Station to meet an incoming supply wagon. Half a mile out, they were attacked by several hundred Indians. During the retreat back to the Station, Collins stopped to rescue a wounded trooper. Collins' horse ran off with him toward the Indians, and he was killed.

In the three years before his death, the youthful Collins, whom the Army honored for his bravery and whose given name inspired the naming of Casper, Wyoming, reported that grizzly bears were numerous on his travels between modern-day Casper and Dubois. John C. Thompson used Collins' letters in this story in his In Old Wyoming series in the Wyoming State Tribune, *March 2, 1948.*

▼▼▼▼

PROTECTIVE devotion of grizzly sows to their young is a theme that runs through [the] history of the Wyoming country from the earliest days. [The] idea of abandoning her offspring in the presence of peril, it appears, seldom was entertained by a grizzly mother. If the cubs could not get away their mothers died in defense of them but very rarely abandoned them. In contrast with the maternal fidelity of a grizzly, the conduct of a host of human mothers of the present is sorry, indeed, to contemplate. A grizzly mother that was false or indifferent to the responsibilities of parenthood was a phenomenon.

Grizzlies still were numerous here when young Caspar Collins, not yet past his eighteenth birthday anniversary, came to the Wyoming country with his father, Colonel William O. Collins, in 1862. Nearly everywhere military duty took the father, there, too, went the youth. He was a seasoned veteran of camp and campaign when cowardice of officers unworthy of the uniform they wore sent him to his death at 21. His experience included opportunities for observation of grizzlies.

In the summer of 1862 the boy accompanied Colonel Collins on an expedition to headwaters of Wind river. There, near where Dubois is located, he witnessed a grizzly mother's devotion to her cub. Writing to his mother from "Upper Crossing of Wind River," under date of August 13, 1862, he related as follows:

"My father and I and a teamster chased two grizzlies about 3 miles and then came upon them in a ravine. I was on my pony, my father on Woodpecker, and the teamster on a mule. I held their beasts while they got behind some rocks within about seventy-five yards of the bear. There was an old bear as big as a cow, and a half-grown cub about the size of a common black bear. It was the night after a rainstorm and not one of the guns would go off. When the old bear heard the snapping, she stood on her hind legs and the cub ran like everything. She would run until she caught up with him, when she would stop until he got ahead again, when she would move on. They got in some rocks where we could not find them anymore."

In an earlier letter from "Sweet Water Bridge," the youngster related: "We see bear every day or two but have shot none yet, they running away too fast. They are the regular grizzly, and one of them was so large that one of our officers mistook him for a buffalo."

A SAVAGE SANTA CLAUS
1860s

 CHARLES M. Russell, one of the Old West's most famous cowboy artists and writers, was born in 1864 and headed west to Montana at the age of sixteen. Although he spent many years as an itinerant cowboy, he was never far from a sketchbook or modeling clay. From his thirties on he made his living as an artist, depicting the Old West from memory—the prairies and mountains, the hard, lonely life of the cowpuncher on the range with his cattle, the game animals, the bears and the wolves, and the lives of the Plains Indians. He was a born storyteller, as demonstrated both in his artworks and in a fine collection of his stories called Trails Plowed Under: Stories of the Old West *(New York: Doubleday & Co., 1927), from which we take this tale of an encounter with a grizzly. Russell's book has, to quote from the book jacket of a 1941 reprint, "more true vernacular, more correct characterization, more faithful, carefully etched portraits, more classical incidental yarns, founded on fact, than can be discovered in any one volume of history, biography, or fiction ever written on the West."*

There is a lingering sense of tragedy in this story. An impossible situation developed, a dilemma: there was no other way for the bear, driven by instinct and interrupted in its hibernation, to have acted, and there was no other way for the men to have responded.

▼▼▼▼

"TALKIN' about Christmas," said Bedrock, as we smoked in his cabin after supper, an' the wind howled as it sometimes can on a blizzardy December night, "puts me in mind of one I spent in the '60s. Me an' a feller named Jake Mason, but better knowed as Beaver, is trappin' an' prospectin' on the head of the Porcupine. We've struck some placer, but she's too cold to work her. The snow's drove all the game out of the country, an' barrin' a few beans and some flour, we're plum out of grub, so we decide we'd better pull our freight before we're snowed in.

"The winter's been pretty open till then, but the day we start there's a storm breaks loose that skins everything I ever seed. It looks like the snow-maker's been holdin' back, an' turned the whole winter supply loose at once. Cold? Well, it would make a polar bear hunt cover.

"About noon it lets up enough so we can see our pack-hosses. We're joggin' along at a good gait, when old Baldy, our lead pack-hoss, stops an' swings 'round in the trail, bringin' the other three to a stand. His whinner causes me to raise my head, an' lookin' under my hat brim, I'm plenty surprised to see an old log shack not ten feet to the side of the trail.

" 'I guess we'd better take that cayuse's advice,' says Beaver, pintin' to Baldy, who's got his ears straightened, lookin' at us as much as to say: 'What, am I packin' fer Pilgrims; or don't you know enough to get in out of the weather? It looks like you'd loosen these packs.' So, takin' Baldy's hunch, we unsaddle.

"This cabin's mighty ancient. It's been two rooms, but the ridge-pole on the rear one's rotted an' let the roof down. The door's wide open an' hangs on a wooden hinge. The animal smell I get on the inside tells me there ain't no humans lived there for many's the winter. The floor's strewn with pine cones an' a few scattered bones, showin' it's been the home of mountain-rats an' squirrels. Takin' it all 'n all, it ain't no palace, but, in this storm, it looks mighty snug, an' when we get a blaze started in the fireplace an' the beans goin' it's comfortable.

"The door to the back's open, an' by the light of the fire I can see the roof hangin' down V-shaped, leavin' quite a little space agin the wall. Once I had a notion of walkin' in an' prospectin' the place, but there's somethin' ghostly about it an' I change my mind.

"When we're rollin' in that night, Beaver asks me what day of the month it is.

" 'If I'm right on my dates,' says I, 'this is the evenin' the kids hang up their socks.'

" 'The hell it is,' says he. 'Well, here's one camp Santy'll probably overlook. We ain't got no socks nor no place to hang 'em, an' I don't think the old boy'd savvy our foot-rags.' That's the last I remember till I'm waked up along in the night by somethin' monkeyin' with the kettle.

"If it wasn't fer a snufflin' noise I could hear, I'd a-tuk it fer a trade-rat, but with this noise it's no guess with me, an' I call the turn all right, 'cause when I take a peek, there, humped between me an' the fire, is the most robust silvertip I ever see. In size, he resembles a load of hay. The fire's down low, but there's enough light to give me his outline. He's humped over, busy with the beans, snifflin' an' whinin' pleasant, like he enjoys 'em. I nudged Beaver easy, an' whispers: 'Santy Claus is here.'

"He don't need but one look. 'Yes,' says he, reachin' for his Henry, 'but he ain't brought nothin' but trouble, an' more'n a sock full of that. You couldn't crowd it into a wagon-box.'

"This whisperin' disturbs Mr. Bear, an' he straightens up till he near touches the ridge-pole. He looks eight feet tall. Am I scared? Well, I'd tell a man. By the feelin' runnin' up and down my back, if I had bristles I'd resemble a wild hog. The cold sweat's drippin' off my nose, an' I ain't got nothin' on me but sluice-ice.

"The bark of Beaver's Henry brings me out of this scare. The bear goes over, upsettin' a kettle of water, puttin' the fire out. If it wasn't for a stream of fire runnin' from Beaver's weapon, we'd be in plumb darkness. The bear's up agin, bellerin' an' bawlin', and comin' at us mighty warlike, and by the time I get my Sharp's workin', I'm near choked with smoke. It's the noisiest muss I was ever mixed up in. Between the smoke, the barkin' of the guns an' the bellerin' of the bear, it's like hell on a holiday.

"I'm gropin' for another ca'tridge when I hear the lock on Beaver's gun click, an' I know his magazine's dry. Lowerin' my hot gun, I listen. Everythin's quiet now. In the sudden stillness I can hear the drippin' of blood. It's the bear's life runnin' out.

" 'I guess it's all over,' says Beaver, kind of shaky. 'It was a short fight, but a fast one, an' hell was poppin' while she lasted.'

"When we get the fire lit, we take a look at the battle ground. There lays Mr. Bear in a ring of blood, with a hide so full of holes he wouldn't hold hay. I don't think there's a bullet went 'round him.

"This excitement wakens us so we don't sleep no more that night. We breakfast on bear meat. He's an old bear an' it's pretty stout, but a feller livin' on beans and bannocks straight for a couple of weeks don't kick much on flavor, an' we're at a stage where meat's meat.

"When it comes day, me an' Beaver goes lookin' over the bear's bedroom. You know, daylight drives away ha'nts, an' this room don't look near so ghostly as it did last night. After winnin' this fight, we're both mighty brave. The roof caved in with four or five feet of snow on, makes the rear room still dark, so, lightin' a pitch-pine glow, we start explorin'.

"The first thing we bump into is the bear's bunk. There's a rusty pick layin' up against the wall, an' a gold-pan on the floor, showin' us that the human that lived there was a miner. On the other side of the shack we ran onto a pole bunk, with a weather-wrinkled buffalo robe an' some rotten blankets. The way the roof slants, we can't see into the bed, but by usin' an axe an' choppin' the legs off, we lower it to view. When Beaver raises the light, there's the frame-work of a man. He's layin' on his left side, like he's sleepin', an' looks like he cashed in easy. Across the bunk, under his head, is an old-fashioned cap-'n-ball rifle. On the bedpost hangs a powder horn an' pouch, with a belt an' skinnin' knife. These things tell us that this man's a pretty old-timer.

"Findin' the pick an' gold-pan causes us to look more careful for what he'd been diggin'. We explore the bunk from top to bottom, but nary a find. All day long we prospects. That evenin', when we're fillin' up on bear meat, beans and bannocks, Beaver says he's goin' to go through the bear's bunk; so, after we smoke, relightin' our torches, we start our search again.

"Sizin' up the bear's nest, we see he'd laid there quite a while. It looks like Mr. Silvertip, when the weather gets cold, starts huntin' a winter location for his long snooze. Runnin' onto this cabin, vacant, and lookin' like it's for rent, he jumps the claim an' would have been snoozin' there yet, but our fire warmin' up the place fools him. He thinks it's spring an' steps out to look at the weather. On the way he strikes this breakfast of beans, an' they hold him till we object.

"We're lookin' over this nest when somethin' catches my eye on the edge of the waller. It's a hole, roofed over with willers.

" 'Well, I'll be damned. There's his cache,' says Beaver, whose eyes has follered mine. It don't take a minute to kick these willers loose, an' there lays a buckskin sack with five hundred dollars in dust in it.

" 'Old Santy Claus, out there,' says Beaver, pointin' to the bear through the door, 'didn't load our socks, but he brought plenty of meat an' showed us the cache, for we'd never a-found it if he hadn't raised the lid.'

"The day after Christmas we buried the bones, wrapped in one of our blankets, where we'd found the cache. It was the best we could do.

" 'I guess the dust's ours,' says Beaver. 'There's no papers to show who's his kin-folks.' So we splits the pile an' leaves him sleepin' in the tomb he built for himself."

MRS. BICTOLL AND THE BIG BLACK DOG
1867

 CAMP life was rigorous in eastern Wyoming during the building of the Union Pacific Railroad following the Civil War, and grub-snatching bears were not tolerated. This amusing story ends, predictably, in death for the grizzly. The account tells of a situation that has persisted to our own day: when bears are drawn into camps by food left out, they are seen as the aggressors and killed. This story by G.E. Lemmon was among the oral histories collected by the Wyoming Works Progress Administration and is filed in the Wyoming Department of Commerce's Historical Research and Publications in Cheyenne. A couple minor changes have been made in the text.

In her textbook, Wyoming: Frontier State *(Denver: Old West Publishing, 1947), Velma Linford offers us a glimpse of the magnitude of the railroad building project and a few of its hardships:*

> *Thousands of men followed the iron trail. In advance of any crew went the surveyors, who, in spite of earlier surveys, resurveyed the route just ahead of work crews. After the surveyors came the grading crew numbering sometimes as many as 10,000 men. They went ahead of the track, set up their tent-and-shack construction towns, prepared the road bed for the track-laying, then moved on. Three hundred freighters were required to carry supplies, the outfits sometimes stretching 100 miles across the desert. After them came the 450 men in the track construction crew. Another 300 came, operating the trains. Every train unloaded its rough-and-ready gangs of graders and track-layers at the end-of-track town.*
>
> *Food for men and livestock had to be hauled 200 to 300 miles beyond the tracks where men were grading. The desert water between Rawlins and Green River was tainted with salt and alkali. One report said that at Bitter Creek (beyond Carbon), it was impossible for cattle to drink the water without dying. The alkali water was even unfit for use in locomotives. . . .*
>
> *Surveying parties, strung out over miles of desert, were perfect prey for Indians. . . .*

From Fort Kearney to Bitter Creek, Wyoming, every mile had to be surveyed, graded, "tied," and bridged under military protection.

▼▼▼▼

MRS. Bictoll was a one-time hired girl of mother's at Liberty Farm on the Ben Holladay stage line to California from St. Joe, Missouri. Shortly after leaving mother's employ, she married. In the migration from the Little Blue to U. P. Construction at Kearney, the spring of '66, the family joined the exodus. There were then two children, a boy of about six and a girl about five. Mr. Bictoll put his few teams on grading work and Mrs. Bictoll cooked for the grading crew that her husband was one of.

Late the fall of '67, they were in a camp west of Cheyenne, Wyoming, near Carmichael's camp at Sherman Pass. James Daugherty, an expert hunter, was furnishing wild meats for the camp. All storehouses were tents, covering, usually, a frame skeleton, out of which it was hard to keep the dogs. Therefore, no dogs were allowed in camp excepting a very valuable hunting dog of Daugherty's and he would absolutely not touch any food except what his master fed him; for Daugherty had taught him thus, on account of his sometimes poisoning grey wolves. Grub was too valuable to be exposed to dogs, so this was practically an established rule in all camps.

One evening, as supper was about ready, Mrs. Bictoll had to go to the grub tent for sugar for supper, so she left six-year old Emma, her daughter, to watch the kitchen in her absence. But soon she heard a scream and rushed back to the kitchen to find Emma flown and what she took to be a large black dog in full possession. Several pans of biscuits were overturned, the slop bucket spilled over the floor and the supposed dog was trying to eat a hot roast he had dragged from the open oven. She seized an ax that was standing beside the outer door and slammed the animal beside the head with the flat side of it and drove him from the kitchen.

About that time the workmen began streaming into the kitchen for supper and she said to them in a loud voice: "You will be in luck if you get enough to eat, for a big black dog has just about demoralized everything." Just then Daugherty stepped in and heard her remark about a dog so he said: "Mrs. Bictoll, there is no dog in camp besides mine and he is not black. Which way did he go for he must be killed before he destroys any more valuable food."

Mrs. Bictoll said he had lumbered off up the side of the mountain; Daugherty grabbed his rifle and started on his trail, for there was sufficient snow for trailing. Soon they heard a shot and Mrs. Bictoll remarked: "I might as well have killed the dog in the first place for he was certainly a goner now as Jim never misses."

Daugherty soon appeared in the entrance to the kitchen and asked Mrs. Bictoll to step to the door and see if it was her dog. As she viewed the remains she answered: "Yes, that is the destructive brute." To which Daugherty replied: "That happens to be a grizzly bear." Whereupon, Mrs. Bictoll promptly fainted and fell backward right into the arms of the walking boss who happened to be in the path of her fall. Just at that moment her husband entered the door, as he was late getting his teams attended to, and beheld his wife in the arms of the boss, he said: "You damn scoundrel! Now that you have her, you can just keep her, for I have been suspicioning this for some time." The boss answered: "Don't be a fool. Come and take her before I let her fall for I am certainly over-matched" (Mrs. B. weighed over 200 pounds). But as Mr. Bictoll made no move, the boss shouted: "For God's sake, relieve me of this livestock." By that time the others had made Mr. B. understand that his wife had fainted from the after-fright from a bear she had just killed and then he wanted to whip the boss for calling his wife "livestock." But the boss, under the circumstances, refused to fight him and it was soon arranged that they were all to claim his wife had killed the bear for demolishing her supper. Mr. B. took great pride in relating to an appreciative audience the circumstances of his wife killing the bear. Daugherty, being an old friend of the family, was allowed to care for the Mrs. in her sleeping tent while Bictoll with the assistance of Emma, gathered up and served the supper. When Mrs. Bictoll had revived enough to understand, Daugherty explained to her that she was to get credit for killing the bear. Of course, she accepted the honor and peace and confidence again reigned in the Bictoll family. Mrs. Bictoll being such a fine cook, the secret was well kept for they did not want a ruction in the family which might deprive them of their excellent bill of fare.

GENERAL SHERIDAN BAGS THE GAME
1870

 GENERAL Philip Henry Sheridan was assigned to the West after demonstrating his leadership and fighting ability as a Union cavalry commander in the Civil War. In early 1870 the General was on an inspection tour of the western part of his Division of the Missouri. In Helena, capital of Montana Territory, after organizing exploratory expeditions to the Yellowstone "wonderland," he learned of the impending war between Germany and France and hurried east with hopes of witnessing it. It was during this journey that his memoirs recount this fairly predictable grizzly bear encounter.

Grizzlies were not only seen as a grand opportunity for sport hunting, but—not surprisingly—this narrative also has the flavor of a military action: the party held "a council of war," "attacked the enemy," and carried off the skins as "evidence of their prowess." Personal Memoirs of P. H. Sheridan, General United States Army, *was first published in 1888 (New York: Charles L. Webster & Co.).*

▼▼▼▼

WE made camp at the end of the day's march within ten miles of [Fort] Buford, and arrived at the post without having had any incident of moment, unless we may dignify as one a battle with three grizzly bears, discovered by our friendly Indians the morning of our second day's journey. While eating our breakfast—a rather slim one, by the way—spread on a piece of canvas, the Indians, whose bivouac was some distance off, began shouting excitedly, "Bear! bear!" And started us all up in time to see, out on the plain some hundreds of yards away, an enormous grizzly and two almost full grown cubs. Chances like this for a bear hunt seldom offered, so there was hurried mounting—the horses being already saddled—and a quick advance made on the game from many directions, Lieutenant Townsend, of the escort, and five or six of the Indians going with me. Alarmed by the commotion, bruin and her cubs turned about, and with an awkward yet rapid gait headed for a deep ravine, in which there was brushwood for shelter.

My party rode directly across the prairie and struck the trail not far behind the game. Then for a mile or more the chase was kept up, but with such poor shooting because of the "buck fever" which had seized most of us, that we failed to bring down any of the grizzlies, though the cubs grew so tired that the mother was often obliged to halt for their defense, meanwhile urging them on before her. When the ravine was gained she hid the cubs away in the thick brushwood, and then coming out where we could plainly see her, stood on the defense just within the edge of the thicket, beyond the range of our rifles though, unless we went down into the cañon, which we would have to do on foot, since the precipitous wall precluded going on horseback. For an adventure like this I confess I had little inclination, and on holding a council of war, I found that the Indians had still less, but Lieutenant Townsend, who was a fine shot, and had refrained from firing hitherto in the hope that I might bag the game, relieved the embarrassing situation and saved the credit of the party by going down alone to attack the enemy. Meanwhile I magnanimously held his horse, and the Sioux braves did a deal of shouting, which they seemed to think of great assistance.

Townsend, having descended to the bottom of the ravine, approached within range, when the old bear struck out, dashing into and out of the bushes so rapidly, however, that he could not get fair aim at her, but the startled cubs running into full view, he killed one at the first shot and at the second wounded the other. This terribly enraged the mother, and she now came boldly out to fight, exposing herself in the open ground so much as to permit a shot, that brought her down too, with a broken shoulder. Then the Indians and I, growing very brave, scrambled down to take part in the fight. It was left for me to despatch the wounded cub and mother, and having recovered possession of my nerves, I did the work effectively and we carried off with us the skins of the three animals as trophies of the hunt and evidence of our prowess.

RANCHERS AND SPORTSMEN

THE nine stories in this section, covering the years from 1878 to about 1915, show that the landscape was indeed being recast by human hands. Lands were fenced and plowed, bison were eliminated and replaced with herds of cattle (the excesses of hide and meat hunters are well known—an estimated 60 million bison were reduced by about 1890 to only a few dozen in Yellowstone National Park), forests were cut on a scale previously unknown, and in this process, predators were targeted for destruction. During this period bear numbers and range shrank dramatically—no match for the seemingly endless bullets, poisons, and traps.

Several basic motives prompted the killing of grizzlies in these accounts, which we feel characterize this period. Many bears were killed by hunters—for bounties, as in our story "Seven Silvertips in Half an Hour," for manly sport, as in "A True Sportsman Speaks," for the "wine of fame" and a bearskin coat, as in "My Last Bear Hunt, by Joe III," for some high-risk fun, as in "Grizzly Roping," or for a sense of domination and control, as in "Dr. Allen." Many bears were also killed by ranchers in order to save their cattle. Future Wyoming Governor B. B. Brooks took retribution on a marauding grizzly in "Big Foot Wallace," as did a ranching community in "Laramie River Grizzly." In addition, simply living on the land occasioned encounters with the big bears, and sometimes these had dread consequences, as in "The Vetter Saga" and "Bear Hugs for Dan Blair."

By the 1890s, the American Frontier was officially declared closed. The dominance of American enterprise was stamped deeply and permanently on the landscape, but in its success, it contained the seeds of a contradictory view that began to emerge at the end of this period.

DR. ALLEN
1878

 IN 1903, Dr. William A. Allen, a dentist in Billings, Montana, published his memoirs, entitled simply Adventures with Indians and Game, or Twenty Years in the Rocky Mountains (Chicago: A. W. Bowen, 1903; reprinted by Time-Life in 1983 in its series Classics of the Old West). This unassuming title, however, belies stories that read today like an archetype of the Old West— monumental scenery, unrestrained hunting (with crusty old characters for partners), brutish predators, and fiendish Indians.

Dr. Allen came west from Ohio in 1877 and joined an emigrant party bound for Bozeman. After an Indian attack and subsequent reorganization of the wagon train, Allen became its leader. The train had other encounters with the Plains Indians, who, by this time, were locked in desperate conflict with the whites. His group spent three days at the site of the battle of the Little Big Horn, little more than a year after it happened. "Each soldier. . . yet lay where he had fallen on that ill-fated day. Each move that was then made could be read by us as from the page of an open book." In the remainder of his book, after the eventful trip to Bozeman, Allen, a keen sportsman and "crack rifle shot," jumped from one game hunt to another for the next twenty years.

Dr. Allen responded fully to the grandeur of the landscape; he often spoke of a need to be in the mountains and described his haunts lovingly. Yet, another need, "the old fever," "the desire to shoot something," came with it. Regarding predators, he claimed, "I had never yet weakened when called upon to rid the world of one of these brutes." He could not tolerate what he saw as pride in any animal. And so it was with the grizzly bear. He respected its strength, grace, speed, keen senses, intelligence. Yet he must have mastery over it, must prove himself against the savage power of this monarch, whom he seemed to regard as an integral part of the mountains he loved.

Here are three incidents from Allen's fascinating book. We have made a few minor typographical corrections in the text.

▼▼▼▼▼

STARTING up Fly Creek, we rode fast all day through the warm sun, and about noon of the next day, we were near the Big Horn mountains.

What a scene lay before us. The verdant hills were covered with hundreds of buffaloes. The sunshine lent luster to their black glossy coats. The calves were at play, running here and there over the grassy slopes. This was not the only picture we looked upon that day. Small herds of antelopes dotted the hills both on the right and left, their white sides glimmering in the distance. The valleys were occupied by elks and antelopes, while, far away near the foothills, strolled a large band of elks, that had just descended from the heights above, to enjoy the grass and warmth of the valley. Nothing could have been added to improve the picture. Men never designed anything half so lovely. Many a hunter of to-day would give much to see the like. All was silent, save that now and then the clear notes of the lark broke the stillness. We let the animals graze, while we sat upon a knoll to feast our eyes. I was trembling from head to foot with contending emotions. I wanted to try my skill with a rifle, yet did not wish to mar the peaceful scene.

"What's the matter with you?" Steward asked. "Did you never see a buffalo before, or are you skeered."

"I am charmed with the buffaloes, elks, antelopes, hills, valleys, and mountains."

"Whar is the elk?" he asked in surprise, straining his failing eyes to see them.

"Look among the foothills to the north and you will see plenty of them," I said.

"Oh, yes, I see them now. Wal, I guess we will be able to load our packs soon."

"We must first find wood and water, then we will take a promenade over that way. Let's be off at once. I am eager for the chase."

Steward needed no further urging. We took our course toward a quaking-asp thicket, about two miles to the northwest. We there found plenty of wood and water. The pack-saddles, blankets, and cooking utensils were torn from the backs of our weary animals, but they kept looking into the thicket, snorting and acting very strangely.

"I'll bet thar's Injuns in thar," said Steward, with a wise shake of his head. "Old John always tells me when thar's Injuns nigh."

"I'll take a turn through the thicket and see what's up, while you picket the horses," I said.

I took my gun and went around the thicket, looking closely, but could find no trail of any kind. I came back and reported to Steward, but he shook his head dubiously.

"John don't lie," he said decidedly. "Go into the hollar and look. Thar's a screw loose somewhar. Keep your hand on your head if you value your scalp."

I took an old game trail and soon saw the tracks of a very large bear. My senses were alert at once; I filled my gun with cartridges and crept forward more carefully. A large hole torn through the fallen pea and hop vines arrested my attention. I raised the hammer of my gun and started to crawl in upon my hands and knees. I followed the opening about thirty yards, and was within ten yards of the opposite bank, when his bearship gave a growl that made me think I had business outside; I did not fly exactly, but bade him a hasty adieu, crawling out much faster than I entered. When I got out to where the air was not so oppressive, I took shelter behind a tree. I attempted to coax the brute out by throwing stones, but failed. Every means was tried in vain. He still refused to leave his vantage-ground. The vines were so dense that I could not see to get a shot at him and, if I ventured in again, he might take me unawares and make a meal of me. In my dilemma I called to Steward that I had run a monstrous rat to earth, and needed assistance. He lost no time in coming and appeared upon the opposite side, with his old Sharp's across his shoulder and his knife swinging from his belt.

"It's a bar instead of Injuns?" he called to me in a questioning tone.

"Yes," I replied, "and you are not far from him; just around that little bank, under those vines, is his castle."

"How do you know?" he asked.

"I was fool enough to crawl in until he gave me to understand my company was not agreeable."

"Wal, I'll soon find him out. He can't run no bluff on me; if I had an explosive ball, I'd jist walk down thar and blow him inside out."

"Try the torpedo racket on him," I said.

"I have a torpedo in old 'reliable' that I'll try on him," said Steward. The bear acted as though he both heard and understood our talk, for at that moment he scattered the vines and uttered savage growls which made me turn cold. Before Steward could fire, the bear was close upon him, but a ball from the rifle struck the brute in the heart while he was crossing a log which gave way, throwing Bruin over backward. Steward put in another cartridge and snapped it, but it did not explode. By this time the bear had regained his feet, and, maddened with rage, was rushing at Steward, who had extracted the shell of the bad cartridge, but not the ball, which stuck fast in the grooves of his rifle. It was a terrible position for a defenseless man, having the bear almost upon him, while, from my position on the other side, I could see only the top of Steward's head, for he was close to the vines and I could not know how the battle was going, although the sounds told me much. I knew my presence was required, but was undecided whether to force my way through the undergrowth, or run around. Either course would have consumed valuable time. Steward intimated what was best for me to do, by dropping his gun and starting up hill, as fast as his lame leg would allow him. I decided to remain perched upon the rock where I was, with the hope that I might get a shot at the bear. Steward rushed up hill, the bear close behind, in plain sight now. Steward's buckskin coat, which was covered with blood, hair, grease, and all kinds of filth, stood out straight behind him. I could not get a shot for fear of hitting him, and began to think he was doomed to be devoured alive.

I called out at the top of my voice, "Run for the rock up hill. Hurry, he is almost on your back."

Steward redoubled his speed and went as I directed him, the bear gaining upon him so fast that I felt sure it would catch him before he could find safety upon the rock. My time for action was come. I sent a ball through the tops of the bushes, which took effect in the shoulder of the bear. He stopped for a moment, roaring with pain and twisting his head to get at the wound; but started again in pursuit of poor Steward. I fired a second time, just as the brute was getting ready to strip the buckskin coat from Steward's back, but did not stop the animal. A thrill of horror ran through me at the thought of what must speedily occur if something was not done to stay the bear. I nerved myself, with great effort, and fired at its head, just as Steward made a leap to grasp the edge of the rock. He caught it, but the frail brink broke and let him down. Luckily for him, however, my last shot had struck the bear in the neck and had broken the spinal cord and they fell together at the same moment.

I could hardly find courage to look. The bear in its deathstruggle did not forget Steward, but caught the old man by the waistband of his elk-skin pantaloons, and threw him twenty feet down the hill. The fearful cry that escaped the lips of Steward as he was tossed through the air unnerved me. I tore through the brush, across the hollow and up the hill. Steward lay motionless, to all appearances lifeless. I feared the bear was not quite dead, and gave it another ball to make sure. The report caused Steward to stir feebly. I examined him carefully and found no marks of violence upon him, but his eyes were encircled by a yellow band, often seen in the face of the dead. I filled my hat with water and bathed his face, which revived him slowly, and looking wildly around, his eyes fell upon the dead bear.

"How did I git away from him?" He asked in a low, feeble voice, a gleam of intelligence lighting up his face.

"He threw you down hill because he did not like your company any better than mine," I replied.

I raised him to a sitting posture. He remained in a profound silence for a time, evidently going through the late adventure in his mind. Finally he said with a great solemnity of manner:

"Great God! Twenty-five years in the mountains, and that's the closest call I ever had yit."

"You are not dead yet," I said, "and you are good for twenty-five years more."

Steward never got over the terrible shock and fright of this affair. It preyed upon his mind continually, his hitherto robust constitution failed soon after. He died alone, in his cabin on Pryor Creek, and his body was found by a hunter two or three days thereafter. Little was known of his previous history, but he told me once, that he had been married in the East and that family troubles had driven him to the mountains to seek peace of mind. It is needless to say that the adventure with the bear terminated our hunt, so I skinned the animal and got one hundred and seventy-six pounds of oil out of the carcass. It was the largest bear I ever saw. The hide was fully nine feet square, just as it was stripped from the body.

▼▼▼

I had gone but a short distance when a skunk stepped boldly into my path, and, forgetting his manners, refused to give the road. This made me angry and the battle commenced. Small stones went whizzing through the air, and my opponent was getting the worst of the battle, when a large grizzly bear appeared upon the scene. She came out of a patch of bushes just beyond the skunk, and stood upon her haunches, looking me over with an air that seemed to forbid further hostilities. There was no tree near, but a high rock offered shelter in case I should need it. I thought I could easily break her neck, but she did not change her position, so I sent a ball at her just as she started to get down on all fours. The ball struck her in the back of the neck, making only a flesh wound. She roared as only a grizzly can roar and made a lunge at me. I ran for the rock, but found that I could not climb it. I then rushed around it and toward the creek, hoping to escape that way. The dodge gave me time to throw in another cartridge, and, as the bear came around the rock, I gave her another ball in the breast. A roar loud and long rent the air, and, before I had time to turn, she was almost upon me. I then ran for dear life, imagining all the time that I could feel her sharp claws and teeth tearing my flesh. She was a knowing brute, and, instead of following in the rear as she rounded the rock, she headed off my retreat.

There was nothing that could be done, but to turn aside and jump into the creek. With one desperate leap I cleared the ice that lay along the bank, and fell into the running water. I was a fast swimmer and got some start of her, but she soon gained upon me rapidly. A large rock was upon the opposite bank, some distance down the stream. My only hope lay in reaching it. Horror! I had not thought of the Devil's Slide, and was almost into the rapids that would dash me to death against the rocks.

Death menaced me on every hand. I threw my side against the waves, and ventured on a little further. The rapids were not so near as I thought, although the waves were strong. One last powerful stroke brought me to shore a little way below the rock, but, while climbing the ste[e]p bank, the big brute came so near, that I was compelled to relinquish my grasp and push her off with my gun. Concentrating all of my strength, I pushed her with so much force as to send her out into the rapids, which bore her to speedy destruction.

Had it been possible to live in the boiling waters, the tall rocks on either side made it impossible for her to get out, and I ran down the bank, trying to catch a glimpse of her but in vain. I was almost ready to die with cold and fatigue. My wet clothes hung upon me like leaden weights. In this condition I reached camp, made a fire, dried my clothes, cooking supper at the same time. A strong cup of coffee strengthened and relieved me at once. . . .

The waning light shone dimly through large cracks in the wall, for darkness was settling around the shack. The sweet, yet mournful, murmur of the stream fell soothingly upon my wearied senses. I could hear the deer as they crossed and recrossed and the beavers slapping the water with their tails repeatedly, while over all sounded the lonely cry of the owl. The snapping of dry sticks aroused me from a semi-conscious state, and I saw a large bull elk dash through the brush and across the creek before I could get my gun. His eyes like two jack lamps as he passed.

John came up through the willows just then, and, after a warm supper, we stretched our weary limbs before the fire and recounted the adventures of the day. John had killed three deer, and I told him of my deer and the skunk, but paused to take breath before I mentioned the bear.

"But what makes you look so lank?" he inquired? "Your clothes fit you closer than they did when we started out."

"Only a swimming race with a grizzly. You should have seen me when it was over," I said. We had a big laugh after all was told, but I assure you that I did not even smile while the performance was going on.

▼▼▼

I... took to the hills, longing to get within shot of deer or elk. The country around was very broken, but, by climbing rocks and holding onto bushes, I managed to keep upon my feet until exhausted. Finally I was compelled to sit down upon a rock for a few moments' rest. Deep-cut canyons, filled with dark green pines, surrounded by massive walls of gray granite, were yawning in the broad noonday light.

A bald eagle, looking as if perched on air, was high above me in the heavens, sailing with pinions spread, while not a quiver or motion of his body was perceptible. As though he would fain express his scorn for a creature so far beneath him, he looked down upon me. Suddenly he bent his body earthward, clapped his wings close to his sides, and came down within one hundred yards. Around and around me he sailed, apparently contemplating the advisability of descending upon me. He paused over my head, scanning the rocks upon which I sat, taking in my position before he should gather me in his talons. The temptation to conquer this proud bird was too strong to be resisted. The power which held him in space was quickly terminated by a ball from my rifle, and he fell to the earth with a force that split his body in twain.

The effects produced by a single rifle-shot in an uninhabited region are wonderful. While the report was echoing from canyon to canyon, ravens screamed, the mountain thrush chattered in his tree, while the squirrels scampered from branch to branch, frisking their tails and chattering in chorus. All were intent upon seeing the intruder and determining what was meant by the unusual commotion. A large bull elk, either fearing for his own safety or curious to learn the cause of the disturbance, came rushing up the canyon, tearing through the small trees and bushes with his horns as he leaped through the air. Anxious to convert him into meat for my own use, I gave him a hasty shot. Alas! he heeded not the summons, but increased his speed, leaving a trail of blood to mark his course.

I followed, as fast as fallen trees and other obstructions would permit, for about two miles, when, covered with blood and foam, he started up from behind a fallen tree. Again the report of my rifle rang through the air, and the animal reeled, fell, and lay prostrate upon the ground, the blood flowing in a stream from his neck. It was no small job to cut him up, but I finally succeeded in securing his hams, and was starting for the ponies, when a terrible roar caused me to look in the direction whence it came.

I saw a large grizzly coming, as fast as it could, to help me dispose of my game, and probably to dispose of me, should I deny its right to a share of the elk. Two cubs brought up the rear, eagerly following the trail of blood, their savage appetites fully aroused. My first impulse was to climb a tree, but the idea of relinquishing my game to these blood-thirsty animals was not to be considered, so I fired at the foremost cub, and had the satisfaction of seeing it drop dead. The mother paused a moment to bewail the loss of her offspring, only to see the other stretched lifeless beside the first.

I now directed a shot at her ear, but missed the mark and slightly fractured her lower jaw. She immediately deserted her dead cubs and rushed at me like a tornado, uttering fierce growls. Another shot, intended for the head, struck her in the neck, and with a deafening roar she leaped toward me.

I attempted to fire again, but she was too quick for me and knocked the rifle from my hands. At the same instant I jumped behind a small tree and swung myself up among its branches.

Vain were her attempts to dislodge me. Her wounds distracted her attention, and, at last, faint from loss of blood, she lay down. I threw stick after stick at her, hoping to drive her to a location more pleasing to myself, but she only rolled her fiery eyes, uttering low guttural growls, until death came to her release. Fearing she might be "playing 'possum," I hurled my knife at her with all my force. Yes, she was certainly dead! Still my hair would stand on end and my teeth chatter, as I stepped down from my retreat, grasped my gun, and put another ball into her, just to make assurance doubly sure.

The spark of life was not quite extinct, but she struggled only for a moment. Tired and somewhat ruffled in temper, I sat down to take in the situation. The earth was torn up in several places, and the grass, but an hour ago so green and beautiful, was dyed with blood. After indulging in a long reverie, I looked around for one of the cubs that was missing, and found it dead in a thicket with an ugly hole through its back.

GRIZZLY ROPING—A GREAT COWBOY SPORT
1884

 GRIZZLY roping was apparently a widespread activity in the Old West. Wyoming Governor B. B. Brooks gives a good account of it in the story "Big-Foot Wallace," and Theodore Roosevelt described it thus in his book The Wilderness Hunter:

Cowboys delight in nothing so much as the chance to show their skill as riders and ropers; and they always try to ride down and rope any wild animal they come across in favorable ground and close enough up. If a party of them meets a bear in the open they have great fun; and the struggle between the shouting, galloping rough-riders and their shaggy quarry is full of wild excitement and not unaccompanied by danger. The bear often throws the noose from his head so rapidly that it is a difficult matter to catch him; and his frequent charges scatter his tormentors in every direction while the horses become wild with fright over the roaring, bristling beast—for horses seem to dread a bear more than any other animal. If the bear cannot reach cover, however, his fate is sealed. Sooner or later, the noose tightens over one leg, or perchance over the neck and fore-paw, and as the rope straightens with a "pluck," the horse braces itself desperately and the bear tumbles over. Whether he regains his feet or not the cowboy keeps the rope taut; soon another noose tightens over a leg, and the bear is speedily rendered helpless.

Roping a 900-pound grizzly, no matter how you look at it, must have been an unparalleled experience. But from the grizzly's viewpoint, an attack by three horsemen meant only one thing: an all-out defense. This story by Peggy H. Benjamin, originally entitled "Grizzly Roping was Great Cowboy Sport," was published in the Wyoming Rural Electric News, *June, 1981. Additional stories about her uncle, Cap Haskell, are recounted in her book* Adventures in Old Wyoming, 1879-1884 *(Lincoln, Nebraska: Midgard Press, 1988).*

▼▼▼▼

ROPING a silver-tipped grizzly was great sport. It could also be dangerous, as Cap Haskell, Lew Williams and Nate Young found out one crisp fall day in 1884.

During the summer roundup for branding, several saddle horses had been lost. It was the cowboys' job to find them before winter set in. Cap and Lew were natives of Ohio; Nate, a Texan, had drifted north with the longhorn cattle drives. But after five years' riding over the rugged terrain, inhabited by wild animals and roving bands of Indians, all three were expert horsemen and equally expert with rope and gun.

Well-armed against the unexpected or possible attacks, the three left their ranch headquarters, the 71 (Seventy-One Quarter Circle) ranch, located at Three Crossing on the Sweetwater, near South Pass City, where many women had been massacred at the time of the Mormon handcart trek to Utah. The vast range covered 2,560,000 acres on which grazed nineteen thousand head of cattle and large herd horses. The ranch manager was John Clay.

Cap figured that the lost saddle horses could be located somewhere in the vicinity of Green Mountain, a well-known landmark to travelers. Fording the Sweetwater, which bordered the ranch yard on the south, the three fanned out. Eyes and ears alert, they searched all day without finding any sign of the missing horses. At dusk they met at the head of Lost Creek, which began about two miles south of the mountain and ran southwest through the Red Desert. At that time of year, the flow was shallow with now and then a deep hole where wild animals watered, then it disappeared into a mile-or-two-long sandbar, followed by another stretch of water with deep holes, then another sandbar, for a distance of fifteen miles.

Gathering armloads of dry sagebrush, the cowboys built a roaring fire. All three were weary after the long day in the saddle. After they had fed, watered and put hobbles on their horses, they boiled a pot of strong coffee. Supper that night was rare beefsteak, fried potatoes and biscuits baked in a small, well-used dutch oven. Oats for the horses, their own provisions and camp equipment had been carried by the packhorse.

As soon as supper was over, they threw more sagebrush on the fire to ward off marauding animals and spread their bedrolls and blankets on the ground, where they slept undisturbed until morning.

At dawn, they were up, ready to resume their search. While Nate went out to bring in the saddle horses, Cap and Lew repacked the packhorse. When Nate returned, he told of seeing a wild hog go across the Red Desert toward Elk Mountain. Since there were no wild hogs in the area, Cap and Lew told Nate that it must have been a young buffalo. But Nate insisted that it was not a buffalo.

Curious, Cap and Lew rode with Nate to where he had seen this supposed wild hog. To their surprise, they found a very large silver-tipped grizzly. By this time the grizzly had reached Lost Creek, pausing to drink at one of the water holes.

Eager for sport, the cowboys decided to rope the grizzly. For Cap and Lew this was to be their last year in Old Wyoming Territory. When spring came, they were heading east to Nebraska. This, they thought, would probably be their last chance to rope a grizzly.

Grizzlies have been known to outrun a horse. This one, however, was old and fat, weighing at least nine hundred pounds. After running a while, it would stop and roll over and over until it had recovered its wind, then run a while longer.

Soon the cowboys overtook the grizzly, but the moment they managed to get a rope on it, it would take it off with its huge, hairy paws. They spent at least half an hour, trying to rope the grizzly and having a lot of fun. Finally, Lew threw his rope, catching the grizzly by one foreleg and shoulder. This sent the grizzly into a rage. Rearing up full height, it made a wild lunge at Lew's horse, barely missing one flank with its long, sharp claws. In the escape, Lew's horse was a little slow getting away. Scared to death, Lew was spurring and whipping his horse when, suddenly, he looked back and saw the grizzly only a few feet behind him. He jerked his six-shooter from the scabbard on his saddle, and fired, hitting the grizzly in one front foot.

At that moment the fun ended. The grizzly went right on the warpath. Charging Lew's horse, it was a terrifying sight, as it reared up full height, baring its ugly fangs. Seeing that Lew's life was in danger, Cap and Nate opened fire with their Winchesters.

According to local Indian legend, Shoshones and Arapahoes wouldn't kill a grizzly or tan the hides. It was also said by some of the Indians that grizzlies never ate during the winter, just sucked their paws.

Cap and Nate took four shots before finally bringing the grizzly down. When they removed the hide, they found a layer of fat as thick as a slab of bacon. They cut away the fat and what meat they wanted to cook, but it was so tough, they couldn't eat it.

"It was tougher than a boiled owl!" Cap exclaimed, after the lost saddle horses had been found, and the three returned safely to their ranch headquarters.

Cap and Lew had the hide tanned, taking it with them to Nebraska as a trophy of their last experience with a grizzly.

SEVEN SILVERTIPS IN HALF AN HOUR
1885

 KILLING bears for bounty was a large-scale, widespread activity throughout the West in the 1880s and 1890s. Grizzly bears, with their low reproductive rate, could not sustain the very high mortality imposed on them as described in this story, and as a result, extinction over most of the species' range was predictable.

The bounty system was among the first wildlife-related laws in America in the seventeenth century. Bounties were offered for wolves, squirrels, crows, and other animals that destroyed crops and livestock. "Almost universal" cash rewards were paid for predators throughout the 1800s by ranchers, livestock associations, and states and counties (see James B. Trefethen, An American Crusade for Wildlife, New York: Winchester Press, 1975). In the 1880s in the West, cattlemen and woolgrowers demanded government help in exterminating rodents (mostly prairie dogs) and predators, and thus were developed enormous federal and state programs of poisoning, trapping, bounties, and compulsory eradication laws. Thomas R. Dunlap writes in Saving America's Wildlife (Princeton: Princeton University Press, 1988) that, by 1915, private hunting and bounty hunting had reduced large predators, including grizzly bears, to remnant populations, yet "the idea of killing off 'varmints' offended no one." Even though it has been widely recognized as bad policy and poor management—"useless, expensive, and open to fraud," bounties are still used today in some places to control "animal damage."

This account by "Bear" George B. McClellan is from the Annals of Wyoming, *January 1954, v. 26, no. 1. It was taken from original manuscripts by Mr. McClellan and contributed to the Department of Commerce's Historical Research and Publications by his niece, Margaret McClellan.*

▼▼▼▼

IN the fall of '85 my partner and I were hunting in the Big Horn Mountains on the head of a small creek called Otter Creek. We had been quite successful that fall, having killed twenty-three bear in about six weeks, but I cannot tell you about all of them. It is my intention to tell you of our big killing that fall.

One evening about 4 o'clock, we left camp and went down to the head of a canyon on one of the prongs of the creek. After wandering around a while, I became tired of that locality and suggested that we go over on another creek about two miles from there.

Billie said, "No, we will go on down until we can look over into the valley."

I did not much like the idea, but I went along. We had not gone very far when we came in sight of an old silver tip and her two cubs feeding in the head of a little coulee. We slipped from our horses' backs in the twinkling of an eye, all thought of dispute about our route laid aside. We made hasty calculations about how to proceed. The bear, when first sighted, were some two or three hundred yards away. On peeking over we concluded to make for a ridge off to our left, which was about 60 or 75 yards from the bear. We crawled up to our position and looked over there.

They were all unsuspicious of danger. The old one had a mane eight or ten inches long, that gave her the appearance of having a hump on her back like a buffalo.

Will said in a whisper, "Now shoot the old one in the head."

We were plenty close enough, so we both took deliberate aim, counted three, and whang went one gun. I looked and did not have any cartridge in the chamber of my Winchester, but when that old bear commenced to roar, it did not take me long to get the gun loaded. Will had hit too low and struck her on the jaw, and how she was bellowing! I fired and she went down. Then we went to shooting at the cubs. One of them was getting close to the edge of the canyon, and while I was working the lever, I turned to look where the old one was. There she was, sitting on her haunches, head turned sideways and uttering the worst roars it was ever my good fortune to listen to. I turned, drew a fine bead on her shoulder, and let her have it. She went down all in a heap like she never would move again. She straightened out, seemed to wake up, pulled herself together, and was into the quaken asp before I could get another shot. The bears were now out of sight.

I asked Will if he got the cub that went into the canyon. He said that he had hit it, but it had gone over the edge. We did not feel very good.

He was inclined to blame me for not killing the old one with the first shot, as he said if I had shot we would not both have missed; while I thought he would have killed her when he had so good a chance. I went back and got my horse and went to where we last saw the cub (I would rather follow a cub on open ground than an old sow in the brush any time). When I got about half way down the hill into the canyon the little fellow heard me and started out above me in the canyon and up the opposite hill. I started after him full tilt, but the ground was too rough for my horses, and the little bear got into a quaken asp patch on top of the hill. I could hear him crying when I first came up to the brush patch, but he soon stopped when he heard me, and I could not find him. I now gave it up and went back to where Will was, but instead of crossing the canyon I went around the head of it, which was a little farther but not nearly so rough.

When I got around, I found that Will had got his horse and followed me over, and was now over where I had left the cub. I thought, "Now if I hurry back over there both of us may be able to get that cub," so back I went as fast as I could go. It did not take us long to make up our minds that we could not find the cub, so we thought we had best go back and see what had become of the old one. We were not in a very good frame of mind. We had every show at three bear and let the old one and one of the cubs get away.

I knew the old one must be badly hurt, for I had taken two shots at her within easy range, and the last one was at her body when she was comparatively still. The cub Will had killed lay in the trail that ran down the canyon, and we wanted to skin it yet that evening as we were saving oil. We started down the hill to go back to look after the old one, when Will said, "Look yonder." I looked up, and he was pointing right the way we were going, and there, coming down the trail on the other side of the canyon were four big old silver tips. Now we must not let them get away. We waited until the bear got down the canyon far enough to be out of sight, then we crossed in behind them and took down the canyon on the same side they were on, but we were on top and we supposed they would go down into the bottom of the canyon where the big game trail led. There we went as fast as our horses would carry us to get ahead of the bears. When we reached about the last place we could get down, we pulled up, jumped off of our horses and started down the steep side of the canyon (just at this place the canyon was very steep). About half way down we came to a wall, and on looking over we could see the game trails in the bottom of the canyon. We were confident that the bear had not passed, and I tell you it has a tendency to raise the spirits of any bear hunter to think that he has a wall 100 feet high between him and four old silver tips.

We were now on a sort of ledge at the top of the wall, and by going a little way above would have an open space with no trees to bother.

We got into the open space and were standing with our guns ready, looking over into the bottom of the canyon, when I heard a slight noise to my right. On looking up I beheld all four of the bear just coming into the opposite side of the open space we were in, which was probably twenty yards across. Well, right then there was the awfullest row I have ever witnessed. All four of those bear bellowing at once, two Winchesters going as though we were trying to tear them to pieces. I shall never forget how those bear looked when we first fired. They acted for all the world like a lot of hogs, when one squeals the rest will run up with bristles raised and ready for war. As soon as they spied us, they made for us, but we were so close and our fire was so deadly that the closest one did not get within ten or fifteen feet of us. One old fellow got knocked over the wall into the bottom of the canyon, but we could not see that he had sustained any great injury, such as breaking any bones or tearing the skin. Of course, he was dead or almost so when he went over the wall. Well, my tale is almost told. There is but little more gore to spill. We did not get through skinning that evening.

Next morning as we came back, we found the wounded cub that had got away. He was not hurt very badly but we soon did him up. We also found the old one dead, so we had seven silver tips to our credit in about half an hour. For fear of the game-hog cry, I will say there was a considerable bounty on bear at that time and that was what made us turn bear hunters. We used the fifty-pound bear traps and have had some very interesting experiences with them of which I may probably tell you some day if you like the story of our best killing.

BEAR HUGS FOR DAN BLAIR
1886

 THIS and other grizzly bear stories from eastern Wyoming show that the great bear was encountered in that part of the state at least until the 1890s. Dan Blair found trouble because he failed to recognize the nearby grunting of a grizzly for what it really was, a warning that the bear's space had been invaded—and he paid the price. This oral history by Mrs. Minnie A. Rietz was collected in 1939 by the Wyoming Works Progress Administration and is from the Department of Commerce's Historical Research and Publications in Cheyenne.

▼▼▼▼▼

DAN Blair had a ranch on Duck Creek in 1886, and it was there this episode took place.

Dan was a bachelor, but not from choice. He built a small claim shack on his place and said he asked every single woman and widow he knew to share it with him, but he was never able to induce any of them to give him a favorable answer.

He was of medium height, about five feet nine inches, tall, with brown eyes and beard. He allowed his hair to grow rather long, and went without a hat so much that it was sunburned to a nondescript shade of leather. One morning he found that his cows had strayed away during the night, so he started out on foot to look for them. Coming to a thicket of wild plums he thought he would gather a few for "sass," so taking off his coat he tied the sleeves at the wrists and proceeded to fill them up with the plums. I shall use his own words as nearly as I can remember them to tell the story.

"I'd heard a queer grunting noise not far from me for quite a spell, but I was so busy picking them plums I never paid no special heed till I'd got the best there was in thet thicket, then I see there looked to be some pretty good plums on a patch of bresh a little ways to the left. There seemed to be some big critter a thrashin' around in there, and I says to myself, now who in tarnation around here has a hog runnin' wild? kicked into the bresh to scare him out, and, oh man! Did I get a surprise? guess that old bear must a had a sore spot an' I must a landed ker plunk onto it, cause he let out a roar and rared up onto his hind feet and come a clawin'. I had a short hunting knife in my belt but no gun. I soon found I couldn't outrun him, so I knew it was to be a fight to the finish and the devil take the hindmost. I squared around and tried to find me a spot on his carcase where I could hit him the worst blow, but he came on so fast I didn't have any choice. His claws ripped into my shoulder and I jabbed with my knife any place I could get it in. He kept trying to get me where he could squeeze the life out of me but I kept a duckin' and diggin' in my knife, and he kept a rippin' the clothes and a lot of the skin offen me. We were both a bleedin' pretty free and both pretty well winded when I made a lucky stab and stuck him in the throat. I must a cut his jugular vein for he sent the blood spurtin' out of his mouth, and began to kinda wheeze when he breathed, but he kept a reachin' for me and I hadn't lost any bear hugs so I kept a dodgin'.

"At last he got down on all fours and sorta staggered and shook his old head, and finally dropped down onto the ground and lay there. I was so weak from loss of blood and my fightin' with him I could hardly crawl, but I could not lay down nor sit down till I was sure he wasn't playin' possum and just restin' for another round. By and by he quit jerkin' and I couldn't hear him breathe so I went over and sure enough he was dead as a door nail. Yes sir!"

I have heard Dan tell this story many times. He crawled back to his shanty and by chance some men looking for strays happened in and found him. They hitched up a team, got the bear and skinned him, then brought Dan into Rock Creek where his sister, Mrs. Bruce Simmons, lived. The men had dressed his wounds as best they could, but he was clawed quite deeply in several places and had lost a lot of blood so he was very weak. They did not get a doctor, as there was none closer than Laramie, which was sixty miles away. Every neighbor had some suggestion as to the care of the cuts and bruises, and all were free with their remedies and help, with the result that Dan was able to be up and about in a surprisingly short time. He had a habit of ending any story with a "Yes sir," the emphasis on the "Yes." The truth of this story can be vouched for by any of the old-time ranchmen of the Duck Creek country.

BIG FOOT WALLACE
1884-87

 MEMOIRS of Bryant B. Brooks: Cowboy, Trapper, Lumberman, Stockman, Oilman, Banker, and Governor of Wyoming *(Glendale, Calif. : The Arthur H. Clark Company, 1939) is the autobiography of one of Wyoming's prominent leaders. The list of Brooks' own careers gives us a quick overview of a critical period of development in western history—from the rugged, individual pursuits of wrangling and trapping to the sophisticated enterprises of oil extraction, banking, and politics. B. B. Brooks was born in Massachusetts in 1861 and spent most of his formative years in Chicago. When he reached eighteen, "tales of the thrilling life of a cowboy, riding the far-flung range of a cattle baron, eating by a blazing camp fire, and sleeping beneath the stars" sent him west. He enjoyed "numerous thrilling experiences" herding cattle in Utah, Idaho, Wyoming, and Colorado. Then, during a stint as a trapper in his early twenties, he acquired a cabin with squatter's rights in the North Platte country of Wyoming territory for the price of "six beaver traps and a sack of flour." This was the start of a large and successful ranching enterprise, based on improving his ranch, adding sheep, and feeding his cattle in winter (instead of letting them roam free on the open range). During his years on the V–V Ranch, the last quarter of the nineteenth century, Brooks witnessed the birth of Casper and the arrival of the railroad, served as one of the original commissioners of Natrona County, saw Wyoming granted statehood, and put an end to that "monarch and terror of the mountains," Big Foot Wallace.*

▼▼▼▼

IN the spring of 1884, as the Platte valley round-up was working down the south side of the Platte river, about eight miles west of my ranch, three of the C Y cowboys, making a circle after cattle in the foothills of Casper mountain, encountered a large silver-tip bear, that was slowly making his way up a shallow ravine. None of the boys were armed, so they decided to rope him.

Now, lassoing a bear may seem a rather hazardous undertaking to people not familiar with cowboy sports, and so it proved on this occasion; yet it is a feat frequently accomplished on our yearly round-ups, and with comparatively slight danger to the boys.

Usually, as soon as the rope tightens about the bear's neck, he begins to tug and hang back, the long hair about the neck prevents the noose from loosening after once being tightened, and in five or ten minutes the bear chokes to death. A buffalo will do the same thing. I have known several instances of cowboys roping and killing full-grown bear and buffalo in this manner.

In this case, two of the boys were riding well-trained cow ponies. As soon as they saw the bear, they made a dash to head him off from the mountains, uncoiling their long grass ropes as they went. The third boy, named Wallace, was riding a large half-broken colt, and had to stop and get his rope uncoiled from the saddle before starting. By the time he was ready his companions had turned the bear down a gulch.

Wallace struck out diagonally down another gully, which joined the one the bear was in about a quarter of a mile below. The colt got rattled at the free use of the spurs and at the dangling noose which Wallace held in his right hand, and made extra fast time down the gulch. In fact, Wallace was scarcely able to control him at all.

Rider and bear reached the point where the two gullies joined, at the same moment. Both gulches were narrow, with steep banks.

Wallace tried in vain to check the horse. The bear reared up on his haunches. Horse and rider shot by and turned up the gulch down which the bear had just come. They passed so close to the bear that Wallace actually struck him on the head with his right hand.

The bear struck both horse and rider with his paws, tearing the horse's flank with one, and the boy's leather chaps with the other. In striking at the bear's head, Wallace had unintentionally dropped the open loop about its body.

When the bear struck the bronco, he commenced bucking and threw Wallace off. The boy was unhurt, and scrambling to his feet, made a dash up the side of the gulch, while the bear turned up the ravine that Wallace had just ridden down.

The other end of the rope was, of course, made fast to the horn of the saddle, and when the bucking horse ran out on it, the weight of the bear threw him. In struggling to get up, he broke the front cinch of the saddle and soon bucked through the flank cinch.

Away went the bear up the gulch, dragging the saddle behind him. The other two boys met the runaway horse and roped him.

Wallace explained as rapidly as possible, and held his own horse while the other two boys went after the grizzly.

Going up the gulch about a half-mile, they found the saddle wedged in between two boulders. The bear had bitten off the rope and was gone. They carried the saddle, which was somewhat in need of repairs, back to Wallace.

In looking at the bear's immense tracks in the sand, they noticed that two toes of the left forefoot were missing. Evidently, the bear had been in a trap at some time.

In rehearsing the story at camp, someone named that bear Big Foot Wallace.

Two years later I had a man herding my cattle back in the mountains, where he lived alone in a tent, some ten miles from the ranch. One day he came in to get provisions. In coming over, he had tried to turn a bunch of cattle and in some way crippled his horse, so he rode back on a little Spanish mule that I had at the ranch. Behind his saddle he tied a miscellaneous assortment of grub, such as potatoes, bacon, canned goods, sugar, coffee, baking powder, etc.

When about halfway on his return, he rode up on a little knoll. Right under him, not fifty feet away, was an enormous bear, eating a calf he had just killed. I had had a number of cattle killed during that year, by wild animals, and this man was carrying a Winchester, slung to his saddle for just such an emergency; but on this occasion it was useless.

The mule saw the bear about the same time the man did, and having previously been spoiled by our trying to pack a bearskin home on her, she whirled and bolted for the ranch. For a mile or so the man tried to check her. Then his arms gave out, and he let her run. She scattered provisions from the brow of that hill clear to the stable door.

The man told his story, and he and I saddled up two horses and started back, hoping the bear had not left. We found my calf half eaten up, but no bear.

The tracks led off up the mountains, showing plainly in the dust of an old cow trail. Two toes were missing from the left forefoot, so we knew that it was Big Foot Wallace that was doing the killing.

My cattle continued to disappear. I set two big forty-pound steel traps, but failed to catch the thief. Once in an October snow I followed his big tracks for miles. They led me eventually into a dense grove of Jack pines and dead-fall timber, where I finally came to the place where he had been lying under some logs. He had either heard or scented me, and had made off, so I gave up the hunt.

The next year he was worse than ever.

There is a small lake that nestles on the side of the mountain, some five miles south of the ranch, and that fall, while up there after geese, I found a two-year-old steer partly eaten up. The tracks of Big Foot Wallace were all about him.

I knew it would be of little use to set traps. My cattle were thick about there and I could not safely set a trap, unless I built a V-shaped pen, as we usually do for bear. This would be useless, for old Wallace was too smart ever to go near a pen. So I returned to the ranch, and that night Post Hole Jack and I took a few blankets and went up and laid for him.

The night was dark, and we could only watch in the evening and early in the morning. We kept this up three nights.

The second night the bear came and ate his fill, but we did not get to see him. The wind was usually from the foothills, and our mode of procedure was to ride up to a certain gulch, about four hundred yards to the east of the dead steer, leave our horses and blankets, and creep over to some rocks about seventy-five yards from the carcass. Here we would lie and watch till it got too dark to shoot, then crawl back, roll up in our blankets, and at daylight repeat the performance.

The fourth day was a busy one at the ranch, Jack and I did not get away until later than usual. At the foot of the mountain it commenced to rain and promised to be such a disagreeable night that we debated strongly about returning home. But the boys at the ranch had been laughing at us about our bear, and we concluded to stay it out.

Darkness came on early, and we were unable to reach our old camping ground. Finally, when about three hundred yards below where we thought the bait lay, it being so dark that we were not certain where we were, we concluded to camp. We unsaddled our ponies and groped about to find a rock to picket them to. Then we put our saddle blankets on the damp ground, unrolled our bed blankets, and putting rubber slickers over these, we turned in and slept like troopers.

It was broad daylight when we uncovered our heads. The new-born day was crisp and beautiful. Our horses had wound themselves up during the night, among the rocks.

As we were so late, we decided to just saddle up our ponies and ride up to look at the bait. We had finished saddling and were in the very act of mounting, when up the mountain-side, not two hundred yards away, came our bear.

I shall never forget how he looked. The sun was not yet up. The faint wind was in our favor. Everything was as still as death. Even our horses, whose heads were turned the other way, seemed to have gone to sleep again; and there, coming, coming slowly, steadily, noiselessly on, like some avenging monster, was the largest grizzly I have ever seen.

He was moving diagonally toward us and would pass within forty yards. We had crouched on the ground beside our horses, slipping our Winchesters out of the scabbards, as we did so. Old Wallace, for I knew him instantly from his immense size, was walking deliberately up the gradual rise of the mountain, his great head hanging low.

He looked neither to the right nor the left, but seemed to think that everything would, of course, get out of his way. On and on he came!

I felt a certain thrill of exultation at the certainty of his death. Here was what we had been waiting and longing and watching for. Here was the destroyer of my cattle. Here was the author of my many troubles, the monarch and the terror of the mountains, marching unconcernedly on and up, to meet us on open ground, in battle royal, in the first bright gray of a September morn.

Now was to come the test between blind, brute fury and strength on the one hand, and nerve, skill, and improved weapons on the other. At last, he was within forty yards.

"Now, Jack! Bust him!"

We dropped our bridle reins, and stepping to one side of our horses, knelt to shoot. The bear never looked up.

Bang! Bang! The great brute suddenly leaped into life. The long hair on the back of his neck stood up like the bristles of an angry boar. He whirled, partly fell, and bit savagely at his shoulder and side where the bullets had struck. Our frightened horses started down the mountains, dragging their bridle reins a trifle to one side to keep from stepping on them.

Bang! Bang! Another tumble. Then a terrible half growl and half roar. He saw us now and tried to charge, but the Winchesters talked fast and furiously. The leaden hail was too much for even his big savage hulk to face. He would fall, roll over, bite himself, struggle to his feet, and would try to come on, only to fall again.

Finally, he lay still.

We advanced and fired one shot into his great head. Not a quiver. He was dead. Then we both hurried up, with the same question in our minds. Yes, there were two toes missing on the left forefoot.

Big Foot Wallace's silver-tipped hide, the long hair on his neck that bristled so at the first fire, his noble, broad, savage head and beadlike eyes, nicely mounted, his three and a half inches of great claws, with two missing on the left paw, all go to form a superb rug that now adorns a certain house in Chicago. I never see it but I wish that I knew the whole story of Big Foot Wallace.

A TRUE SPORTSMAN SPEAKS
1887

 UNTIL the middle of the 1800s, hunting was done largely for the purpose of getting meat or removing predators or other destructive beasts in any manner possible. In mid-century, however, argues Thomas R. Dunlap in his book Saving America's Wildlife *(Princeton: Princeton University Press, 1988), hunting was adopted by the American upper classes as a sport. As such, it was felt to be a democratic pursuit that developed strong manly virtues and male camaraderie, provided "pleasant and invigorating relief" from daily life, and instilled a knowledge of the "greater reality" of nature. A sportsmen's code developed: a true sportsman gives a fair chase to game species only, treats his dogs and horses well, shares shots and bags with his hunting buddies, and leaves some game for the next hunter and the next year.*

In his excellent history, American Sportsmen and the Origins of Conservation *(New York: Winchester Press, 1975), John F. Reiger summed up the code thus: "In order to obtain membership in this order of 'true sportsmen,' [gunners and anglers] had to practice proper etiquette in the field, give game a sporting chance, and possess an aesthetic appreciation of the whole context of sport that included a commitment to its perpetuation." It was out of this code, which viewed wildlife (or at least game) as a resource to be husbanded, that late nineteenth-century hunters helped lay the foundations for a wildlife conservation ethic.*

Predators were the last to benefit from these efforts, not receiving any sympathy, any understanding of their ecological role, nor any legal protection until well into the twentieth century. Bears, however, have always held an unusual position—despised as predators and esteemed as the greatest of game animals. This ambivalence toward them continues to this day.

The present author, George O. Shields, was an ardent hunter, staunch wildlife conservationist, and successful writer and magazine editor. He crusaded against "game hogs" (those who take indecent numbers of game animals) and against the use of automatic shotguns, and he was instrumental in getting many early wildlife protection laws passed at national and state levels. In the article excerpted here, which appeared in the 1887 Harper's New Monthly Magazine, *(v. 75, pp. 368-372), Shields gives us his philosophy of hunting and his high regard for grizzly bear hunting in addition to his adventure tale from Wyoming's Shoshone Mountains. Compare Shields' closing comments with those of Theodore Roosevelt, quoted by Paul Schullery in* The Bear Hunter's Century: Profiles from the Golden Age of Bear Hunting *(New York: Dodd, Mead & Co., 1988): "The most thrilling moments of an American hunter's life are those in which, with every sense alert, and with nerves strung to the highest point, he is following alone into the heart of its forest fastness the fresh and bloody footprints of an angered grizzly; and no other triumph of American hunting can compare with the victory thus to be gained."*

▼▼▼▼▼

THE grizzly bear possesses greater vitality and tenacity of life than any other animal on the continent, and the hunter who would hunt him must be well armed and keep a steady nerve. Each shot must be coolly put where it will do the most good. Several are usually necessary to stop one of these savage beasts. A single bullet lodged in the brain is fatal. If shot through the heart he may run a quarter of a mile or kill a man before he succumbs. In the days of the old muzzle-loading rifle it was hazardous indeed to hunt the grizzly, and many a man has paid the penalty of his folly with his life. With our improved breech-loading and repeating rifles there is less risk.

We were hunting in the Shoshone Mountains in northern Wyoming. I had killed a large elk in the morning, and on going back to the carcass in the afternoon to skin it we saw that Bruin had been there ahead of us, but had fled on our approach. Without the least apprehension of his return, we leaned our rifles against a tree about fifty feet away, and commenced work. There were three of us, but only two rifles, Mr. Huffman, the photographer, having left his in camp. He had finished taking views of the carcass, and we were all busily engaged skinning, when, hearing a crashing in the brush and a series of savage roars and growls, we looked up the hill, and were horrified to see three grizzly bears, an old female and two cubs about two-thirds grown, charging upon us with all the savage fury of a pack of starving wolves upon a sheepfold.

They were between us and our rifles when we first saw them, and we sprang to our horses, which were picketed a few yards below, supposing, of course, that when the bears reached the elk carcass they would proceed to eat it, and pay no further attention to us. Strange to say, it was the carcass to which they paid no attention. They still came after us; we had no time for flight, and could not even release and mount our terror-stricken horses. Our only chance was to fight for our lives, and with one accord we all three grasped our hunting-knives and dashed at them. We threw our hats and yelled like Comanches, and the savage brutes, seeing themselves thus boldly confronted by equal numbers, stopped, raised on their haunches, growled, snapped their jaws for a few moments, and then walked sullenly back up the hill into the brush. This gave us an opportunity to get hold of our rifles, and then it was our turn to charge. To make a long story short, we killed the old female and one cub; the other escaped into the jungle before we could get a shot at him. The resolute front we put on alone saved our lives.

The best localities in which to hunt the grizzly bear—that is, those most accessible and in which he is the most numerous—are the Big Horn, Shoshone, Wind River, Bear Tooth, Belt, and Crazy mountains, in Wyoming and Montana, all of which may be easily reached by way of the Northern Pacific road.

There are several methods of hunting him, the most common being to kill an elk, and then watch the carcass. Shots may frequently be obtained in this way early in the morning or late in the evening, and on bright moonlight nights it is best to watch all night, for the immense size of the grizzly renders him an easy target at short range even by moonlight. Another method is to still-hunt him, the same as is done with deer. This is perhaps the most sportsman-like of all, and if a coulee or creek bottom be selected where there are plenty of berries, or an open, hilly, rocky country where the bears are in the habit of hunting for worms, or any good feeding ground where bear signs are plentiful, and due care and caution be exercised, there is as good a chance of success as by any other method. Many hunters set guns with a cord running from the trigger to a bait of fresh meat, and the muzzle of the gun pointing at the meat; others set large steel-traps or dead-falls. But such contrivances are never used by true sportsmen.

Game of any kind should always be pursued in a fair, manly manner, and given due chance to preserve its life if it is skilful enough to do so. If captured, let it be by the superior skill, sagacity, or endurance of the sportsman, not by traps which close on it as it innocently and unsuspectingly seeks its food.

Grizzly bear hunting is unquestionably the grandest sport that our continent can afford. The grizzly is the only really dangerous game we have, and the decidedly hazardous character of the sport is what gives it its greatest zest, and renders it the most fascinating of pursuits. Many sportsmen proclaim the superiority of their favorite pastime over all other kinds, be it quail, grouse, or duck shooting, fox-chasing, deer-stalking, or what not; and each has its charm, more or less intense, according to its nature; but no man ever felt his heart swell with pride, his nerves tingle with animation, his whole system glow with wild, uncontrollable enthusiasm, at the bagging of any bird or small animal, as does the man who stands over the prostrate form of a monster grizzly that he has slain. Let the devotee of these other classes of sport try bear hunting, and when he has bagged his first grizzly, then let him talk!

THE VETTER SAGA
1892

 THE mauling of Phillip Vetter by a grizzly bear is one of the grimmest stories from the Greybull River region of northwestern Wyoming, an area rich in history. We give three published versions of the Vetter saga here: The first, which eloquently describes the details, appeared in Thompson's "In Old Wyoming" column in the Wyoming State Tribune *on February 19, 1948. It is based largely on "Tragedies of the Hills," a chapter in Tacetta B.* Walker's Stories of Early Days in Wyoming: Big Horn Basin, *(Casper: Prairie Publishing Co., 1936). The second account is from Bob Edgar's and Jack Turnell's history of the Pitchfork Ranch,* The Brand of a Legend *(Cody, Wyoming: Stockade Publishing, 1978); it is recorded in the words of Tom Osborne, who worked for Otto Franc, owner of the nearby Pitchfork. The third version is a brief mention of the incident from* Experiences and Impressions, *the autobiography of A. A. Anderson, another ranch owner in the area and author of one part of the story "Wahb." According to Thompson's account, the bear that killed Vetter was Wahb, and according to Anderson, Wahb was a cattle killer that he himself eventually shot.*

The powerful pathos of Vetter's story is perhaps best marked in his deathbed notes, which each author records differently. Perhaps each author—and each reader—profoundly moved by such suffering, can only imagine what Phillip Vetter's last words might have been.

▼▼▼▼

Thompson

WILD plums were lusciously ripe in thickets along the Greybull river in September, 1892. This was the proximate cause of an incident among the most grisly in the Wyoming country's grizzly bear lore. Bears loved plums, resorted to the thickets to gorge on them, fiercely resented any interruption of their feasting. That's why P. H. Vetter's supper dishes were not washed; why Vetter linger[ing]ly came to the end of his trail in his lonely cabin beside the river. He went for a walk in the vesper hour of a lovely day—and ran into grizzlies! Three weeks passed and there came a visitor from the "outside," to find the dishes unwashed, Vetter's decaying corpse on a blood-blackened bed, a poignant message from a dying man scrawled on a margin of a newspaper.

This message was in four installments, the intervals between them measuring the flow of Vetter's life blood.

First: "All would have been well had I not gone down the river after supper."

Second: "Should go to Frank's [Otto Franc's Pitchfork Ranch] but too weak."

Third: "It's getting dark. I'm smothering."

Fourth: "I'm dying."

A fifth instal[l]ment, not written, mutely was told by Vetter's body. An prologue was supplied by tracks of a bear with only 18 toes.

Vetter was a hunter and trapper whose crude abode was on the ranch of A. A. Anderson, locator and supervisor of the first federal forest reserve. His trap lines were along the river, a tributary of the Stinking Water (later christened "Shoshone" by legislative fiat), and up a creek called "Mee-tee-tse," a Shoshone word meaning "near-by." This creek ran through the "spread" now known as the "Pitchfork" ranch. Grizzly bears were numerous on this range. So lonely was Vetter's abode that it rarely was visited by a "neighbor." The trapper was not lonesome when alone: he lacked gregariousness even more than the bears which roamed the region around his home. Sufficient unto himself, he did not yearn for companionship.

Among Vetter's neighbors was a man-hating bear made famous by Ernest Seton Thompson (who later juggled his name to make it Ernest Thompson Seton) in his book, "Wahb, the Autobiography of a Grizzly." This book now is a "collector's item." This ghost-written story depicts Wahb as a creature embittered by the loss of two toes in a trap. Tacetta B. Walker, in her book, "Stories of Early Days in Wyoming," is authority for assertion that it was Vetter's fatal misfortune to encounter Wahb in his evening walk through the plum thickets.

What happened when Vetter allegedly met Wahb, and two ursine companions, and during the brief remainder of the trapper's lifetime, is a matter of deduction. The trapper's gun and hat were found some distance from his cabin; a trail of blood led from the spot to the cabin. One of his arms had been mutilated, the principal artery severed. He had staggered back to the cabin, collapsed upon the bed. Suspenders and a bloody handkerchief provided evidence that unsuccessfully he had endeavored to stanch the flow of blood. As he hemorrhaged to death he waveringly scrawled his message on a margin of a newspaper which lay on the sill of a window above the bed.

Vetter probably flushed the three grizzlies whose tracks were found at the point where the blood trail began while his thoughts were far away; had been set upon and mangled without an instant's forewarning. Tracks of an 18-toed bear and a trail of blood led to a tree which the man probably had endeavored to climb. One shot had been fired from his gun. Why the bears abandoned their attack could not be deduced; possible the shot had frightened them. An erratic trail of gore led from the tree to the cabin.

Condition of Vetter's body made it necessary to bury it on the spot. Possibly the grave has been unviolated to this day; probably the remains of the victim of a grizzly's might were moved when A. A. Anderson built a palatial ranch home nearby.

▼▼▼
Edgar and Turnell

John Corbett left Arland for John Gleaver's over on Wood River. As Corbett neared the Greybull, he could see that a cloudburst was near so he started for Phil Vetter's cabin. Upon reaching Vetter's cabin, he rapped on the door. As there was no reply, he opened the door. The first thing that he spied was a stream of blood on the floor. Glancing at the bed he saw Vetter lying dead. He found two notes. One stated he had tried to go to Otto Franc's. The other was blood stained so that he couldn't make it out. Corbett went on to Gleaver's and reported what he had found at Vetter's cabin. Gleaver, Corbett, and others started back to see if they could find what had happened to Vetter. They tracked Vetter from the cabin down to the bank of the river. There sat his water bucket. His track then led back to the cabin, where he had gone for his gun, as he had spotted a bear lying under the bank next to the river, below the bucket. The tracks showed that Vetter went back down to the river bank and took a shot at the bear. The bear came for Vetter, striking him in the chest, after knocking Vetter down the bear left him. Vetter's chest was caved in, but he managed to get back to the cabin where he died from hemorrhages. He was taken upon the hill a little southwest of his house and buried.

▼▼▼

Anderson

At one time I had a neighbor named Vedder who, in partnership with another man, owned a ranch a few miles below mine. One day his partner went to a near-by town to obtain provisions while Vedder remained at the cabin. Just before dark he happened to look out of the cabin and saw a grizzly bear coming down the mountainside. He went out with his rifle and shot at the bear, but failed to bring him down. The bear attacked him, tore out his left arm, and apparently left him for dead. The man came to, however, crawled back to the cabin, and wrote with a pencil on the fly-leaf of a book a short account of what happened. His last words were "My God, how I suffer!" His partner returned and found him dead.

LARAMIE RIVER GRIZZLY
1894

 IN this brief oral history by Mrs. Minnie A. Rietz, collected by the Wyoming Works Progress Administration, we may well be witnessing the demise of one of the last grizzly bears in southeastern Wyoming. Grizzly bears may have suffered in the previous ninety years of conflict with the encroaching white people, but killing homesteaders' livelihood, their livestock, sealed the great bear's fate once and for all.

▼▼▼▼

BEAR were not very plentiful along the Laramie River valleys in 1894, so when cattle were found dead with great claw marks on them, it was believed to be the work of a mountain lion. The carcasses were seldom found until all the tracks were covered by those of coyotes and other small animals. Cattle were turned out on the open ranges in May, gathered again once during the summer for branding the calves, and not again until November, when they were turned into the winter pastures.

There were no fences for miles. Often the milch cows would be three or four miles from home and have to be driven in by a man on horseback.

T. J. Cramer had taken up a claim in 1893; C. F. Rietz in 1894; and C. A. Morrison in the same year (1894). These were the only ranches on the upper part of the river at that time. Mr. and Mrs. Padgett and daughter Georgia lived on the Morrison place, and all the group were cattlemen.

A cow of Rietz's was killed just above the house on the Morrison place, not more than fifty yards from the house and out in the open where the ground was soft, and being so close to the buildings, she was found at once while Bruin's tracks were still plain to be seen. Traps were set at once. A brown claw was found in one trap, and after that only rabbits and skunks were caught. A few weeks later a cow belonging to Mr. Cramer was killed back in the hills west of the ranch. Traps were again set, but for several days without result: then one morning Mr. Padgett went up to see how they were and found a big grizzly bear firmly caught by a hind foot and greatly enraged. He stood on his hind feet and roared, lunging the length of the chain with which the trap was fastened. Mr. Padgett came back to the ranch and then called at the

Cramer and Rietz ranches so all could get a look at the bear before he killed it. As there were no telephones this took some time, and when they got back the bear was eating on the carcass, but stopped at once to growl and show fight. He was quickly dispatched with a well-aimed shot. He was nice and well rounded, so was in fine condition for eating, and generous portions were distributed to all the neighbors. Dr. Culley of Texas came up that fall and bought the hide, which Mr. Padgett had dressed for a robe. This bear must have been alone, as there was no further trouble from bears after that.

MY LAST BEAR HUNT, BY JOE III
ca. 1912-15

 THIS account, from Wyoming's Big Horn Mountains, tells of a hunt for old Three-Toes, the man-killing grizzly bear. We believe it comes from the Lovell Chronicle in Wyoming, but we have been unable to learn the date it was published or the end of the story—our copy is cut off in mid-sentence.

We are very pleased that Lovell historian Anna Parks was able to supply more information. As a child, she knew some of the people mentioned in the story, including Dan Olson and Jack Kocherhans, owners of a blacksmith shop. After conferring with life-long Lovell residents Burl Cox (whose brother Orlan is mentioned in the story) and Sophie Johnson, Mrs. Parks learned that Joe III was actually Joel Johnson and that his encounter with the grizzly took place about 1912 to 1915. Mrs. Johnson, wife of Joe III's nephew, remembers hearing this story many times.

This is a good account of the peer pressure that existed to enforce the killing of bears and the status that accrued to a man who killed a bear.

Typographical and punctuation corrections have been made in the text.

▼▼▼▼▼

TWENTY years! It won't make any difference, as time can never erase that picture from my mind. Those two old birds, Dan Olson, fat and swabby with that Danish grin, Jack Koker, hook nosed and important as the village gossiper, were always goading or coaxing me to take the name of Nimrod. If Cody could become famous by killing a few harmless buffalo, how historical a man could become by trailing the mighty grizzly or bearding a mountain lion in its den.

From the chain of Dan's and Jack's waterbury [sic] hung an old bear claw which was full of notches numbering the lions and bears that they had slain and with each one there was a tail, also a tale. The tail they would spin night after night to in- [missing words] sold with the pelt but the tale they would spin night after night to interesting crowds.

"Get in the game Joe, get in the game, you're western, a good shot and the sport is grand if you once get started. These bears are going to chase your log cutters from the timber if you don't get busy."

"Here, count my notch stick and make one of your own," said Dan. "Be a sport," said Jack. "I'll put you on a track that you can become famous in one day." This was their chatter night after night 'till I become drunk with this wine of fame and decided to wear a bearskin coat taken from a grizzly that I had slain in single combat.

I owned and operated a saw mill in the Big Horn mountains in Wyoming at this time, and game of all kinds that was native of that region was very plentiful and I often rode out and brought in a deer or sheep but I had never cared to trail the lion or bear until Dan and Jack made the mill their head quarters.

One day after a light skift of snow had fallen, Dad Johnson and Frank Asay came rushing to the mill very excited and told me how a large bear had nearly run over them while they were cutting timber. This decided me so I said, "Well, boys, show me the track and I will have me an overcoat before night."

"Make out your will and will me your notch stick," said Sid Johnson. "The bear is the one that will need the notch stick," said foxy Orlan Cox.

"Leave it to me boys, and his scalp will be dangling to my belt by night," said I as a little choking sensation came to my throat. I meant to ask Dan about a few things but as he and Jack were away I must take the track immediately before the snow melted.

With my faithful Marlin strapped to my saddle I followed the track to the edge of Shell Canyon and as the timber and rocks were too thick for me to ride farther I dismounted and took the trail on foot. I followed the tracks through the timber and with every step they seemed to grow fresher and larger when to my amazement I found that I was following old Three Toes, the man killer. Old Captain Jack, the famous bear trapper had caught him in his trap and he had lost some of his toes in making his escape. He had killed one Bill Thompson, hence the name Man Killer.

When I saw the track was minus two toes I started back to my sweet little Sawmill Home and I hummed "Be it ever so humble." "What will I tell those ginks at the mill?" I queried as I slowed my steed towards home. "I can't tell them that I lost the track as they were too plainly marked in the snow." I would have to tell them that I lost my nerve, and that I could not do. Besides, what a great honor it would be to wear an overcoat made of the only bear on the mountain that had killed a man. I turned again on the track as I said, "I'll get that bear or he'll get me." To settle my nerves I took the cartridge from my gun and snapped it a time or two at an imaginary bear in the distance and then quietly set out again on the trail.

Over fallen rocks and trees, through bushes and briars he led me until I was tired, and wet to the skin, but still that overcoat was uppermost in my mind. "I will send that man killer to hades and his hide to the best tanner in New York," I cogitated as I rounded a large rock when to my horror seven feet of bear weighing nearly a ton, stood within two feet of me.

The old fellow opened his mouth and growled and I think I murmured, "Mother, come get your boy." I thought of the Sunday Schools I had attended so I mumbled, "Give us this day our daily bread," but I saw this did not fit the situation so I tried some more scripture by saying "Thou shalt not kill." But he gave me another growl and the echo seemed to come back, "Thou shalt have no other Gods before me."

I remembered the thousand pictures I had seen of Daniel facing the lions, but he was not docile like Daniel's lions so I could not be calm. I thought of asking to be excused, in fact everything imaginable passed through my mind those few seconds that I faced him when my mind rambled to Dan, Jack and the notch stick. I grabbed my gun by the barrel and batted the old fellow over the head. The gun snapped in two like a piece of chalk and I saw that I may as well hit the rock of Gibralter as the man killer. I found myself tumbling over and over through the brush and rocks for a hundred feet with the killer in pursuit. I stopped, hanging to a tree within three feet of a ten feet ledge, but the bear rolled over, and forty or fifty feet below me he gained his feet, looked around and hit for tall timber as fast as he could go. I did not throw a kiss at him but I always wish I had. He had given me a tremendous blow and I had gone down....

▼▼▼

Although the story ends here, Sophie Johnson reports that at this point Joe III decided that he could do without a bearskin coat.

YELLOWSTONE
The Last Refuge

These eight stories take place from 1899 to 1929; they are arranged by their original publication date, except for the final story, an oral history of an event that took place in 1929. The loss of the great American wilderness and its premier symbol, the grizzly bear, spawned calls for preservation and conservation.

People came to understand that the great western wilderness and all it represented could only be preserved through establishment of extensive national parks and other managed federal lands. In these haunts the grizzly was to make its last stand. Yellowstone National Park was the focus of both wilderness and grizzly bear attention and a symbol of the magnificence of a land that was once vast and untamed. Some basic arguments for grizzly bear and wilderness conservation were laid during this period.

We begin with a look at the life of a wilderness king, Meeteetsee Wahb: "He had but one keen pleasure in his sombre life—the lasting glory in his matchless strength." Other authors in this period expressed a new appreciation and admiration for the once-maligned grizzly, as shown in "New Environments" and "Wildwood Test," while some serious study of bear behavior was undertaken by the author of "A Photographic Expedition for the Yellowstone Grizzly." "The Yellowstone Sanctuary" and "A Wildlife Crusader" illustrate bear life in the Park, while "Oh, Ranger!" shows the familiarity between bears and people taken a bit too far. The second part of "Wahb" and "A Death in Yellowstone" provide evidence that bears continued to die at human hands.

These protective values clashed dramatically at first with the mass destruction that took place in the preceding decades. As time passed, the new outlook gained currency, and a growing portion of the American public came to understand the many positive values the bear embodies.

WAHB
1899

 IN the late 1800s, an enormous grizzly bear named Wahb lived and died in Meeteetse country along the upper Greybull River in the western Big Horn Basin, just east of Yellowstone National Park. Our first account of his life is a fictional one, written by Ernest Thompson Seton and based upon real events (as related in our second account). It tells of the hardships for a bear living in a country rapidly filling with settlers and ranchers. It is rare to have a story from the grizzly's point of view, and this one clearly reflects Seton's sympathy for the great bear.

Artist, naturalist, author of more than forty books, lecturer, social reformer, and "master storyteller," Ernest Thompson Seton was almost a folk hero, a man who—like Buffalo Bill—had legendary appeal, especially to children, for many decades. The Biography of a Grizzly *(New York: Grosset and Dunlap, 1927) is a delightful, small book, first published in 1899, and should be read in its entirety. This excerpt describes Wahb's prime and his discovery of Yellowstone National Park.*

Our second account of Wahb's biography brings us back to the reality, however, that grizzlies and ranches simply could not coexist. It is provided by another artist, A. A. Anderson, owner of the Palette Ranch (named for his artist's palette, of course) along Piney Creek where Wahb lived. He was also instigator and first superintendent of the Yellowstone Forest Reserve, as described in his memoirs, Experiences and Impressions—The Autobiography of Colonel A. A. Anderson *(New York: Macmillan Co., 1933). He wrote about the real Wahb, or Wab, as he knew him.*

▼▼▼▼
Seton

He had forgotten what a fine land the Piney was: plenty of food, no miners to spoil the streams, no hunters to keep an eye on, and no mosquitoes or flies, but plenty of open, sunny glades and sheltering woods, backed up by high, straight cliffs to turn the colder winds.

There were, moreover, no resident Grizzlies, no signs even of passing travelers, and the Blackbears that were in possession did not count.

Wahb was well pleased. He rolled his vast bulk in an old Buffalo-wallow, and rearing up against a tree where the Piney Cañon quits the Graybull Cañon, he left on it his mark fully eight feet from the ground. In the days that followed he wandered farther and farther up among the rugged spurs of the Shoshones, and took possession as he went. He found the sign-boards of several Blackbears, and if they were small dead trees he sent them crashing to earth with a drive of his giant paw. If they were green, he put his own mark over the other mark, and made it clearer by slashing the bark with the great pickaxes that grew on his toes.

The Upper Piney had so long been a Blackbear range that the Squirrels had ceased storing their harvest in hollow trees, and were now using the spaces under flat rocks, where the Blackbears could not get at them; so Wahb found this a land of plenty: every fourth or fifth rock in the pine woods was the roof of a Squirrel or Chipmunk granary, and when he turned it over, if the little owner were there, Wahb did not scruple to flatten him with his paw and devour him as an agreeable relish to his own provisions.

And wherever Wahb went he put up his sign-board:

Trespassers beware!

It was written on the trees as high up as he could reach, and every one that came by understood that the scent of it and the hair in it were those of the great Grizzly Wahb.

If his Mother had lived to train him, Wahb would have known that a good range in spring may be a bad one in summer. Wahb found out by years of experience that a total change with the seasons is best. In the early spring the Cattle and Elk ranges, with their winter-killed carcasses, offer a bountiful feast. In early summer the best forage is on the warm hillsides where the quamash and the Indian turnip grow. In late summer the berry-bushes along the river flat are laden with fruit, and in autumn the pine woods gave good chances to fatten for the winter. So he added to his range each year. He not only cleared out the Blackbears from the Piney and the Meteetsee, but he went over the Divide and killed that old fellow that had once chased him out of the Warhouse Valley. And, more than that, he held what he had won, for he broke up a camp of tenderfeet that were looking for a ranch location on the Middle Meteetsee; he stampeded their horses, and made general smash of the camp. And so all the animals, including man, came to know that the whole range from Frank's Peak to the Shoshone spurs was the proper domain of a king well able to defend it, and the name of that king was Meteetsee Wahb.

Any creature whose strength puts him beyond danger of open attack is apt to lose in cunning. Yet Wahb never forgot his early experience with the traps. He made it a rule never to go near that smell of man and iron, and that was the reason that he never again was caught.

So he led his lonely life and slouched around on the mountains, throwing boulders about like pebbles, and huge trunks like matchwood, as he sought for his daily food. And every beast of hill and plain soon came to know and fly in fear of Wahb, the one time hunted, persecuted Cub. And more than one Blackbear paid with his life for the ill-deed of that other, long ago. And many a cranky Bobcat flying before him took to a tree, and if that tree were dead and dry, Wahb heaved it down, and tree and Cat alike were dashed to bits. Even the proud-necked Stallion, leader of the mustang band, thought well for once to yield the road. The great, grey Timberwolves, and the Mountain Lions too, left their new kill and sneaked in sullen fear aside when Wahb appeared. And if, as he hulked across the sage-covered river-flat sending the scared Antelope skimming like birds before him, he was faced perchance, by some burly Range-bull, too young to be wise and too big to be afraid, Wahb smashed his skull with one blow of that giant paw, and served him as the Range-cow would have served himself long years ago.

The All-mother never fails to offer to her own, twin cups, one gall, and one of balm. Little or much they may drink, but equally of each. The mountain that is easy to descend must soon be climbed again. The grinding hardship of Wahb's early days, had built his mighty frame. All usual pleasures of a grizzly's life had been denied him but *power* bestowed in more than double share.

So he lived on year after year, unsoftened by mate or companion, sullen, fearing nothing, ready to fight, but asking only to be let alone—quite alone. He had but one keen pleasure in his sombre life—the lasting glory in his matchless strength—the small but never failing thrill of joy as the foe fell crushed and limp, or the riven boulders grit and heaved when he turned on them the measure of his wondrous force.

[A few chapters later, Wahb discovered Yellowstone National Park.]

Many years ago a wise government set aside the head waters of the Yellowstone to be a sanctuary of wild life forever. In the limits of this great Wonderland the ideal of the Royal Singer was to be realized, and none were to harm or make afraid. No violence was to be offered to any bird or beast, no ax was to be carried into its primitive forests, and the streams were to flow on forever unpolluted by mill or mine. All things were to bear witness that such as this was the West before the white man came.

The wild animals quickly found out all this. They soon learned the boundaries of this unfenced Park, and, as every one knows, they show a different nature within its sacred limits. They no longer shun the face of man, they neither fear nor attack him, and they are even more tolerant of one another in this land of refuge.

Peace and plenty are the sum of earthly good; so, finding them here, the wild creatures crowd into the Park from the surrounding country in numbers not elsewhere to be seen.

The Bears are especially numerous about the Fountain Hotel. In the woods, a quarter of a mile away, is a smooth open place where the steward of the hotel has all the broken and waste food put out daily for the Bears, and the man whose work it is has become the Steward of the Bears' Banquet. Each day it is spread, and each year there are more Bears to partake of it. It is a common thing now to see a dozen Bears feasting there at one time. They are of all kinds—Black, Brown, Cinnamon, Grizzly, Silvertip, Roachbacks, big and small, families and rangers, from all parts of the vast surrounding country. All seem to realize that in the Park no violence is allowed, and the most ferocious of them have here put on a new behavior. Although scores of Bears roam about his choice resort, and sometimes quarrel among themselves, not one of them has ever yet harmed a man.

Year after year they have come and gone. The passing travellers see them. The men of the hotel know many of them well. They know that they show up each summer during the short season when the hotel is in use, and that they disappear again, no man knowing whence they come or whither they go.

One day the owner of the Palette Ranch came through the Park. During his stay at the Fountain Hotel, he went to the Bear Banquet Hall at high meal-tide. There were several Blackbears feasting, but they made way for a huge Silvertip Grizzly that came about sundown.

"That," said the man who was acting as guide, "is the biggest Grizzly in the Park; but he is a peaceable sort, or Lud knows what'd happen."

"That!" said the ranchman, in astonishment, as the Grizzly came hulking nearer, and loomed up like a load of hay among the piney pillars of the Banquet Hall. "That! If that is not Meteetse Wahb, I never saw a Bear in my life! Why, that is the worst Grizzly that ever rolled a log in the Big Horn Basin."

"It ain't possible," said the other, "for he's here every summer, July and August, an' I reckon he don't live so far away."

"Well, that settles it," said the ranchman; "July and August is just the time we miss him on the range; and you can see for yourself that he is a little lame behind and has lost a claw of his left front foot. Now I know where he puts in his summers; but I did not suppose that the old reprobate would know enough to behave himself away from home."

The big Grizzly became very well known during the successive hotel seasons. Once only did he really behave ill, and that was the first season he appeared, before he fully knew the ways of the Park.

He wandered over to the hotel, one day, and in at the front door. In the hall he reared up his eight feet of stature as the guests fled in terror; then he went into the clerk's office. The man said: "All right; if you need this office more than I do, you can have it," and leaping over the counter, locked himself in the telegraph-office to wire the superintendent of the Park: "Old Grizzly in the office now, seems to want to run hotel; may we shoot?"

The reply came: "No shooting allowed in Park; use the hose." Which they did, and, wholly taken by surprise, the Bear leaped over the counter too, and ambled out the back way, with a heavy *thud-thudding* of his feet, and a rattling of his claws on the floor. He passed through the kitchen as he went, and, picking up a quarter of beef, took it along.

▼▼▼

Anderson

One summer Ernest Thompson Seton, whose animal stories are known throughout the world, visited the ranch. . . . I told Mr. Seton about an unusually large grizzly bear that had been frequenting the country about my ranch for many years and had been most destructive to my cattle. There was but one marauder; I knew this by the track, which measured thirteen inches in width. Bears' feet often vary in size, like women's; I have killed large bears with small feet, and small bears with large feet. I knew that this was an unusually large bear not only by the size of his track but by the depth it would sink down into the soft earth.

I told Seton about this bear, and some of my other experiences bear-hunting, and, with his literary ability, he wove them into an entertaining story called "Wab, or the Biography of a Grizzly," and dedicated it to the Palette Ranch. In this account he had Wab deliberately commit suicide in Death Valley. This is poetic license, as Wab met a different end.

As Wab had killed a number of my cattle (one day his trail led me by the carcasses of five cows he had killed) and was rather an expensive boarder, I decided to get rid of him. Wab only came down to the ranch in the early spring and pulled out usually in the month of April. He probably went over to Yellowstone Park, only twenty-five miles distant, to live on the refuse of hotels. Although I did not usually go to my ranch until midsummer or fall, I decided to make an exception and go in the month of May in the hopes of having an interview with Wab.

That year, . . . Mayor John Purroy Mitchell was asked to open the Universal Exhibition in San Francisco and on his way out I invited him to visit my ranch. The Mayor was a good sport, and was delighted at the prospect of getting a shot at a bear. We arrived at my ranch one afternoon about four o'clock. My foreman told me that a bear had killed a cow the night before, two miles above the ranch house. Knowing that a bear will often return a second time to the place of his prey, I thought I was going to be fortunate in giving the Mayor a shot at the bear immediately.

A bear is a nocturnal animal, spending his day hiding in some deep shade of the forest and coming out only at dusk in search of food. Just before sunset, therefore, we mounted our horses and rode up the valley to the spot where the bear had killed the cow.

We found the carcass partly eaten; so the Mayor and I concealed ourselves behind a near-by rock to await his coming. But our waiting was in vain. The veil of night came down, and no bear appeared. After a bear has gorged himself the night of his kill, he seldom shows up the following night, but almost invariably returns the second evening. So I was not discouraged at his non-appearance, feeling sure that we would be successful the next evening. On that day, unfortunately, Mayor Mitchell was taken with one of the dreadful headaches to which he was subject, and for two days was not able to leave the house. As I was anxious that the Mayor should kill the bear I did not go to the bait. When Mr. Mitchell was able to ride out with me, we discovered that the cow had been completely devoured. And not by one, but by three bears. I then decided to put out another bait.

My house is situated on a small stream called the Piney, the dearest little stream that ever tumbled down a mountain side. It rises in a large spring some six miles above my ranch and, tumbling down over the clean boulders, is aërated, and makes the most delightful drinking water I have ever discovered, as cold as ice-water all summer long. About five miles above my ranch a game trail comes down the side of the mountain and crosses Piney. It is frequently used by bears. On the north side of Piney at that point is a small, open meadow. There I decided to place my bait. I had an old horse, no longer of any use, and as bears are more fond of horse meat than any other kind, I decided to use the horse for that purpose. I directed one of the cowboys to take the horse to that spot, shoot him, and let me know if the carcass was found by bears. On the second day he told me that a bear was using the bait. We had an early dinner that day, and the Mayor and I rode up Piney, secreting ourselves behind some sagebrush a short distance from the bait.

Snow covered the ground. The air was cold. But we patiently waited in hopes of a visit from the bear. Finally just before dark I saw an immense bear which I recognized as Wab coming directly down the creek towards us. I waited until he was not more than fifty yards away, and, turning to the Mayor, who was behind me, whispered, "Jack, he's coming."

The Mayor rose to his feet as if he were going to make an address, and said, "Where?"

The bear saw him, jumped behind some willow brush and disappeared. He never saw him again.

We returned the following evening, but the bear, having been frightened, did not return again to the bait until after dark. A few days after, the Mayor was obliged to go to San Francisco, where he was to open the World's Fair, and, I am sorry to say, never got his bear.

I was very anxious to get rid of Wab, and, as I did not see him come out before dark, I decided to trap him. I do not consider trapping a very manly sport, and would not have resorted to it in this instance had not the bear been so destructive of my cattle. I set the bear trap beside the carcass. A bear trap is a large steel trap weighing some forty pounds, with a chain and a ring, by which it is attached to a movable log. If it were not attached to a movable object, when the bear first placed his foot in it, he would certainly tear loose; but as the log is movable, this does not happen. I carefully placed the trap beside the bait, covered it with leaves and grass so that it was invisible to the eye, and returned to the ranch.

The following morning with great curiosity and anticipation, I returned to see if the bear had been at the bait. I found that he had been there. And now I am going to tell you something that I would not have believed, had I not seen it myself. The trap had been sprung! It was in the same spot, and the jaws merely closed. There was no hair in it, and not the slightest evidence as to how the trap had been sprung.

That day I placed a second trap on the other side of the bait, carefully concealed. On returning the following morning, I found that both traps were closed. I was somewhat discouraged but again set both traps. When I returned the next day, one trap was sprung. The other, having been exposed to the rain and the damp air, had become rusted so that, although the pedal had been pushed down, the jaws had failed to close. But, strange to relate, the bear had turned the trap over so that the teeth were on the ground. Thus, if the trap did close, it would do no harm. This sounds incredible but it is absolutely true.

As I found that the bear was too cunning to be trapped, and the carcass was nearly consumed, I decided to watch for him again at dusk. The following evening I went to the bait, and hiding behind some sagebrush twenty-five yards from the carcass, I waited. As I have said, there was a small meadow between me and the stream, and directly opposite, on the other side of the stream, the game trail went up the mountainside among the pine trees.

I waited and waited, and had almost given up hope of seeing the bear, when I looked up on the mountainside, and there between the openings in the trees I saw two bears wandering about, gradually making their way down the mountain. As it turned out, one of them was a female bear; the other, who was following her, was Wab. This love affair was the cause of his destruction.

Presently the female bear came down the trail, rushed up to the bait, and commenced to eat. She was only twenty-five yards away and I could easily have killed her then and there, but I waited in hopes of the larger bear joining her. The female bear at that particular point evidently got a whiff of air and scented my presence, as she threw up her head and started on a run across the meadow, splashed across the stream and headed up the trail. I then saw it was my last chance, and, taking careful aim, cut loose. The bullet went true, and she rolled down dead at the bottom of the trail.

I then saw Wab crossing a small opening among the trees at a fast walk. I took aim and fired, and going up there I found the bear dead only a few yards from the spot I had shot at him. I rather congratulated myself that I had killed two grizzlies moving, one 100 yards and the other 150 yards distant, in two shots. This was the last chapter in Wab's history of destruction. His skin now decorates my studio. During the morning of the same day I had been successful in killing two other grizzlies; a total of four grizzlies in one day.

A PHOTOGRAPHIC EXPEDITION FOR THE YELLOWSTONE GRIZZLY 1906

 WILLIAM Wright's book of grizzly bear adventures, first published in 1909, is "one of the best all-around books ever written on the grizzly bear," according to Frank Craighead, Jr., who wrote the foreword to the 1977 reprint of The Grizzly Bear: The Narrative of a Hunter-Naturalist *(Lincoln: University of Nebraska Press). Wright's purpose in writing the book was, as Craighead pointed out, conservation. Wright spent many years hunting the bears himself, then gave hunting up for study and photography.*

William Wright must have been quite a man. His engaging book shows a sensitive and thoughtful naturalist, a man truly at home in the forests and mountains, an unschooled scientist, a lover of the grizzly bear. The emerging conservation ethic of this era was fueled not only by observations that, within a single generation, species such as the great bear had gone from plentiful to rare, but also by the growing appreciation and love of nature based on increased knowledge of it.

▼▼▼▼

A great many years ago my interest in natural history, which grew out of my interest in hunting, caused me to give a certain amount of attention to photography. Little by little, as I became more expert in this, I took to carrying a camera with me on my various expeditions, and finally I came to making excursions with no other end in view than the photographing of game. It was a long time, however, before I developed a definite ambition to photograph a grizzly, because the difficulties which presented themselves in that field were so many that at first I saw no way of overcoming them.

Much hunting has not only made the grizzly very shy, but has caused him gradually to become even more nocturnal or, to be accurate, crepuscular, than he was originally. It follows that in these latter days the chances of obtaining a daylight picture of a grizzly are almost negligible, and though by some lucky chance one might meet a bear in a snap-shotting light when one had a camera ready, the coincidence would be too unlikely to depend upon. When, therefore, I began to think seriously of attempting to photograph these bears, I of necessity turned my mind to flash-light, and for several years I worked and experimented to that end. The most favorable time to operate being between sundown and dark, it was impracticable to set up a camera and leave the lens open and provide for the exploding of a flash when the bear came along, and I therefore set about perfecting an electrical device which at the same time would explode the flash and spring the shutter of the camera. My first idea was to have this apparatus operated by the bear himself, and to that end I constructed it so that the trigger could be tripped by pressure applied to a fine thread or wire, which could be stretched across the trail; but though I soon succeeded in getting this mechanism to work well at home, actual practice in the field developed a succession of difficulties which had to be overcome little by little, and as field trials were scarce and expensive, it took me a long time to arrive at satisfactory results.

By the time my camera was in working order, the bears on which I had expected to use it were all but things of the past; and having heard for a number of years that the grizzlies of the Yellowstone National Park had become comparatively tame, and that it was no difficult task to photograph them, and having hunted grizzlies in all the country round the park without finding the bears there different from what they were in other parts of the country, I determined to take my camera to the park and study the grizzly in this field. This was in 1906.

I was armed with a permit from Major Pitcher, the acting superintendent, which allowed me to photograph and study the grizzlies, provided I did not molest them in any way. I went first to the Grand Cañon. I found there quite a number of grizzlies feeding in the evening at the garbage dump back of the hotel, and for a few evenings I watched them there in order to determine the direction from which they came, and to ascertain how many were using this feeding ground. After watching for a few evenings I found that there were about thirty grizzlies all told that came there. There were several old she bears with litters of cubs, several litters two and three years old that had left their mothers, but were still running together, and several old fellows that came and went by themselves.

While I was watching the dump in the evening, I travelled the surrounding country by day to see if any of these bears could be seen by daylight, and though I scoured every thicket and gully, not a grizzly did I thus see during some two weeks' sojourn there. In this respect they were much more timid than they were in a great many places throughout the Selkirk and Rocky Mountain ranges.

My next move was to find out where these bears hid when they were not feeding, for I have never yet seen a grizzly that did not have a home, either in some dense thicket or in some heavy timber or in some high mountain. I followed some of the more travelled trails for several miles and found that nearly all of these grizzlies had their headquarters in the range of mountains around Mt. Washburn. I then selected their largest highway, and after setting up my camera, concealed myself one evening about a hundred feet from the trail and to leeward of it, and watched for the coming of the grizzlies. Across the trail I had stretched a number forty sewing thread, one end attached to the electric switch and the other to a small stake driven into the ground beyond the trail. Just below where I had located, there was an open park in which the bears had been feeding, as was shown by the grass that had been nipped and the holes that had been dug for roots.

For some hours I waited in the bushes and fought gnats and mosquitoes. I saw several black bears pass along the hillside, but not a grizzly showed his nose until after the sun had set and the little marsh in the park was covered with a mantle of fog. Suddenly then, far up the trail, appeared what at first looked like a shadow, so slowly and silently did it move. But I knew at once, by the motion of the head and the long stride, that a grizzly was coming to the bottom for a few roots and a feed of grass.

I watched closely to see if he acted differently from bears elsewhere that are supposed to know less of man. I could not, however, detect the slightest difference in his actions from those of bears that had never seen Yellowstone Park. All his movements were furtive and cautious, as if he expected to meet an enemy at every step. He would advance a few feet, and then stop, turn his head from side to side, scent the air, and peer in every direction.

I was, of course, very anxious to see what he would do when he came to the thread across the trail, and I had not long to wait, for he came on steadily but slowly and, when within ten feet of the thread, he stopped, poked out his nose and sniffed two or three times, raised up on his hind feet, took a few more sniffs, and then bolted up the trail in the direction from which he had come. This bear did not seem to have been very successfully tamed.

A few minutes after he had gone three more appeared. These were evidently of one litter and appeared to be between two and three years old. They came on with the same cautious movements, and when they were close upon the thread, they also stopped and went through a similar performance. The one in front pushed out his nose and sniffed gingerly at the suspicious object. Those in the rear also stopped, but being curious to learn what was causing the blockade, the second one placed his forefeet on the rump of the one in front, in order to see ahead, while the third one straightened up on his hind legs and looked over the other two. They made a beautiful group, and just as they had poised themselves, the one in front must have touched the string a little harder than he had intended to, for there was a sudden flash that lit up the surroundings, and I expected to see the bears go tearing off through the timber, but, to my utter surprise, nothing of the kind happened. They all three stood up on their hind legs, and looked at each other as much as to say, "Now, what do you think of that?" and then they took up their investigation where it had been interrupted, followed the thread to where it was fastened to the stick, clawed up the spool, which I had buried in the ground, sniffed at it, and then went back to the trail, where they had first found the thread. Here they again stood up, and then, having either satisfied their curiosity or becoming suspicious, they turned around and trailed away through the timber. As far as I could see them they went cautiously, and stopped at frequent intervals to stand up and look behind them to see if there were any more flashes or if anything was following them. Unfortunately this picture was utterly worthless. I had failed to use enough flash powder, and when I came to develop the plate, it showed only the dimmest outline of the animals.

Soon after this an old she bear with three cubs came down the trail, but they were just as cautious as the others had been. Every few feet the mother would stop and sniff the air, and the cubs, fascinating little imitators that they are, had to copy her every move. If she stood up on her hind feet, they also stood up on theirs. If she stopped to sniff the air, they would run up and, placing their tiny feet against her sides, would peer wisely and anxiously ahead, until the old lady started on again. When she came to the thread she stopped short, and while she was making her investigations the cubs stood with their forefeet against her and awaited the verdict. It was sudden and apparently surprising, for, after satisfying herself that the obstacle was placed there for no good, she gave a lively snort that could have been heard for a hundred yards, and without waiting for her youngsters to get down, suddenly turned tail and, upsetting the whole lot, disappeared up the trail like a whirlwind, with the cubs trying their best to overtake her.

After this last delegation had gone I waited for an hour or more, but got no more photographic opportunities. Several bears came out, but it was too dark for me to follow their actions, and none of them saw fit to run into the thread. However, just before I was about to leave, I heard something coming down the trail as if pursued by the devil, and it occurred to me that whatever it was would be in too much of a hurry to stop and examine the string, and so it proved. There was a bright flash, and for an instant the forest was lighted up, and I saw an old black bear travelling as if for dear life. I had thought that he was at his best gait before he struck the string, but in this I was mistaken. He had only been fooling along before. Now he got down to business, and in less time than it takes to write it he was out of sight and beyond hearing. When I developed the plate it looked as though a cannonball of hair had been shot across it.

This was my first evening, and it did not pan out very heavily in practical results. But I had a lot of sport, and had begun to find out, as later on I was to prove more thoroughly, that the Yellowstone Park grizzlies differ in no material respect from others of their species.

A WILDLIFE CRUSADER
1913

 WILLIAM T. Hornaday was a well known and vocal crusader for wildlife in the first decades of this century. We give here two brief excerpts from his 1913 book Our Vanishing Wild Life: Its Extermination and Preservation *(New York: New York Zoological Society). Unlike the other stories, these excerpts do not recount encounters with the grizzly, but they show that Yellowstone had national prominence as a refuge for wildlife, and that, clearly, its bears were considered one of the primary beneficiaries of this safe haven.*

Although the American public was becoming more aware of the plight of native birds and mammals and more favorable toward conservation, "[m]arket hunting was still practiced in many states; plume hunting had not been entirely eliminated; spring shooting of waterfowl, shorebirds, and upland game birds was a nearly universal practice; game laws were extremely liberal; and the automobile and rapid social change were beginning to have their first direct and indirect impacts on the wildlife resource" (James B. Trefethen, An American Crusade for Wildlife, *New York: Winchester Press, 1975). Our Vanishing Wild Life played an important role in the enactment of many laws and regulations to protect wildlife. However, it demonstrates the ubiquitous hatred of predators held even by scientists and wildlife supporters (Hornaday would write, as late as 1931, "The gray wolf should always be killed. No danger of his extermination.").*

It is striking that, in the historically complex arena of conservation, many of the same arguments we hear today for and against wildlife had already been articulated in Hornaday's time and in his book. Although much sound scientific research has informed and improved wildlife regulation and management since 1913, the battle lines had already been drawn. Hornaday used the old argument that sportsmen wanted the grizzly bear preserved for hunting (he himself was a hunter; see his exciting grizzly hunt in Camp-Fires in the Canadian Rockies, *1906). Yet he also articulated two more contemporary notions: first, that the grizzly bear has the power to inspire us as no other North American animal does and should, for that reason, be preserved, and second, that refuges such as Yellowstone National Park are valuable in preventing the extinction of species.*

▼▼▼▼

To many persons it may seem strange that anyone should feel disposed to accord protection to such fierce predatory animals as grizzly bears, lions and tigers. But the spirit of fair play springs eternal in some human breasts. The sportsmen of the world do not stick at using long-range, high-power repeating rifles on big game, but they draw the line this side of traps, poisons and extermination. The sportsmen of India once thought,—for about a year and a day,—that it was permissible to kill troublesome and expensive tigers by poison. Mr. G. P. Sanderson tried it, and when his strychnine operations promptly developed three bloated and disgusting tiger carcasses, even his native followers revolted at the principle. That was the alpha and omega of Sanderson's poisoning activities.

I am quite sure that if the extermination of the tiger from the whole of India were possible, and the to-be or not-to-be were put to a vote of the sportsmen of India, the answer would be a thundering *"No!"* Says Major J. Stevenson-Hamilton in his "Animal Life in Africa:" "It is impossible to contemplate the use against the lion of any other weapon than the rifle."

The real sportsmen and naturalists of America are decidedly opposed to the extermination of the grizzly bear. They feel that the wilds of North America are wide enough for the accommodation of many grizzlies, without crowding the proletariat. A Rocky Mountain without a grizzly upon it, or at least a bear of some kind, is only half a mountain,—commonplace and tame. Put one two-year-old grizzly cub upon it, and presto! Every cubic yard of its local atmosphere reeks with romantic uncertainty and fearsome thrills.

A few persons have done considerable talking and writing about the damage to stock inflicted by bears, but I think there is little justification for such charges. Certainly, there is not one-tenth enough real damage done by bears to justify their extermination. At the present time, we hear that the farmers (!) of Kodiak Island, Alaska, are being seriously harassed and damaged by the big Kodiak bear,—an animal so rare and shy that it is very difficult for a sportsman to kill one! I think the charges against the bears,—if the Kodiak Islanders ever really have made any,—need to be proven, by the production of real evidence.

In the United States, outside of our game preserves, I know of not one locality in which grizzly bears are sufficiently numerous to justify a sportsman in going out to hunt them. The California grizzly, once represented by

"Monarch" in Golden Gate Park, is almost, if not wholly, extinct. In Montana, outside of Glacier Park it is useless to apply for wild grizzlies. In the Bitter Root Mountains and Clearwater Mountains of Idaho, there are grizzlies, but they hide so effectually under the snowbent willows on the "slides" that it is almost impossible to get a shot. Northwestern Wyoming still contains a few grizzlies, but there are so many square miles of mountains around each animal it is now almost useless to go hunting for them. British Columbia, western Alberta and the coast mountains at least as far as Skagway, and Yukon Territory generally, all contain grizzlies, and the sportsman who goes out for sheep, caribou and moose is reasonably certain to see half a dozen bears and kill at least one or two. In those countries, the grizzly species will hold forth long after all killable grizzlies have vanished from the United States.

I think that it is now time for California, Montana, Washington, Oregon, Idaho and Wyoming to give grizzly bears protection of some sort. Possibly the situation in those states calls for a five-year close season. Even British Columbia should now place a bag limit on this species. This has seemed clear to me ever since two of my friends killed (in the spring of 1912) *six* grizzlies in one week! But Provincial Game Warden A. Bryan Williams says that at present it would be impossible to impose a bag limit of one per year on the grizzlies of British Columbia; and Mr. Williams is a sincere game-protector.

▼▼▼

The most charming trait of wild-life character is the alacrity and confidence with which wild birds and mammals respond to the friendly advances of human friends. Those who are not very familiar with the mental traits of our wild neighbors may at first find it difficult to comprehend the marvelous celerity with which both birds and mammals recognize friendly overtures from man, and respond to them.

At the present juncture, this state of the wild-animal mind becomes a factor of great importance in determining what we can do to prevent the extermination of species, and to promote the increase and return of wild life.

I think that there is not a single wild mammal or bird species now living that can not, or does not, quickly recognize protection, *and take advantage of it.* The most conspicuous of all familiar examples are the wild animals of the Yellowstone Park. They embrace the elk, mountain sheep, antelope, mule deer, the black bear and even the grizzly. No one can say precisely how long those several species were in ascertaining that it was safe to trust themselves within easy rifle-shot of man; but I think it was about five years. Birds recognize protection far more quickly than mammals. In a comparatively short time the naturally wild and wary big game of the Yellowstone Park became about as tame as range cattle. It was at least fifteen years ago that the mule deer began to frequent the parade ground at the Mammoth Hot Springs military post, and receive there their rations of hay.

Whenever you see a beautiful photograph of a large band of bighorn sheep or mule deer taken at short range amid Rocky Mountain scenery, you are safe in labeling it as having come from the Yellowstone Park. The prong-horned antelope herd is so tame that it is difficult to keep it out of the streets of Gardiner, on the Montana side of the line.

But the bears! Who has not heard the story of the bears of the Yellowstone Park,—how black bears and grizzlies stalk out of the woods, every day, to the garbage dumping-ground; how black bears actually have come *into the hotels* for food, without breaking the truce, and how the grizzlies boldly raid the grub-wagons and cook-tents of campers, taking just what they please, because they *know* that no man dares to shoot them! Indeed, those raiding bears long ago became a public nuisance, and many of them have been caught in steel box-traps and shipped to zoological gardens, in order to get them out of the way. And yet, outside the Park boundaries, everywhere, the bears are as wary and wild as the wildest.

The arrogance of the bears that couldn't be shot once led to a droll and also exciting episode.

During the period when Mr. C. J. Jones ("Buffalo" Jones) was superintendent of the wild animals of the Park, the indignities inflicted upon tourist campers by certain grizzly bears quite abraded his nerves. He obtained from Major Pitcher authority to punish and reform a certain grizzly, and went about the matter in a thoroughly Buffalo-Jonesian manner. He procured a strong lariat and a bean-pole seven feet long and repaired to the camp that was troubled by too much grizzly.

The particular offender was a full-grown male grizzly who had become a notorious raider. At the psychological moment Jones lassoed him in short order, getting a firm hold on the bear's left hind leg. Quickly the end of the rope was thrown over a limb of the nearest tree, and in a trice Ephraim found himself swinging head downward between the heavens and the earth. And then his punishment began.

Buffalo Jones thrashed him soundly with the bean-pole! The outraged bear swung to and fro, whirled round and round, clawing and snapping at the empty air, roaring and bawling with rage, scourged in flesh and insulted in spirit. As he swung, the bean-pole searched out the different parts of his anatomy with a wonderful degree of neatness and precision. Between rage and indignation the grizzly nearly exploded. A moving-picture camera was there, and since that day that truly moving scene has amazed and thrilled countless thousands of people.

When it was over, Mr. Jones boldly turned the bear loose! Although its rage was as boundless as the glories of the Yellowstone Park, it paused not to rend any of those present, but headed for the tall timber, and with many an indignant "Woof! Woof!" it plunged in and disappeared. It was two or three years before that locality was again troubled by impudent grizzly bears.

And what is the mental attitude of *every* Rocky Mountain black or grizzly bear *outside* of the Yellowstone Park? It is colossal suspicion of man, perpetual fear, and a clean pair of heels the moment man-scent or man-sight proclaims the proximity of the Arch Enemy of Wild Creatures. And yet there are one or two men who tell the American public that wild animals do not think, that they do not reason, and are governed only by "instinct"!

"A little knowledge is a dangerous thing!"

THE YELLOWSTONE SANCTUARY
1916

 SOME thoughtful people, very early in this century, recognized the grizzly's vulnerability to extinction by overhunting and other conflicts with man. The value of Yellowstone National Park to bear conservation was appreciated, and it is clear that the primary reason grizzlies remain in this region today is because of the Park. This essay by Stephen N. Leek was published in May 1916 in In the Open *(Pittsburgh, Pennsylvania); it is the first part of an article originally entitled "Grizzly and His Sanctuary," a transcript of which was filed in the Works Progress Administration collection in the Wyoming Department of Commerce's Historical Research and Publications in Cheyenne.*

Stephen Leek was an early homesteader in Jackson Hole, Wyoming, just south of Yellowstone. He arrived in 1888, when there were fewer than 40 settlers in the valley, later built a dude ranch/hunting lodge (which still bears his name) on Jackson Lake and, in the early years of the new century, served in the state legislature. He took it upon himself to document and publicize the plight of Jackson Hole's starving elk herd, which had been pushed from its traditional wintering grounds by ranching activities. His writings, lectures, and especially his photographs galvanized public opinion and led to Congressional action providing the elk with hay and establishing the National Elk Refuge in 1912. This event is considered a milestone in the history of American wildlife conservation. From this essay, we see that Leek fully understood the value of setting aside land for numerous wildlife species.

▼▼▼▼

THE Yellowstone Park was established at a time when many of our big game animals were threatened with extinction. Their extreme plentifulness but a few years before had led people to believe (that is, if they even thought of it at all) that the extermination of the myriads of big game animals was impossible. However, they were rudely awakened to the fact that if even a few individuals of some of the species were to be saved, they must act at once. This was the case with the antelope, grizzly bear, beaver, mountain sheep, and buffalo. A few of all of these were included in the park, and now it contains the only herd of wild buffalo in the United States; it saved the beaver from practical extermination in the west, and it may be the means of saving the antelope. To all the above animals, to which may be added, moose, black-tail deer, white-tail deer, and elk, it has been a refuge and breeding ground, and now the extra numbers of some of these animals can be spared, are being captured and shipped to other localities for exhibition or stocking purposes.

The park has been of no more benefit to any one of these animals than it has been to the bear, and were they exterminated now, the park would lose one of its great attractions to the eastern tourist. Outside the park, all men's hands have been turned against these noble game animals. They were killed at all seasons of the year, in all manner of ways, even had a bounty put on their heads, and added to this was the price of their fur. Every means was employed to outwit and capture or destroy them until but for their cunning and sagacity, and the impenetrable nature of some of their retreats not one would be left today.

Absolute protection in the park, (except a few cases of where a cross-tempered bear has become dangerous and been shot, or the few that have been shipped to other localities for exhibition purposes,) has made them very plentiful and tame, so much so that they are a source of amusement and interest to the park visitors, and of much annoyance and alarm to others.

For generations the bear have had to rustle for a living. In the wild state this consisted of food supplied by nature, such as different roots, nuts, berries, tender vegetable growths, insects, and such, but the great number of bears in the park has made the natural food supply insufficient, and they are natural pilferers, as the visitations to the pig styes of the Pilgrim Fathers, demonstrate, and they thereby acquired an appetite for pig meat that has been handed down, generation to generation. Therefore with the park bear the longing is hereditary. They have the craving for sugar-cured hams and bacon, and they regard the "sage-brush tourists," as their legitimate source of supply for the hams and bacon necessary to supply this craving.

Now I suppose I must explain a "sage-brush tourist," but first I will tell you what a "dude" is. Out west, every man from the east entering the Rocky Mountains on a hunting, camping, fishing, or sight-seeing trip is called a "dude" by the natives. And any of the natives who make a trip through the park with horses, and camp out along the roads in the park, are called "sage-brush tourists" by the "dudes". So sometimes a "dude" can be a "sage-brush tourist," but a "sage-brush tourist" can never be a "dude." As there are poor chances of obtaining uncooked food in the park, these "sage-brush tourists" must take a supply with them. Fresh meat is very hard to take on such a trip, so a good portion of the food is carried along in sugar-cured hams and bacon. The sweet aroma from this sugar-cured pig meat attracts the bears to the camp. They are generally harmless, but a person feels sort of queer to be awakened from a sound slumber, to hear a bear drinking from the water pail near the camp fire, or hear the dutch-oven lid knocked off during the night.

One party thought it would be fine to take a flash light picture of a bear near their wagon. So they got everything set before dark. During the night they heard a noise at the wagon and sprang the flash. They didn't think much more about the picture till they developed the plate; on it they found 13 bear, some in the wagon, some part way in and others around it.

Once, while camping near the River-Side geyser, at the upper geyser basin in the park, I had two young men with me, who were both "sage-brush tourists" and "dudes." Uncle Jack, an old trapper, was our cook. We had a saddle-horse each, and four pack horses, and one big tent where we all slept, and in which our food was placed at night. We had only one ham left and during the night the bear got that, that is, we supposed he did though nobody saw or heard anything. At the Upper Basin in the park there is a store and I went up and got another ham. That night when we turned in, Uncle Jack said, "Here Steve, I will let you take care of this ham." I told him all right, I would watch the ham if he would watch the balance of the food. He said all right he would, and placed it all in the packing sacks. These he placed in the tent, then roofed them over as if he expected rain, with our dish camp outfit on top of the roof. These were expected to rattle if disturbed by bear. I placed the ham near my pillow and every time I woke up during the night I felt for the ham. No tin dishes were heard to rattle during the night, and in the morning the ham was still there. Uncle Jack came for it to cut some for breakfast and soon called us out to feed. We were jollying about getting the best of the bear, but Uncle Jack was sort of quiet and cranky for him, until finally after breakfast one of the boys said, "What's the matter Uncle Jack, what makes you so cranky?"

"Oh," he said, "the damn bear got the bacon."

A little later in the season after we concluded the park trip, we went bear hunting. Then we wished them a little more plentiful and more sociable.

Our hunting ground was a beautiful place high in the mountains, possible to reach only with saddle and pack-horses. If you would see nature at her best, this is the way to go, leave the man-made trails and roads, cabins and camps, and follow the dim trails of the wild creatures back to their hidden retreats, and see them at their best.

When first I visited the location of our intended camping ground, I was alone with saddle-horse, riding through heavy open timber, when I saw before me passing glimpses through the timber of a great canyon, heavily timbered for a distance, then breaking off in sheer descent. I wondered where the canyon could lead to, and hurried through the timber to the brink. A trout leaped in the air and the spell was broken, but the illusion had been complete, I was gazing across a beautiful little lake. On the opposite shore rose a hill timbered at the base, broken and rocky near the summit. Even as I looked, it appeared inverted and mirrored in the lake, and in imagination I again saw the opposite wall of a great canyon. Then a band of elk crossed a shallow grassy neck of the lake on the opposite shore, and as I looked in the cold transparent depths, numbers of speckled trout could be seen. I snapped bits of limbs in the water and they rushed for them. Never before had they seen a man or artificial bait. I rode around the lake shore to its outlet, a sparkling little brook that went tearing down the mountain side among the boulders.

On returning toward camp a few hours later, I rode out on the brink of the hill above the lake and dismounted. On the edge I sat for a long time drinking in the beautiful sight. Back of me my pony grazed upon the abundance of grass. Barring my companion at our camp below, I knew of no human being within 25 miles in any direction. As I lingered there the sun got lower in the west and the hill on which I sat began to cast its shadows across the view below. Then I saw an old bear appear, sniffing and feeding about the springs at the head of the lake. Soon two more appeared, little black fellows, the old bear's cubs. They put in their time wrestling, playing, and running about, but the old bear was very busy with the evening meal, among the rank vegetation near the springs. The trout were now jumping continuously all over the lake. Regretfully I turned back from the edge, and mounting my pony took my way over the log-strewn route to camp leaving the beautiful view undisturbed.

NEW ENVIRONMENTS
1919

 THE battle to protect Yellowstone's wildlife lasted decades, as Colorado author Enos A. Mills records in this chapter from his book, The Grizzly: Our Greatest Wild Animal, *first published in 1919 (Sausalito, California: Comstock Editions, 1976). The Act of Congress that created Yellowstone National Park in 1872 had authorized regulations to be made for its protection but had not authorized any means for their enforcement. When, after several years, Congress stopped appropriating even minimal funds for protection of the Park's wildlife, timber, and geological features, the cavalry came to the rescue—literally. Yet, the Army too "labored under severe legal restrictions and impossibly vague orders" in trying to protect Yellowstone, as James B. Trefethen wrote in* An American Crusade for Wildlife *(New York: Winchester Press, 1975). It was not until 1894 that the Lacey Act was signed into law to protect the Park against growing threats from poachers, loggers, vandals, tourists, the mining interests, and real estate developers who were lobbying for a railroad line through the Park.*

But even when the slaughter stopped inside the Park, the increasing numbers of both grizzlies and tourists created management problems that were not easily resolved. Although there have been many who have shared the vision and ecological understanding of Enos Mills, bear management remains a stubborn challenge to this day.

▼▼▼▼

A rock fell from a high cliff and struck upon solid granite near a grizzly whom I was watching. There was a terrific crash and roar. Unmindful of the flying fragments and pieces bounding near, the grizzly reared up and pressed fore paws over his ears. Just as he was uncovering them the echo came thundering and booming back from a cliff across the lake. Again he hastily covered his ears with his paws to soften the ear-bursting crash.

On another occasion a wounded bear took refuge in a small thicket where the hunter was unable to get a shot at him. After failing to force the bear into the open, the hunter gave a wild, ear-splitting yell. With a growl of pain the bear at once charged furiously through the thicket toward the hunter.

A grizzly has supersensitive ears, and loud, harsh sounds give his nerves a harrowing shock. Through his higher development the grizzly probably suffers more intensely and enjoys more fully than other animals. The clashing city noises must be a never ending irritation and torture to a bear who has been sentenced to end his days in a riotous environment. How he must yearn for the hush of the wilderness! And, as his sense of smell is also amazingly developed, perhaps he longs for a whiff of pine-spiced air and the wild, exquisite perfume of the violets.

Experience in many zoos has shown that subjecting caged grizzlies to close contact with people is unusual cruelty to animals. Often they become cross, and a number of crowd-worried grizzlies have died prematurely from resultant apoplexy. Modern zoo bear-pens are constructed so that the bear is beyond the wiles of visitors—so that he can have much privacy—one of the needs of any grizzly. Perhaps we too often think of the bulky grizzly as being coarse and crude. But he is an animal of the highest type, sensitive, independent, and retiring. The normal bear is good-tempered and cheerful.

A grizzly placed in new environment in association with men will respond happily only to considerate handling and proper feeding. Tell me what a bear is fed and how, and I will tell you what the bear is—his disposition and health. A grizzly should be fed by no one except his keeper. If any one and every one feed a bear, he is likely to receive food that he ought not to eat and to have it given in a manner annoying to him. Feeding is the vital consideration for grizzly pets, for grizzlies in zoos, and for grizzlies in National Parks.

When I arrived in Colorado, in 1884, grizzlies were still common throughout the mountain areas of the State. They were numerous in a few rugged sections where there were but few people and plenty of food. In the Long's Peak region around my cabin, I early discovered the tracks of five grizzlies. One or two missing toes or some other peculiarity enabled me to determine the number. Two of these bears ranged near, and I had frequent glimpses of them.

During the autumn of one year, 1893 as I remember, I crossed the mountains between Trapper's Lake and Long's Peak. Snow covered most of the ground. During the eight days which this trip occupied I must have seen the tracks of between forty and forty-five grizzlies. I counted the tracks of eleven in one half-day. But grizzlies decreased in numbers rapidly. Numerous hunters came into the State annually. Stockmen and settlers hunted grizzlies for fun and for their hides, and professional hunters for revenue. Altogether, the grizzly had little chance for his life, and only a few survived.

In the settlement of the West many of the grizzlies had to go. Men came in with flocks of sheep and herds of cattle. The grizzlies' food was taken or driven off. Rarely did a grizzly kill any of the invading stock. Usually he worked harder for a living and took things philosophically. Many grizzlies were killed and a few sought homes elsewhere. But in the West there are still many wild regions, and in these there is room for the grizzly.

There is a wonderful unwritten story of the making of an empire—the Yellowstone—into a wildlife reservation. Big game had long been hunted in this region. The grizzly bear, since his discovery, had been relentlessly pursued; man with every conceivable contrivance was on his trail day and night; there was no quarter and no hope for peace. But suddenly firing ceased and pursuit stopped. This was epoch-marking. "What can it mean?" the grizzlies must have instantly asked. They must have asked it over and over again. But they quickly accepted it as a fact and as an advantage, and came forth to associate peacefully with man. This has made a change worth while for man. Since shooting has stopped, thousands have seen the grizzly and enjoyed him where only one saw him before. The grizzly is easily the most popular animal in the National Parks. He really is the greatest animal on the continent. The grizzly walks: there is a dignity, a lordliness of carriage, and an indifference to all the world that impress themselves on the attention. Some one speaks quietly to him: he halts, stands on hind legs, and shows a childlike eagerness of interest in his expressive face. His attitude and responsiveness are most companionable and never fail to awake the best in every one who sees him in these moments.

Some one told me the following amusing incident concerning a grizzly. In the southwest corner of Yellowstone Park a number of boys were bathing in a steam, when a young grizzly came along and for a moment stood watching their pranks. Then he slipped quietly behind some trees upon the bank of the stream. When the boys approached this spot, with a wild "Woof, woof," he leaped into the water among them. This caused great excitement and merriment, plainly just what he desired. As he swam hurriedly away, he looked back over his shoulder with satisfaction.

Another amusing incident also happened in the Yellowstone. As the stage arrived at the Canyon Hotel, one of the passengers, who had been having much to say concerning bears, put on his raincoat and got down on all fours, proceeding to impersonate a bear. While this demonstration was on a grizzly arrived. He made a rush at the man and chased him up a tree, amid laughter and excitement. The bear made no attempt to harm any one and plainly enjoyed this prank merely as a prank.

A grizzly mother in Yellowstone Park was catching trout for her cubs one June day of 1891, when a friend and I came along. We went near to watch them. Mother grizzly charged; we fled. After one leap she stood still and appeared to be almost grinning at us. We went back, she charged, and again we ran, although she stopped at the end of the first leap. But the third time she leaped at us we stood our ground. She growled but came no nearer. Although her threats did not appear to be in earnest, we did not risk going closer; nor would I have risked standing even at that distance if we had been outside of the Park boundary....

In the Yellowstone the environment of grizzlies was radically changed when it became a wild-life reservation. The numerous bear-population quickly discovered that in the Park it would not be shot at. Grizzlies at once wandered about near people with no attempt to conceal themselves and with the best of manners; there was no annoying of people, no crossness, no ferocity. This ideal association of people and grizzly bears went on unmarred for years.

Numbers of bears from far outside Park boundaries came to spend two or three months of each summer there, returning to home territory during the autumn. Other grizzlies left their homes outside the Park and moved in to stay. Whether the summer migrant bears or the recent residents came to the Park because of the food, the safety, or both is difficult to say. Unusual opportunities were furnished Park visitors to study and observe the grizzly, with beneficial influence on themselves. But their worrying of the bears in time proved harmful.

The bears were thoughtlessly betrayed. Increasing numbers of visitors produced large garbage-piles. People came to the garbage-piles to watch the bears feed and often teased them. The bears became cross. Sometimes there were fights among the assembled bears over the smelly feasts. The charity of the garbage-pile led them into bad habits, upset their digestions, and ruined their dispositions. But their appetite for garbage increased until they became food pensioners and garbage drunkards. Like some humans they enjoy being pensioners and insist on being supplied. If there wasn't enough garbage they raided camps and hotels. If their raid was interrupted they resented it. In due time a few of the most dyspeptic bears became bold and defiant raiders.

The Park is visited by thousands for whom the bears should be a source of relaxation and furnish new interests and enjoyment. But the bears are becoming unhealthy and are a menace to people. Now and then some official tries to cure the bear trouble by having a number of bears roped, tied, and whipped. Occasionally a bear is shot. There are those who advocate that the guides and officials of the Park carry guns; and still others are advocating the extermination of the grizzly. We need the grizzly. Most cures proposed are worse than his trouble. But there is a prevention in simply no garbage-piles.

In the Glacier National Park, which has been a wild-life reservation only since 1910, the grizzlies have not yet become demoralized by garbage. The grizzly bear situation in the Yellowstone is a serious and even an alarming one, and what exists here is certain to develop in other Parks. The demoralizing factors are likely to be expanded and not diminished. Then, too, in the Yellowstone this continuous eating of garbage may ere long bring on a pestilence among the grizzlies, or possibly put a check on the number of cubs born. The whole situation appears to be embraced in what I have previously said about what a grizzly is fed and how.

The grizzly has not lost all his old instincts in the Park. Around the garbage-piles he is a lazy, cross pensioner. But away from them, and especially where he ranges outside of the Park, the same bear is as alert and as energetic as ever in getting a living and watching out for his safety. They are tame near garbage-piles but a short distance away are wild. They are comparatively easy to trap near the garbage-piles, where they will enter a trap-door; but the same bear outside the Park is extremely wary and avoids going near a trap....

The ability to comprehend a new situation or incident and readjust one's self to it is the act of an open and a thinking mind. The food, religion, politics, and personal habits of an individual are changed slowly and with difficulty. Progress is constantly being held back by old customs—the inability of the race to form new habits meeting new conditions. Many species of extinct animals have perished because of over-specialization. "Leave your prejudice at home" was the best advice I received just prior to a trip to Europe. Prejudice and its allied mental conditions are binding and delaying. The grizzly does not allow old prejudice to prevent his exploring for new information, and he is ever ready for something new in his environment.

In a generation or two the grizzly has become expert is eluding the pursuer; he rivals the fox in concealing his trail, in confounding the trailer and escaping with his life. That he has developed this trait since coming in contact with the white man and the repeating rifle—out of necessity—there can be no doubt. Formerly, the rightful monarch of the wilds through superiority, he roamed freely about, indifferent as to where he went or whether or not he was seen. He has been wise enough to readjust himself to the evolutionary and revolutionary forces introduced by man. The king of the wilderness has survived through retreat; he has become the master of strategy. Instinct hardly accounts for this swift evolution. The readjustment—avoiding man—does not indicate cowardice; it indicates brains. In the warfare of existence, in changing, exacting environments, the grizzly bear has risen triumphant.

WILDWOOD TEST
1925

 THE author of this account, Milton P. Skinner, first worked in Yellowstone in 1896 while he was a college student. Working in the Park again some years later, he seized on the idea of establishing an official educational service, to include "guiding, lecturing, information bureaus, and a museum." He was able to generate some interest but no money for the project. But in 1919, new Superintendent Horace Albright embraced Skinner's ideas, asked him to set up such a program, and designated him the first "park naturalist." By the time Skinner left a few years later to continue his research and writing, he had started a small nature newsletter, set up a summer informational program, and his museum exhibit consisted of "47 pieces of igneous rock, 43 pieces of geyserite, 41 pieces of petrified wood, 2 mounted animal heads, 1 mounted eagle, 4 pieces of wood cut by beaver, 1 contorted tree trunk, 2 mineral specimens, and pressed flowers representing 80 species" (Aubrey L. Haines, The Yellowstone Story: A History of Our First National Park, Colorado Associated University Press, *1977, 2 v.).*

In his book, he introduces the grizzly by recalling its reputation of the previous hundred years:

What of the great, gray, grizzly fellows, the reported scourge of the western plains and mountains? We are beginning to feel that this wonderful animal has been greatly misunderstood and misrepresented. Instead of a raving monster eager to maim and destroy every living thing, we, in the Yellowstone, know the grizzly as a peaceful, self-respecting animal that asks only to be let alone. And we have found that if he is let alone, he rewards us with many an interesting scene and many amazing instances of the marvelous intelligence and agility of this most interesting, to me, of all animals. But if we forget our good manners and either tease or molest this monarch of the forest, then the scene rapidly changes. For once aroused, the grizzly is a fearful antagonist indeed. And no visitor to the Park should forget for an instant that both the grizzlies and the black bears here are wild bears, quick to resent any seeming unfairness or any undue familiarity.

A better understanding of the bear in its environment had finally appeared. Skinner demonstrates his high regard for the grizzly in this excerpt from his book, Bears in the Yellowstone *(Chicago: A. C. McClurg & Co., 1925).*

▼▼▼▼

I know of nothing that gives one a better idea of bear sagacity and cunning, as well as individuality, than to trail up an old grizzly, wise in his years of discretion. To trail such a big animal by his tracks in the snow seems a simple task. And so it would be if it were not the track of a resourceful, intelligent animal with limb and wind sufficient to carry him anywhere he may elect to go. Old Eph cannot be treed, and he will not travel in circles, or follow any other rule that gives one a chance to forestall or get ahead of him. Grizzlies that are followed use their brains all the time and apparently never become panic-stricken. They can travel the roughest of rocky, mountainous regions with surprising agility and speed. And, furthermore, the following of a trail and working out its tangles, its turns, its counter-turns, and its various eccentricities is a liberal education for the trailer. He who matches himself against this past master of woodcraft, he who pits his skill, his care, and his endurance against the grizzly, will learn much, will acquire much new respect, for bruin. And in the learning will enjoy much in the way of entertainment and satisfaction.

When I was but a boy in college, I began hunting the grizzly. I learned a great deal of him, of his ways and habits, of his courage and sagacity; and I learned to respect his sturdy qualities. I persevered, at times I was successful—more often I was not. I steadily acquired woodcraft; I often returned to camp dirty, wet, and tired out, but I never regretted those days in the forest. As for the grizzly, I began by respecting him and then I came to admire him. For many years now I have not used a rifle; sometimes I take a camera, but more often I spend days studying the great bear, and still my wonder and respect increases the more I learn. I have found that the trailing of Old Eph, wise and wary in his old age, is the most difficult, the most exhaustive of all wildwood tests.

One autumn when the snow fell just right and lay two or three inches deep for five days without melting, or crusting so as to be noisy, I took a blanket, a little food, a light pack, and a camera to track down a grizzly. I found his trail in a small meadow where the remains of a squirrel burrow still covered the snow with fresh dirt and the long grass was still rising from bruin's footsteps in a way to indicate only two or three hours' start. He was not traveling fast and I had high hopes of catching up. Soon after I started I noticed that most of the time he traveled into the face of the wind. This, of course, was to be informed of what was in front of him as far as possible. In a way this made my work lighter, for any noise I made could not so readily reach those keen ears and no telltale scent could give me away. But Old Eph knew that as well as I did and it made him still more watchful of his rear; in fact, he apparently never felt safe about his back track and was always alert to possible approach from that direction. As the day wore on, the snow told me that he frequently stopped and rose on his haunches to look and listen and probably sniff in all directions. Since the snow was fairly well melted in such places from the heat of the body, it was evident he spent many minutes in each survey, although I was quite sure it was not until two days later that he felt he was being followed. If these ordinary investigations did not fully satisfy him, he made a slow circle, stopping whenever he saw something he wanted, but nevertheless, eventually getting back across his trail before going on again. Once or twice during the day he back-tracked along his trail, possibly to see if all was well. He did not by any means travel straight away, nor even in any general direction. He was unalarmed, he was attending to his ordinary business of securing enough to eat; he cropped grass, he dug mice, squirrels, and woodchucks, he tore up logs, and he overturned many stones. But, as a grizzly habitually does he watched his back track to prevent surprise.

On a small plateau where almost every stone was turned, he crossed and recrossed his own trail so repeatedly I could not follow its tortuous ways, and only by making a big circle myself could I pick up the onward trail again. At times he climbed a rock or a hillside to look back, and again he turned at right angles to his trail for a sufficient distance to have sound or scent come from his back trail. He used a number of methods to deceive anyone that might be on his trail, so that I could not foretell what was coming next. Sometimes he went straight across an open meadow or "park" only to "stop, look, and listen" in the far edge of the woods; sometimes he passed around the opening to the left, sometimes to the right; and once or twice he right-angled in the middle of a meadow and went out to one side.

Although years of trailing and tracking had long since raised me out of the novice class, I could not foresee and anticipate his movements, and I had to risk his seeing me in the openings or else lose time circling to pick up his trail again. On the third day his trail started diagonally down a canyon wall and I assumed he was going to the bottom, and accordingly let myself down over an easier course than his, to the creek. Failing to cross and pick up the trail there, I was obliged to climb back. There I found the bear had gone two-thirds of the way down, then turned sharply and climbed to a shelf and bedded down for several hours. Afterward he climbed to the ridge, went back a mile, recrossing his old trail, then down to the creek bottom, and, turning away from his previous course, climbed to the far ridge and on again. But now he seemed to be aware I was following, and I believe he had seen me in the gulch, for I crossed the creek so soon after him that his tracks still contained muddy water. I followed him two days longer, but he did not vary his tactics at all except to travel fast enough to keep well ahead. I actually saw him twice during the last two days, neither time within rifle shot, and still more hopeless for my camera. At no point did I outwit him completely, and he defeated most of the plans I made to cut across on his trail and forestall him; yet he did not seem to eat less than usual or to hurry to any extent.

"OH, RANGER!"
1928

 HORACE M. Albright was superintendent of Yellowstone from 1919 to 1929. As Richard A. Barlett says in his history of the Park, "[Albright] arrived in the park with hard-set notions of his role. He was to run Yellowstone as smoothly as possible 'for the people,' protect it from damage, keep its land, waters, animals and thermal phenomena absolutely inviolate, and be a public relations man enhancing at every opportunity the park's world wide reputation" (Yellowstone: A Wilderness Besieged, *Tucson: University of Arizona Press, 1985). Albright's book "Oh, Ranger!" A Book about the National Parks (co-author Frank J. Taylor, Stanford: Stanford University Press, 1928), from which these excerpts are taken, certainly met this last goal.*

Here, once again, as in the Indian legends, grizzly bears have become personified—but how very differently!

▼▼▼▼

"Oh, Ranger! Where can I see a bear?"

The bears are, without doubt, the greatest single attraction in the parks, at least from the visitor's point of view. Geysers, waterfalls, mountains, canyons, great trees centuries old, all fade into secondary importance in the visitor's interest when a bear ambles into sight. Furthermore, they remain of secondary interest as long as the bear continues his antics. The rangers say that in Yosemite National Park a visitor will look at Yosemite Falls, half a mile high, one minute and then turn around and watch a bear one hour.

This amazing interest of the American public in bears goes back to childhood days. Boys and girls are raised on bears. They are brought up on Little Goldilocks and the Three Bears, and numerous other bear tales. Bears are no longer wild animals to us. They have become personified. They are like people, and the visitors to the parks want to treat them as such. That probably explains some of the foolish things people try to do with the national park bears.

"Fooling a bear" is something that just shouldn't be done. We had a bear in Yellowstone known as Mrs. Murphy. There had been several complaints about Mrs. Murphy, who was accused of nipping visitors' hands and feet, so a ranger was assigned to shadow her for a day and see what was happening. He reported as follows:

One Sagebrusher, for the sake of a picture, held some bacon in his mouth and coaxed the bear to remove said bacon from his mouth. He got his picture and also escaped without injury. That Sagebrusher was lucky.

Another tourist tried to make Mrs. Murphy jump for candy, like a dog. Mrs. Murphy reached up, knocked the man's hand down so that she could reach the candy. That frightened the tourist considerably, but he escaped without injury. He, too, was lucky.

A Dude, with no candy or food, held out his hand as though there were candy in it. That made Mrs. Murphy angry and she nipped the man on the toe. He retaliated by kicking Mrs. Murphy on the nose, which is a bear's most sensitive spot. She responded by whacking the Dude with her paw. He was bruised but not badly hurt. He was lucky.

Fully two score people fed Mrs. Murphy and her cub that day in the proper way, by throwing candy to her, and were entertained for hours by the bears with no incidents nor accidents.

The only innocent visitor to suffer injury was a Dude who, disregarding a ranger's warning, insisted upon walking between Mrs. Murphy and her cub, to take a snapshot of the cub. Apparently believing her cub in danger, Mrs. Murphy rushed the Dude, tore out the seat of his ice-cream pants, and, as she thought, saved her cub. The Dude rode the rest of the day in a blanket to seclude a certain blushing and over-exposed portion of his anatomy.

After receiving this report, the rangers decided that Mrs. Murphy was no more guilty than the Dudes and Sagebrushers who attempted to fool her with food that did not exist.

There are two kinds of bears in the national parks, grizzlies and black bears. The grizzlies can be seen only in Yellowstone National Park and occasionally in Glacier and Mount McKinley National parks. Otherwise, they are almost extinct, being much prized by hunters and trappers for their fine gray fur, tinged with silver tips. The grizzly is a wonderful animal, perhaps the strongest and most ferocious beast of the American forest.

Indirectly Yosemite National Park was named after the grizzly. "Yo-semite" was the Indian word for "the Grizzly." It was chosen as the tribe name following a valiant fight by a brave, who, single-handed and unarmed, slew a ferocious grizzly on a trail near Yosemite Valley. The Yosemites themselves were a fierce, warlike tribe, and they were well named after the grizzly. It is greatly to be regretted that the grizzly bear has entirely disappeared from Yosemite National Park, hunted down and exterminated before the territory became a protected area.

Grizzlies are true animals of the forest. They avoid human habitations, roads, camps, and are seldom seen by the average visitor to the national parks. At the Canyon in Yellowstone, as many as twenty-five of them can be seen at dusk, feeding at the garbage pit. They are shy and take to the forest upon sight of humans. This seems strange in view of the fact that the grizzly is master of the forest. The other bears fear him, and flee to the tree tops as soon as a grizzly approaches. The grizzly cannot climb trees because his claws are too long to give him purchase in the bark. The grizzly can be recognized by his broad head and by the hump over his shoulders, as well as by the silver tips of his fur.

At the Canyon, two grizzlies, while but cubs, became separated from their mothers and fell in with the black bears. From the black bears they learned strange ways, including familiarity with humans. They frequented the camps of the Sagebrushers and learned to beg, something that a self-respecting grizzly will never do. These two grizzlies, as they matured, have given the rangers some worry because a grizzly when "fooled" or provoked is a dangerous animal, and we have trembled to think what they might do if some foolish tourist attempted to tease them.

The black bears are the bears that most people know. In spite of the popular belief to the contrary, there is no species known as the brown bear. Black bears may be either blonds or brunettes, just as are humans. The blonds of the bear family are brown, or cinnamon. There are various color phases ranging from light brown or tan to the deep black.

The black bears are the clowns of the forest. They are full of tricks and their antics never fail to give the Dudes and Sagebrushers a thrill. After all, a bear does seem terribly human, and when he sits on his haunches, his fore paws spread out before him, his head up like that of a human, he almost invites you to talk to him. As a matter of fact, most people do talk to the bears, just as though the animals could understand, and the things that are said by the Dudes and Sagebrushers are as funny to us as the bears must be to them....

Bears are always doing unexpected and perverse things. That is one of the reasons they seem so human. There is always a surprise in a bear. There is always some play in him. He loves to fool somebody else, but he doesn't like to be fooled himself. That is human. He wants his own way. He has his moods when he is sulky, when he is friendly, or when he is just plain ornery. The way to a bear's heart is through his stomach, the female of the species being just as susceptible in this as the male. Another human attribute, poets to the contrary! When a bear is hungry he is cross. When he is full of "salad" he is sleepy; when he is eating he doesn't want to be bothered. So there you are!...

We have often thought of offering complaining Dudes the opportunity to spank the bears that they wanted shot, on condition that they capture the bears as did Buffalo Jones [by lassoing it—this incident is recounted in the story "A Wildlife Crusader"]. Not long ago, when the man who dumped the "salad" at the Canyon complained that a bear had bitten him and insisted that the animal be punished, the rangers said, "Point out the guilty bear and we'll punish him."

Just then a bear came out of the woods.

"There he is," said the man. "That's the one that chewed me."

"No, it's this fellow over here," insisted his companion, as another bear approached on the opposite side.

They fell into a heated argument as to which was the bad bear.

"Well, we can't shoot all the bears," the rangers told them. "First you'll have to get the evidence to convict the bear."

A bear is presumed to be innocent until proved guilty. The rangers call the witnesses against the bear and question them about the alleged damage or injury, then seek to establish the identity of the bear. If the bear can positively be identified by the complaining witnesses, and there is general agreement on one bear, the bear is in a fair way to be convicted, but if, as almost always happens, the witnesses cannot agree on the identity of the bear, the rangers refuse to touch any bear or hold any one bear responsible for the trouble....

It has been but a few years since the bears of the national parks were harrassed by visitors and regarded as menaces. When the National Park

Service was formed, it was decided to exclude dogs from the parks. That was really the beginning of the era of friendship between mankind and the bears. The rangers were criticized then, and still are for that matter, for permitting the bears to roam at large through the parks. Now, of course, there would be a tremendous protest from the public if we did anything to interfere with the opportunity to see the bears. The Dudes and the Sagebrushers demand their bears. The present generation has been raised on bear stories, and real, live bears give them the thrill of their vacation. That is why they are the greatest single attraction in the national parks.

A DEATH IN YELLOWSTONE
1929

 ATTITUDES and actions toward Yellowstone's grizzlies changed repeatedly over the decades—fear of a monster, annihilation of a "bad" predator, amusement at the once-dread-now-foolish road-side beggars, appreciation as natural animals, scrutiny as objects of research, termination after "conflicts." Policies concerning bear management are not fixed or clear-cut even today. Our final story reminds us that, although grizzlies had received protection and appreciation in the Park by 1929, and although the author of this narrative regretted the incident, bears still sometimes died there at human hands, as they do even today.

Dave Aaberg tape-recorded this bear story by Dudley Hayden in 1967. The tape was transcribed and filed in the Wyoming Department of Commerce's Historical Research and Publications in Cheyenne. We have edited it extensively to make it easier to read.

▼▼▼▼

MY name is Dudley Hayden. I am at the present time about 69 and one half years old. Years ago I was a ranger in Yellowstone Park in Wyoming.

In the winter of '29, I was doing some game survey work with a very famous biologist by the name of Murie in the neighborhood of the southeast corner of the Park. A friend of mine, who was one of the early Yellowstone scouts (he'd been in the Park practically all of his life), told me that I was tempting providence by leaving a haunch of venison hanging outside my cabin. He said the bears would get it. Snow at that time was about a foot deep all over the country and I hadn't seen a bear track for a week or so, and so I didn't think there was any danger in losing my meat. It hung on a ridge spike outside the door of the cabin, and we had been doing all right with it. It wasn't but half eaten.

One night, about 2:30 in the morning, I woke up. The whole cabin was shaking. I realized, of course, even though I was only half awake, what had happened. A bear had come out of hibernation, or hadn't gone in. I jumped up out of the bunk and grabbed my rifle and ran to the door. Without thinking too overly long, I jerked the door open with the idea of scaring the bear away from the meat and getting it back in the cabin where it would be safe. Well, I swung the door open and there was the bear. He had considerable difficulty getting the meat off the spike, so I yelled at him a time or two. He let go of the meat and backed off a ways.

It was a windy night, and there were quite a few clouds in the sky, although there was a moon intermittently, and I could see him going away. But he only went to the top of the bank, possibly thirty, forty feet from the door. I didn't think that was quite far enough for me to chance going out and getting a hold of the meat. So I pulled the rifle up and fired at him from my hip and didn't even take aim.

The next time the clouds moved away from the moon, I saw the top of the bank was clear. I went outside in my practically-nothing-on and took the meat off the ridge spike, brought it back in the cabin, closed the door, and went back to bed.

The next morning, I had to get up early because I had some horses out in the pasture and, to keep them from wandering away in case they got loose, I was in the habit of feeding them every morning the first thing with a little oats. I filled the pan about half full of oats and started up the hill, my eyes still heavy with sleep. I turned at the spring at the bottom and started on toward the pasture. Pretty soon I saw this great big enormous black shape in front of me leaning up against a tree. It dawned upon me that there hadn't been a rock there the night before. A little puzzled, I finally opened my eyes wide so I could see, and it was a bear looking at me—rather glaring at me, I would say. Of course, I was quite a bit startled, so I dropped the pan and went back to the cabin for my rifle.

When I returned, I could see that the bear was dead although his eyes were wide open, and he was in kind of a sitting position leaning up against this tree. I had heard the bullet thump when I had fired the rifle, but it never occurred to me that I'd hit the bear. There were so many trees around that I figured I had probably hit a tree. For some strange reason, the bear didn't make any outcry when he was hit.

Well, that bear was quite a bear, a real silver tipped grizzly—jet black with the ends of his hairs white, maybe a half inch of white on them. I had to do something about this bear, and that meant skinning it out for the skull and getting a specimen. I'd seen plenty of them alive in Yellowstone Park, of course, being a ranger, but that was my first experience of having skinned a bear. I realized that I was going to have to be very careful, I didn't dare cut the hide or anything.

It took me five hours to skin that bear. After I got it skinned, I tried to drag the skin up to the cabin, but, my gosh, it was too heavy. I had to get one of my saddle horses and a saddle rope, and the horse towed it up to the cabin. I laid it up on the horse rack we had tied between several trees, and I measured that hide with a spool tape. It measured 11 feet from its nose to its tail.

Then I realized that I couldn't very well leave the carcass on the trail because—I don't know if too many people know it—horses are desperately afraid of the skinned-out carcass of a bear. It really spooks them. I got a rope on the carcass and I tried to get my saddle horse to drag it out in the marsh. And by george, the carcass was too heavy for him to move, so I had to get an ax and cut it into pieces before I could move it out in the marsh even with the horse dragging it.

I think that bear skull was one of the very largest ever on record in the history of Yellowstone Park. I was quite concerned having killed it. I wanted my meat pretty bad, though.

SELECTED READING

STORIES OLD AND NEW

Gowans, Fred R. 1986. *Mountain Man & Grizzly*. Orem, Utah: Mountain Grizzly Publications. 210 pp.

Haynes, Bessie Doak, and Edgar Haynes, eds. 1966. *The Grizzly Bear: Portraits from Life*. Norman: University of Oklahoma Press. 370 pp.

Hubbard, W.P. 1960. *Notorious Grizzly Bears*. Chicago: The Swallow Press, Inc. 205 pp.

McCracken, Harold. 1955. *The Beast that Walks like Man: the Story of the Grizzly Bear*. Garden City, New York: Hanover House. 319 pp.

Rockwell, David. *Giving Voice to Bear: North American Indian Myths, Rituals, and Images of the Bear*. Niwot, Colorado: Roberts Rinehart Publishers. 224 pp.

Schullery, Paul, ed. 1983. *American Bears: Selections from the Writings of Theodore Roosevelt*. Boulder: Colorado Associated University Press. 193 pp.

Schullery, Paul. 1988. *The Bear Hunter's Century: Profiles from the Golden Age of Bear Hunting*. New York: Dodd, Mead & Co. 252 pp.

Schullery, Paul. 1991. *Yellowstone Bear Tales*. Niwot, Colorado: Roberts Rinehart, Inc. 212 pp.

Shepard, Paul, and Barry Sanders. 1985. *The Sacred Paw: The Bear in Nature, Myth, and Literature*. New York: Viking Press. 243 pp.

Young, F.M. 1980. *Man Meets Grizzly: Encounters in the Wild from Lewis and Clark to Modern Times*. Boston: Houghton Mifflin Company. 298 pp.

CONTEMPORARY MANAGEMENT, ETHICS, CONSERVATION, AND SCIENCE

Brown, David E. 1985. *The Grizzly in the Southwest: Documentary of an Extinction*. Norman: University of Oklahoma Press. 274 pp.

Calicott, J. B. 1982. *Traditional American Indian and Western European Attitudes Toward Nature: An Overview*. Envir. Ethics 4:293-318.

Craighead, Frank C., Jr. 1979. *Track of the Grizzly*. San Francisco: Sierra Club Books. 261 pp.

Herrero, Stephen. 1985. *Bear Attacks: Their Causes and Avoidance.* New York: Lyons & Burford. 287 pp.

Interagency Grizzly Bear Committee. 1987. *Grizzly Bear Compendium.* Washington, DC: U.S. Fish and Wildlife Service.

Laycock, George. 1986. *The Wild Bears.* New York: Outdoor Life Books. 272 pp.

Mattson, David J., and Matthew M. Reid. 1991. *Conservation of the Yellowstone Grizzly Bear.* Conservation Biology 5:364-372.

McNamee, Thomas. 1984. *The Grizzly Bear.* New York: Alfred A. Knopf. 308 pp.

McNamee, Thomas. 1987. *Nature first.* Boulder, Colorado: Roberts Rinehart, Inc. 54 pp.

Peacock, Doug. 1990. *Grizzly Years: In Search of the American Wilderness.* New York: Henry Holt and Company. 288 pp.

Russell, Andy. 1967. *Grizzly Country.* New York: Alfred A. Knopf. 302 pp.

Rolston, Holmes, III. 1981. *Values in Nature.* Envir. Ethics 3:113-128.

Schneider, Bill. 1977. *Where the Grizzly Walks.* Missoula, Montana: Mountain Press. 191 pp.

Schullery, Paul. 1992. *The Bears of Yellowstone.* Worland, Wyoming: High Plains Publishing Company. 318 pp.

U. S. Fish and Wildlife Service. 1990. *Grizzly Bear Recovery Plan.* U.S. Fish and Wildlife Service, Missoula, Montana.